I can't help but be amazed by the almost 20-year convoluted trajectory that Abba's life took from the moment he fled his home at the end of August 1942, up until the court's verdict against Nazi villain Adolph Eichmann at the close of May 1962.

During those years, Abba, my father, went from being a cruelly treated Nazi slave to being the SS-Obersturmbannführer's personal guard – ensuring his safety until the verdict was implemented.

The narrative of Abba's life reflects an important principle, and for that reason alone it was worth filling page after page with ink, organizing the pages, and binding them into a book so that others reading it can learn from this ethical stance and internalize it for the future.

I dedicate this book

To its hero, my dear late father, Shmuel Blumenfeld, who during the tender and formative second decade of his life watched his family disappear and who, in May 1945, had no choice but to face the fact that he was now an orphan, bereft of family and friends, and lacking a home to which he could return.

As both the protagonist and hero of *Grasping at Life*, he repeatedly chose the tough path of recovery. He devoted the remainder of his life to nurturing our small family: my mother, my sister and me. He educated us to diligence, love of others, and integrity. With hard work, piece by piece and step by step, he rebuilt a family heritage and interwove the memory of his own family and victims of the Holocaust.

I am grateful to G-d that Abba enjoyed a long life, saw his life's work come to fruition, and watched his children grow, establish their own families and raise his grandchildren and great-grandchildren.

Although focused on rehabilitation, never for a moment did he forget his vow to "remember and commemorate his family, his neighbors, and his friends, who were unable to oppose their Nazi overlords and were horrifically murdered by the most odious of men during the Holocaust."

Abba directed his energies into perpetuating the memories of the people impacted by that era of terror. This project is my modest contribution to upholding his vow.

To my dear mother, Rivka Blumenfeld, who always stood by me, supporting me unconditionally even as a very "mischievous" boy, as she'd call me. She was our family's "Rock of Israel," so to speak, and we all knew that she could always be depended upon. She was the one who encouraged me throughout, metaphorically carrying me on her back on days when I could barely crawl, and releasing me when the time came, letting me race ahead and blossom. My mother's Holocaust story is of a different nature, but bears a parallel chronology to that of Abba's, but through the cities and forests of Lithuania.

To Iris, my incredible wife, whose partnership walked me through life and who cast a light on how to differentiate between good and evil. With loyal devotion, she cleared the obstacles; with hard work, she paved the way for our shared journey. Together we built a warm home filled with love, supported our children lovingly, and cared for each other with mutual respect.

To my three wonderful children, Mor, Ashley Hashla, and Daniel, who are of supreme importance in my life. They know the degree of responsibility we hold relative to the chain of future generations. Together with Iris, they help me bear our individual and collective torches of memory in Israel, ensuring that they will be passed on to future generations and underscore our independence in Israel, which can never be taken for granted and which we are obligated to safeguard under all circumstances.

To Oren Cohen Ninio, artist and sculptor, who listened patiently yet keenly to my stories, urged me on, kept driving me even when I felt exhausted, and whose contribution to this book has been essential. Oren has his own Holocaust stories, yet he helped shape this book, turning Abba's adolescent experiences, as those were seared into my heart, into a visual, moving work, and adding illustrations that expand and deepen the connection to the events described. Without Oren, I would never have reached the finish line and gotten this book into print. My heartfelt thanks.

To the Proszowice Jewish community, eradicated by the Nazis in the summer of 1942; it is one of thousands of similar communities wiped out in the Holocaust. As Proszowice community descendants, it is our duty to tell the stories of our community's people to ensure that listeners will continue to learn of the horror inflicted by the Nazis with their so-called "enlightened ways" throughout Europe as well as northern Africa, even though many prefer to forget those times. We will continue to fulfill our obligation to those whose lives were cut short by remembering and commemorating them forever.

Contents

Glossary of Jewish Words 13

Introduction 17

Foreword 21

The Final Journey 29

A Dance of Love and Hate 31

Proszowice Township's
Conquest by the Germans in WWII 41

Meeting the Proszowice Mayor 45

Proszowice under Nazi Occupation 48

Occupation's New Routines 52

Reb Getzel Pińczewski, Head of the Proszowice Judenrat:
How He Was Chosen, His Role, and His Bitter End 57

Fleeing the Forced Labor Camp for Proszowice 63

Farewell to the Family Forever 66

Fleeing Home 70

"If You Want to Know…" 74

Slomniki: The Hellhole of the Michów District's Towns 77

After Fleeing Home 83

The Ceremony 86

The Second Deportation from Proszowice 91

My Last Visit to My Childhood Home in Proszowice 97

Wicek Wincenty and His Wife Jadwiga:
A Ray of Light in Poland's Darkness 102

The Meeting in Kraków 107

The Kraków Ghetto Up Until Its Liquidation 110

The Kraków Ghetto's Liquidation 115

The Murder of Proszowice's Righteous Rabbi Wachs 118

The Path to Hell on Earth 126

The Jeruzulimskiej Forced Labor Camp
and Heshel Blumenfeld's Bitter End 131

Hell on Earth: Day One at Birkenau (Brzezinka) 133

Auschwitz-Birkenau: Learning the Ropes 138

Camp Routine 158

The Jawiszowice Coal Mining Camp:
Auschwitz's Hellish Satellite 165

The Brzeszcze Area 2 Coal Mine 169

The Camp Work Routine 175

The First Death March:
Jawiszowice, Buchenwald, Ramsdorf........................ 183

The Second Death March: Ramsdorf to Theresienstadt......... 189

Release, and Returning Home. Or Not..................................... 200

Eichmann: The SS Officer I Dream About in Birkenau 206

Eichmann: Abba's Nightmare 208

The Oppressor in Prison.. 214

Tough Days 217

Abba and the Murderer 220

The Oppressor's Daily Schedule 224

Attorney Robert Servatius.. 232

The Stain on the Wall 233

The Appeal 239

The Real Eichmann 242

Kurt Gerstein, Nazi, Exposes the Truth to the World 245

The Protest...250

The Legendary Satan's End 255

The Last Visit to Proszowice 258

Abba's Home in Proszowice 259

The Cemetery 262

Shmuel Blumenfeld's Memoirs 263

The Final Chapter of Abba's Life 266

Glossary of Jewish Words

A note on Jewish terms used in this book.

The word "G-d" is written this way since in Hebrew we never write the name in full; this ensures that the sacred written name can never be desecrated, either accidentally or intentionally. Writing the word "G-d" throughout this book respects that Jewish tradition, cherished and carefully kept by Abba and our family, as well as Abba's childhood community.

Other words commonly used include:

Abba	Father in Hebrew. The word I grew up with and use to refer to my own father
Aliyah	Hebrew: immigration to Israel
Gemara	Rabbinic commentary on the Mishnah, forming the second part of the Talmud
Haggadah	The text read on the first night of Pesach
Kaddish	The mourner's prayer

Kheider	A school for young children where studies focus on Jewish texts
Kippah	Skullcap
Magen David	Star of David
Matzah	Unleavened bread eaten during Pesach (Exodus 12:39)
Mezuzah	A small, rolled parchment containing specific Biblical verses, inserted in a decorative holder and affixed to doorposts in Jewish homes and buildings (Deuteronomy 6:9)
OBM	of blessed memory
Pesach	Seven-day festival of Passover (Exodus 12)
Rosh Hashanah	Jewish New Year (generally falls around mid-September) (Leviticus 23:24)

Sabba	Hebrew: grandfather.
Shabbat	Sabbath, which Jews observe on Friday night and Saturday
Shoah	Hebrew word for Holocaust
Siddur	Jewish prayerbook
Tallit	Prayer shawl (Numbers 15:38)
Tateh	Yiddish: Father. This is how Abba referred to his father.
Tefillin	Phylacteries for arm and head, made of leather, containing Biblical verses and worn during weekday morning prayers (Exodus 13:9, 16)
Tzitzit	Garment with four corners, each holding threads knotted in a specific way (Numbers 15:38)
Yom Kippur	The Day of Atonement, which falls 10 days after Rosh Hashanah (Leviticus 16:29)

Introduction

Put everything you typically know about the Holocaust aside. Yes, my family's – and my – Holocaust story is, like so many others, one of coping with sorrow and death, of crumpled memories that are nonetheless as sharp as a razor, and on occasion sound monotonous, exhausting, shrouded in fear, horror, and uncertainty. Even so, I invite you to go on this often complicated journey with Abba and me as we zigzag through the boundaries of time and space, look deep into the eyes of evil, and long for compassion. Our path ahead is complex, but I promise that it will carry value and meaning.

The deportation of Jews from the township of Proszowice, Poland, took place on August 29, 1942, corresponding to the 16th of Elul 5702, according to the Jewish calendar. It was a Saturday: for Jews, that is the holy Shabbat, a day of rest. Abba swore then, as a young boy, that if he remained alive, he would do all he could to perpetuate the memories of his family, his friends, and the town's Jewish residents.

Proszowice's destruction is a symbol of the destruction of Poland's entire Jewish population, in place for generations prior to WWII. Some 2,000 Jewish residents of Proszowice – more than half the town's population – were rounded up and killed in one way or another. The war over, it was discovered that only about 150 Jews survived – of whom, as I write these lines, only three are still alive today, among them Abba. These survivors have devoted their lives to telling their town's story. I grew up hearing Abba recount these events, which show how closely his life was woven into the town's existence.

When the 78th anniversary of Proszowice's obliteration was marked, I decided to present Abba's stories to him in an early draft form, explaining that this is how I absorbed and understood them as I grew up. I wrote them down for several reasons: firstly, for the children of the second, third, and fourth generations who would want to explore, question, and discover, and would have no one with first-hand experience to ask.

A second reason was the fact that recent years have seen survivors' families taking part in the discourse on the importance of openness on the part of Holocaust survivors. Countless children of survivors face parents who pursed their lips and obstinately, although understandably, refused to describe the horrors. Nonetheless, the second generation has absorbed the immense sorrow and has a need to hear the details that have had such a colossal influence on their lives.

By contrast, Abba never stopped talking about those events, actively involving himself in perpetuating the victims' memories. As a child, I absorbed these stories for years but lacked the tools to cope with the horror and shame. I stored the stories in my consciousness. Now I'm trying to air them, to digest them, but perhaps too late? Abba's mantra was, "Anyone who was there doesn't need an explanation, and anyone who wasn't will never be able to understand."

The third reason is my own sense of commitment to our historic truth, as well as my commitment as an educator to make this truth accessible to the generations that follow, ensuring that they fully comprehend the message of those dreadful years and will continue working to guard and preserve what we have, which we unwisely presume can be taken for granted.

Many years ago, Abba penned his testimony, sharing it with

me and making me promise to publish it upon his death. I decided to tell my story, based on his – but from my perspective – while he is still alive. He has meanwhile passed away, so this book is a testimony to his life.

To make these events more accessible, I've opened a Facebook page called "From Holocaust to Revival" where comments can be added and activities of the town's survivors can be followed.

Lastly, I am fully aware that the stories contained herein are what I heard and understood, as told to me by Abba, and bear my own interpretations drawn initially from my thoughts as a child and later as an adult. Those additions cannot be ascribed to him.

Arie Blumenfeld

Shmuel Blumenfeld, June 1945

Foreword

As a child, and like so many of my friends at the time, I didn't hear in-depth details about what the Holocaust inflicted on Europe's Jews. Messages were primarily covert, yet powerful enough to seep into our awareness. I was skinny, naughty, blond, and blue-eyed. Countless times I heard my parents' friends, most of whom also bore blue tattooed numbers on their arms, say, "He looks so much like a non-Jew that he'd have managed to survive," or "He's so thin that he looks sick." Both messages hold back-door comparisons that are nonetheless sharp and clear.

Both my parents lost their entire families in the Holocaust. Abba was the firstborn, followed by five siblings, all murdered by the Nazis. As a child, the lack of family bothered me so much that I called all my parents' friends "aunt" or "uncle." In the building next to ours lived a large Tunisian family with many children and two grandmothers – all in the same house – with countless relatives coming and going. That made the absence of my own extended family even more poignant. I was very envious.

As an adult, I married a woman with seven siblings and in an instant gained an extended family. My compensation.

It's not surprising that as a kid I took no great interest in the Holocaust. It was simply an inherent component of my life. Abba was a survivor who talked about coping with harsh trauma. He spoke a lot about his family, about life in the town, and named his firstborn, my sister, after his mother, murdered in Poland by the Germans. I was named for my maternal grandfather, murdered in Lithuania.

As a teacher in Israel, I joined a 1993 March of the Living delegation to Poland, accompanying my students. Abba came, too, as a survivor able to provide living testimony. At the time, school excursions to Poland weren't nearly as well put together as they are now, and the idea of taking a survivor with us doubled as an opportunity for me to go with Abba to his town of birth.

We picked a day during the school trip and, outfitted with our video camera, hired a driver. We set out for Proszowice, some 30 kilometers from Kraków, to where Abba and his family had moved during the Holocaust. The closer we got to Proszowice, the narrower and less well maintained the road became. It was as though we'd entered a time tunnel and were flying backwards through the years.

It was very evident that we were using a rural road, as Kraków's multi-story dense apartment blocks were no longer visible. Instead, farm fields spread before us. Vast swaths of land were planted with crops, interspersed with anything from densely growing clumps of trees to thick forests. Here and there, small clusters of farmhouses could be seen. For good reason, Proszowice was known to Kraków's wealthy residents as a top destination for summer holidays. The air was fresh, the atmosphere typically Jewish, and nothing, Abba frequently reminded us, was like the taste of "Matzah Proszowinka," the unleavened Passover bread famous throughout Poland.

At the town's entrance we see the Jewish cemetery, a not overly large area enclosed by a neglected fence made of metal bars, broken in places. An equally neglected path leads from the road to the gate's three stone pillars coated with white plaster. Scratch the plaster a bit and it peels away to reveal the old green paint. Between the pillars are two gates: the narrower one leads to the visitors' entrance, and the wider one, composed of two wings, allowed vehicles to drive through. Three large Stars of David, each positioned inside a circle, were welded to the gates.

One pillar bears a sign in Polish cautioning visitors: "This is a UNESCO protected site." The sign was affixed following pressure by Nathan Yoshkwice, born in pre-war Proszowice, who moved to Germany after the war. Between 1942 and 1986, no Jews had come to the region; he was the first to visit in 1986 when diplomatic relations between Poland and Israel were renewed. Nathan worked tirelessly to restore the local cemetery, looted during the war and post-war period. He restored seven gravestones, which he set along the cemetery's main path as a silent testimony to an entire community eradicated during the Holocaust. Funds were raised from the town's survivors who had meanwhile emigrated to the USA and who also worked with him to have UNESCO recognize and protect the site. Abba was the second Jewish person to make a post-war visit to the Proszowice Jewish cemetery. Showing just how much the area still reeks of hatred, a large swastika and revoltingly worded graffiti against the Jews – the work of local anti-Semites – were on barefaced display when we visited.

Our visit is the third time Jews have gone to the town, and Abba's second. With a bit of effort we manage to climb over the locked gates. The sight hits us hard in the gut and clearly shows how the locals relate to the Jews who lived there for so long. The area is overgrown. It's almost as though the weeds want to hide the shame: smashed headstones, exposed graves, bits of tombstones scattered around, and – worst of all – the row of restored headstones has also been smashed. Chunks of stone line the path where the stones had been. I'm aware that I suddenly feel shocked. I try to comprehend the barbarism. And I'm searching for the perspective that Abba might have.

"Arie," he addresses me, "it's because no Jews have lived here since 1942."

His rationale reflects the difference between us: He experienced the most virulent type of anti-Semitism and is therefore able to categorize anti-Semitic acts by degrees of severity. Although he finds the desecration of the graves sacrilegious, the act itself is directed at stones, whereas he has clear memories of the same types of acts being directed at fellow humans. By contrast, I know what an enemy's hatred feels like but haven't really experienced anti-Semitism driven by blind hatred simply because I'm Jewish, or because some inanimate object represents Judaism.

Walking around the cemetery, I carefully turn stones over and read the engravings, trying to cope with the images as they are revealed. I peek at Abba. I see his intuitive spark in action, the same strong instincts that kept him alive throughout the Holocaust. I see that he's physically here, but his mind has already raced ahead. I can almost hear the whirring of the cogs in his brain. While I'm mourning the townsfolk's past, he's building the future. No doubt it's this ability that helped him survive the extermination camps, an ability that must surely be inherent but was finely honed in the school of hard knocks until he excelled at it.

We say the Yizkor memorial prayer and conduct a kind of memorial ceremony. Abba also says Kaddish, the prayer of mourning for the deceased. As we leave the cemetery, I can clearly see that Abba's got a plan of action. Outside the gates, he turns back; in his mind the vision is absolutely clear: it's in the way he looks at those gates. Unlike him, all I see is destruction and hatred in abundance.

"Arie, there in the hell that was Auschwitz, I made a vow: If I stay alive despite everything, I'll work my whole life to perpetuate the memories of those who didn't make it through. Later, when I was at what I thought must be the very lowest of lows that humans could ever reach – depressed, sure I had no chance of making it – two things kept me clinging to life. The first was my mother's request. The second was my vow. I wanted to stay alive, if not for my own sake, then at least for them. Who'll come here? Will we come here again?"

Knowing Abba as I do, when he asks a question in two formulations, his answer is evident in the second question.

A pragmatic man, Abba took on the job of restoring the cemetery, collecting the chunks of stone, ordering replacements for any missing parts, getting the fence painted, clearing and replanting the grounds, and setting up a monument at the center of the site. This was all topped off by a decision to make the site enticing to the Polish locals – predominantly devout Catholics – while putting into play the brilliant move of recruiting the local Patriarch by having him play a key role at the monument's dedication and sanctifying the site for Christians, too. In one fell swoop, Abba's clever plans would instantly put an end to displays of anti-Semitism and the ensuing destruction of the Jewish cemetery, and ensure that the site enjoys the respectful sanctity it deserves from the local population.

On future occasions when Abba joins trips to Poland to provide a survivor's testimony, he insists on one condition being fulfilled: that the itinerary include a visit to the Proszowice Jewish cemetery. As a result, since 1993, and at least three times a year, delegations of Israeli youth and adults visit the cemetery and pay their respects. They hold ceremonies accompanied by an impressive display of Israeli flags. The visits leave leading city officials in wonder at the Jewish nation's strength and they see how Jewish youth who never knew Proszowice's residents or have no direct blood relationship to the victims, deeply and authentically identify with the memories of the town's Jewish population. These visits present Jews as wonderful, caring people.

As time passed, these visits led the mayor to accept Abba's gently prodding requests: Cut back the wild grass, re-plaster the entrance pillars, paint the fence black and the Star of David symbols white, plant rows of flowers, and collect the pieces of broken stone. Abba sets the stones in a row, representing the Proszowice residents buried here, forgotten by all except Abba. It's as though he's implemented the phrase, "My beloved has a vineyard ... which he dug, and cleared of stones, and planted with choicest vines" (Isaiah 5:1-2).

Reining in Abba's activities comes from a very unexpected direction. Opinions of survivors in Israel are divided over the idea of establishing a monument to Holocaust victims in the old Proszowice Jewish cemetery. Fierce opposition is voiced primarily by a core group of veterans who lost families and children. For them, Polish land is cursed and anyone who goes there desecrates the name of G-d and the victims. The argument becomes volatile and threatens to split the survivor community into two camps.

The opposition is authentic, honest, principled; legal threats are bandied about. Abba, a man of peace and compromise, had never imagined such an outcome. The idea is dropped from the survivors' agenda for the sake of empathy and harmony. The idea is let go but not forgotten. Instead, the monument is raised in the cemetery of the city of Holon, and first-generation survivors, accompanied by their families, gather once a year to conduct a memorial service marking the day that Jews were deported from Proszowice. That date was declared the "yahrzeit" (literally "year day" or anniversary), by the older survivors, and it is diligently observed each year.

In 2004, having brought hundreds of high school students to Proszowice over almost a decade, conditions began to align that would make it possible to put up a monument inside the cemetery. The dedication was attended by the Proszowice mayor, the head of Kraków's Jewish community, the regional cemetery groundskeeper, heads of synagogues and of Jewish properties in Poland, and the local Catholic bishop – who not only accepted Abba's invitation, but spoke at the ceremony, announcing that the site was sacred to all, Christian locals and Jewish visitors alike. How wise Abba was to give the bishop a central role; since that event, there hasn't been even one anti-Semitic incident or desecration in the Proszowice Jewish cemetery. On the contrary: locals come to pay their respects.

Abba, guiding gently, proved that closeness helps prevent acts of hatred. How sad that no one among the locals thought of that earlier.

The Final Journey

My cell phone rang, breaking the thoughts whirling in my mind. This can't be anything good, I was thinking. I always think that when the phone rings. One day I need to explore why I react that way. I peek at the screen. It's Abba. Let's hope nothing's wrong.

"Arie, we've received an invitation to a special meeting of the Proszowice City Council. They want to award me a municipal medal for my work on commemorating the town's Jews."

Abba's voice is justifiably proud and gratified. He conveys the main details of his conversation with them, skipping the niceties of asking how I am. Before I manage to congratulate him, he concludes, "I need you to accompany me to the ceremony."

I stutter; I mumble. On the one hand, yes, of course, this is a very important event for Abba. On the other hand – why me? How will I deal with it?

Anyone who knows me well knows that I have a hard time with flights. Top psychologists have diagnosed the problem as a type of complex abandonment anxiety, blended with a few other issues. Experts have tried various techniques to help me overcome the barriers, but nothing was very successful. I make a point of distancing myself from anything to do with flying or any commitment to fly.

But I know my Dad. He doesn't view "No" as a reasonable response. Without recourse to "No," I find myself charging headlong into a situation that leaves me no choice, is against my wishes, makes me fear that my anxiety will break out any second, and has me trying to plug it up fast and hard, keeping the bad little demons well bottled up.

Preparations went fairly smoothly. And then, here we are, the three of us, fastening our seatbelts: Abba, me, and my son. First-, second-, and third- generation Shoah survivors speeding down the tarmac. Abba's already dozing off after calming down from this exciting situation – his return to his town, to Poland. He once told me that every trip there has him facing his separation from his family once again, and that every time it happens, he hopes he'll reach a different level of closure than on the previous occasion, perhaps even meet a family member who returned. When that doesn't happen yet again, he comforts himself by thinking that perhaps it will next time. And so the cycle of hope, dashed hope, and new hope, goes on.

This time everything is different. It seems that Abba also understands that this will be the last time he'll "travel back in time," so to speak. He is 92, healthy, and functioning well. When a young woman stood for him in the bus we took to the airport, he politely refused. "I'm still young. The time hasn't come for that yet," he said to her, smiling.

My son joined us for reasons of his own. Firstly, he wanted to be part of this exciting chapter in exploring his family's roots, but it was also a chance to go touring and shopping, to see and learn about another place in the world. Maybe the proverbial "wandering Jew" gene was at play.

I had my own very different reasons: Beyond my commitment to Abba and his express wishes, at that point I felt, more than ever, that I was ready to delve deep into my soul in search of desperately needed answers. I was accompanying Abba and simultaneously accompanying myself. I was sure that this was the time and place where I'd discover the key and solve the tightly twisted knots that Abba's stories had caused in my soul as a child and as a teenager.

A Dance of Love and Hate

Thinking about that brought to mind one of Abba's stories. It related to a fellow Proszowicer, Beirel Feifkofe.

"As a kid, I disliked Beirel intensely."

That comment surprised me even before hearing the tale unfold. I'd never heard Abba express such a strong negative opinion about anyone; on the contrary, he always stood up for fellow Jews. But right away he reassured me, "Don't worry, I made up with him towards the end, several days before he was murdered at the Auschwitz-Birkenau gas chambers by the accursed Nazis and returned his soul to G-d."

"Well, what did Beirel do?" I asked.

"Beirel had a long, ginger-colored beard. He wore the round cap typical of Jewish men at the time. Highly respected in the town, a scholar with a good heart and good traits, there was one thing this wonderful man simply couldn't do: Forgive your grandfather, Heshel Blumenfeld, may his soul be blessed. Beirel wanted to be head of the community in town, competing for the job against Rabbi Wachs. But the rabbi earned the prestigious position by the one vote that determined the election's outcome: your grandfather's."

Abba was 11 when, in the winter of 1937, he was sent by his family to Beirel, requesting that Beirel provide a note to the doctor on behalf of Shmuel's two younger, very ill brothers. The boys were at home, suffering from severe pneumonia and hovering between life and death. Their parents were desperate. Clearly, their prayers weren't sufficient but they lacked the funds to pay for a doctor.

"That day," Abba detailed, "my mother burst into the synagogue during morning prayers, pulled open the doors of the

Holy Ark, and with heart-rending cries, begged G-d to cure her sick children and take her instead."

As the oldest child, Shmuel was sent on behalf of the family to request a note for the doctor. It was one way that a community could help the ill, using money from a fund of donations and disbursed according to written recommendations by one of the community's leaders. Abba described his meeting with Beirel.

"A wintry sun lightly lit the town's blanket of snow. My cheeks and nose burned from the cold. The clip-clop of hooves, the whinnying of horses harnessed to sleighs, people chattering … my ears caught all those sounds echoing around the marketplace. Life's going on as usual here, I remember thinking, and only in our house it feels like life is fading, crumbling, and death is fast approaching."

Abba stepped inside Beirel's store, eyes downcast as he stood among the shoppers. Beirel knew who the boy was. Abba and his family had been Beirel's neighbors, on good terms, until Shmuel was eight years old.

"What do you want, boy?" the voice of Beirel, owner of the shop and a community leader, rang out.

Abba looked up and spoke very shyly. "Something terrible is happening at home. My parents are asking for compassionate aid. Please give me a note to the doctor that will save my very sick younger brothers' lives."

Beirel fumed. "I'm not a doctor!" Aggravated, he rebuked him, "Don't bother me now with notes, boy. Go to David Shidlowski, your important uncle, the one who convinced your father to support my competitor. Let him give you a note. He's also a big shot in the community," he said, refusing to help.

Shmuel's skin turned into goose bumps. Ashamed and miserable, he left Beirel's store, bursting into tears outside. Ever since, he bore a grudge against Beirel, but fate, bringing them face to face years later, would turn things around.

Crying and in despair, Shmuel raced off to Dr. Skorchinsky, a local Christian doctor. He was an older man, his hands shook, and his body was partially paralyzed. The elderly doctor visited the boys in their home, caring for the two young brothers and healing them.

But Abba never forgot that humiliation. The pain was evident on his face even when he told me the story so many years later. As always, I stayed silent, identifying with the shame he could still feel when stepping back into his own childhood shoes. A few minutes later, during which he had clearly relived the incident and the hurt, he took up the story as though he'd never paused.

"And then we came across each other once again, more than five years later, in the Auschwitz-Birkenau hellhole," he added.

Abba arrived in Auschwitz five days before the festival of Purim, when the Scroll of Esther is read. That same transport from Kraków also held Beirel Feifkofe and his sons. Abba described their face-to-face encounter.

"Outside, a light snow was falling. We stood together, a group of camp prisoners, next to Block 19. We were sort of jumping up and down, trying to keep ourselves warm in the fierce cold. Suddenly I noticed a group of people gathered together, and wondered if some food was being handed out since the group seemed quite lively. Some of the faces were familiar: Israel Goldstein, Kalman Shidlowski, Kalman Pińczewski, and others. And Beirel, head of the community, among them. I hated him so much but now the reason for my loathing, in light of the conditions in the camp, seemed so petty. Over a note to the doctor! I clearly remembered my mother begging me to go and get that note. I clearly remembered him refusing, mocking me, shaming me before others because of a political disagreement with Tateh. I remember having been sure that I wouldn't forgive him for the rest of my life."

After the demeaning humiliation Abba experienced in Auschwitz at the hands of the Nazis, his anger towards Beirel paled by comparison. Fate had them meet in Auschwitz – Abba as a skinny teenager, and Beirel with his two sons – all sharing a snow-covered bench, surrounded by other Proszowice Jews. Beirel read the Scroll of Esther to the group, the familiar words like a beacon of hope and light in the thick darkness of that place.

Recognizing Shmuel, Beirel called him "my son" in a clear loud voice in front of everyone there. "I lacked for nothing in my life. I had a wife, children, wealth, respect. Let us keep together as one family, and G-d willing, we will be freed and go our own ways."

Others joined Beirel in voicing these hopes, and read the scroll with him that Purim of 1943, the sky lit by the flames from burning furnaces.

"Reb Beirel," Abba addressed him, using the term of respect for an older, well-studied man, "because of a note, I've hated you for years. But now here you are, like our shepherd, guiding our township's Jews through the darkness by keeping our traditions. May you always be blessed as a righteous person," he added, kissing the scroll.

"Reb Beirel!" Abba addressed him

"My son," Beirel repeated, "Proszowice has sunk into oblivion together with all its arguments and quarrels. Did you not see how our two holy leaders, Rabbi Horowice and Rabbi Wachs, made their peace during the war, swearing that from then on, all the Jewish people are like one? It's better that we don't talk of that incident anymore," he summed up, waiving off the unpleasantness between him and Abba, and making peace with him.

Beirel had barely finished talking when the booming voice of Avraham, the man in charge of the prisoners' wing, rang out. "You there, what are you all standing around for?" was accompanied by a stream of vulgar words as he took hold of a metal rod near the doorway and flung it like a javelin. The crowd dispersed in no time; only Reb Beirel remained seated in his place, holding the scroll. Blood burst forth from him, staining the parchment. Abba took over, reading the words "For how can I endure seeing the evil that shall come to my people, or how can I endure the destruction of my kin?" (Book of Esther 8:6).

How useless sanctity is here, Abba remembered thinking to himself. Beirel survived that event, but just barely. After great torment and difficulties, Reb Beirel passed away, together with his two sons, during one of the selections at the Birkenau extermination camp.

But until Birkenau, Beirel had been hopeful. As Nazi domination expanded, and with the experience of a community leader, it was clear to him that the end of Proszowice was near. He packed up and left for the big city, Kraków, and the Jewish ghetto, believing that his chances of survival would be better there, but left his very elderly father-in-law, Itche Meir, behind. He also did two more things, considered important to Orthodox Jews. The first was taking the Scroll of Esther with him. It accompanied him from Kraków to Auschwitz, allowing Jews in the camp to hear his public reading that winter of 1943. The second was taking the Torah scroll with him from the Chęciny Hassidic community's synagogue where Abba's family also worshipped in their pre-Holocaust days.

Due to its size, Beirel hid the Torah scroll, taking the secret of its location with him when he was murdered, and so no one had any inkling of where it might be. That Torah was very important to Abba, having been handwritten by his own grandfather, the ritual scribe Yehezkel Blumenfeld, himself a Chęciny Hassid, one of many Hassidic sects flourishing at the time. Yehezkel had donated that Torah to the Proszowice community during an auspicious ceremony. Unlike the hefty Torah, the Scroll of Esther was relatively small and easily carried. Clearly Beirel had assumed that he'd return when the war was over – which he was sure would be very soon – and retrieve the Torah, restore it, and rededicate it to the synagogue.

A woman named Golda lived in Proszowice. She was Polish, but the townsfolk couldn't help wondering, by virtue of her name, whether she wasn't Jewish. For years Golda ran a simple restaurant in the town center, serving the Polish Christian locals. Towards the ends of the 1990s on one of his many visits accompanying Israeli groups visiting the area, Abba sat down in Golda's restaurant. In no time her son appeared and told Abba that he'd found "one of your books" in his family house. He couldn't really describe what was written there, and had no idea of its importance.

Abba suggested that the young man bring it to him, because Jews indeed have "all kinds of written materials." Off the young man went, but on the way changed his mind and refused to show it to Abba. Over the course of the very many visits Abba made to Proszowice, he visited Golda's son each time until the young man learned to trust Abba.

Meanwhile Golda passed away, and her son continued to manage the restaurant, maintaining a good relationship with

Abba. Every time he visited, Abba brought Golda's son a small gift of Judaica: a prayer shawl, a shofar, a Chanukah candelabrum, and so on. The young man decided to set aside a spot to memorialize the Proszowice Jews who had filled the town before WWII. Displayed in the restaurant were the items Abba brought, as well as photos of pre-war Proszowice Jews that Abba provided. And what was the main feature of the display — if not the Torah scroll?

On the trip with Abba, we visited the restaurant owner and offered to buy the scroll, under the assumption that if it had indeed been hidden by his mother in their family home, it was most likely the one written by my great-grandfather. He refused to sell it, saying that ever since displaying it, the restaurant had become hugely successful, as though the Torah brought good fortune to the business.

He did allow me to examine it, however. I noted that it was one roll of parchment, constituting half the Torah. The parchment's last words belonged to the reading of the portion called "Tzav" (Leviticus 8:36). A thought came to mind: Could it be that a Jewish person had been hiding where the scroll was, was forced to flee, and therefore split the Torah's two sections, sewn together, into separate parchments, since the whole one would have been too bulky and heavy? Could he have taken the section beginning with Tzav because that would match the readings for the coming weeks and months? Did the person perhaps think that the war would soon be over, and he'd return and sew the pieces of parchment together again?

I was weighing the amazing fact that Beirel Fcifkofe had read the Scroll of Esther at Auschwitz. That scroll is read on the Jewish date of 14th Adar, which corresponded that year to March 22, 1943. On the Shabbat immediately afterwards, the weekly Torah reading was indeed "Tzav." Coincidence? That, too, was knowledge that probably disappeared along with the murder of the person who'd known it. Beirel Feifkofe's plan was to flee Proszowice for Kraków, integrate there, and return for his father-in-law. I wondered why he hadn't taken Itche Meir in the first place.

One reason for leaving him behind may have been that the old man was so strictly religious that he simply wouldn't shave his beard, despite the Nazis' express instructions and the punishment they promised. Not even the threat of death could sway Itche Meir, so he chose never to leave his house rather than shave his beard.

Beirel was certain he'd return for Itche Meir, but in the cruel Nazi world, it was made abundantly clear that plans could be made and promises could be given, but not necessarily kept. Beirel didn't come back, and his father-in-law may have stayed at home the entire time, immersed in his Gemara books, waiting to be collected by his family.

Two rounds of deportation were carried out in Proszowice, the old man in his house completely unaware of the destruction that befell the community. One day after the second deportation November 9, 1942, and when it was clear that Beirel must have gotten stuck in Kraków and was unable to return, the head of the local police force, Videle, together with his officers, did house-to-house searches for Jews because of a rumor that some were still hiding in the town.

Tsayevski, the new local police chief, together with several policemen, were sent to search the houses of the Adler family and Itche Meir Kaizer. Four Jews lived in that house, located right next door to the town's Jewish police offices. On entering, they came face to face with old Itche Meir, packed and ready to leave but surprised to find that the person taking him was a Polish policeman rather than Beirel. He was seated at the table studying the Talmud, his tallit over his coat, a heavy woolen hat on his head, boots on his feet. Next to him lay a bag with his tefillin and several other items. Everything was ready for him to accompany whichever messenger Beirel sent to fetch him.

Bursting loudly into the room, the police were stunned by this old man, who showed no fear, but sat nobly, not trying to hide his Jewish identity. They demanded that he accompany them to the local police station.

Closing his Talmud, he set it gently on the corner of the table. His head raised, tears streaming from his eyes, he walked over to the doorpost's mezuzah, which contained holy writings, and spent so long kissing it and praying that the Polish police officer began to lose his patience. Itche Meir left his home for the last time in his life. Outside, driving rain and icy cold painted a very grim image.

As they trudged to the police station, Itche Meir mumbled in Polish that he was leaving his home in Proszowice according to the will of G-d, and that despite this situation, G-d is great and holy, and this, too, will be a blessing, just as G-d blessed him in better days. The next day he and several other Jews caught then were urged up onto a horse-drawn wagon and taken to Miechów, and from there to the Belzec extermination camp where he was killed like so many others from his town. May his memory be a blessing.

* * *

So there we were, boarding El Al flight 5119, when a man of about 35 came over; grinning broadly and excitedly, he pointed to Abba. "Shmuel! You were our living witness on our school's trip to Poland. The ORT Shomron School from Binyamina. I'm Eran Levi." For years Abba accompanied the ORT Shomron student delegations to Poland. I couldn't help thinking what a small world we live in: 17 years since Eran had traveled there as a teenager, and now as a young man, the memory was still strong and clear.

Smiling, the emotion visible on his face, Abba turned to me. "See that? He remembers me!"

The boy-that-was pulled his cell phone out of his pocket and scrolled through the photo gallery. He found the photo from 2002 with Abba in Poland. Just look at how much that trip meant to the 17-year-old Eran! It had such an impact that he'd kept the photo of the living witness. On the other hand, I was thinking about how I've been carrying these stories around in my memory since earliest childhood, how every meal was accompanied by some story from Abba's childhood or adolescence, and I tried to make sense of it all in my mind. Insights left painful scars on my soul. In my helplessness, I buried them deep within and don't know where they are anymore. But Eran was thrilled to take a selfie with Abba.

Now I'm thinking ahead to what awaits us, concentrating hard on the present, attempting to ignore the jet's acceleration in readiness for takeoff. Abba's excited. He's heading to his hometown once again. To distract my attention from the flight, he tells me about the night that the Germans conquered Proszowice.

Proszowice Township's Conquest by the Germans in WWII

The night of September 7, 1939, is one that Abba remembers in the finest of details. It was the night that the Nazis conquered Proszowice. He decides to retell this story during the flight, simply ignoring the fact that he's told it to me dozens of times. But I won't let yet another repetition upset me. I listen intently, checking my own memory against his story-telling.

"In the house of Uncle Moshe the slaughterer, there was a relatively well- protected basement. We hid, several of us, including my family. Don't forget that our house was made of wood and about to collapse any day even without the earth-shaking bombings. That night a bloody battle raged between the German and Polish armies for control of Proszowice. The Poles preferred to handle the battle outside Kraków to avoid damaging the beautiful old city, which was much more important to them. That's how Proszowice's residents found themselves right in the range of fire at the heart of the battle out in the town's fields."

"Among the people hiding there, in addition to our family, was David Shohat and his family and the house's owners, Yisrael Goldkorn, Beileh Izbicki, and Moshe Shohat. Later on, we were all joined by Leibish Bendiner and his wife Perl. They came in the middle of the night, bundles of bedding slung over their shoulders. The bedding had holes where bullets had grazed but had not penetrated the bundles as they zigzagged their way through the town's streets. They burst into the shelter, hysterically screaming, "Fellow Jews! The town is surrounded by flames. The whole town is burning!"

The men began reciting Psalms, praying to G-d to protect them, to save them from the hands of their enemy, "Though I walk through the valley of the shadow of death, let no harm come to me for You are always with me," they cried from the depths of their hearts, hoping for the best, and not knowing that what they were going through was barely the beginning of what would yet be.

For over five hours the battle raged in Proszowice. Jewish soldiers also fought. At 6 a.m. the next day, as dawn broke, the shooting faded. The Germans had fully conquered the town.

Children were the first out on the streets. Fearful adults preferred to remain hidden a while longer. Abba was 13. Leaving the basement, he climbed the street's stairway, heading for the town center where the acrid stench of burning filled the air. Thick smoke carried the smell of burning flesh, tires, and fuel. In the market square Abba saw, for the first time in his life, German soldiers, one of whom was chasing a Jew who was desperately trying to flee. The soldier gave up the chase and simply shot at him but the Jewish man darted away and disappeared around the street corner. Tanks filled the market square. Their cannons were aimed at Abba and at a group of children who'd also come out from their hiding places.

Young German soldiers sat on the tanks. One played with a puppy, caressing it as though it were a baby. Other German soldiers just looked around at the burning houses, blank looks on their faces. Abba glanced at the houses in flames; knowing which house belonged to whom, he began to feel very anxious about his neighbors. Were the families still inside? German officers in knee-high black boots and binoculars hanging on their chests, wandered about. Further up Slomniki Street was a long line of German trucks packed with armed soldiers. The trucks pulled field cannons mounted on racks with rubber wheels. The German military was taking a brief respite as it waited for their next batch of orders. One officer, tall and with a pleasant face, signaled to Abba.

"I remember him saying, 'Come here, young fellow.' So, I climbed up hesitantly onto the truck. The German officer held out a loaf of bread. 'Here, take it, young man. Are you hungry?' I nodded, took the bread and pulled a chunk off, to show him that I was about to eat. But I halted for a moment, remembering that at school we'd been warned about taking food or sweets from the Germans because of the very real fear that it could be poisoned. Immediately afterwards, logic kicked in. The way the officer had offered it to me seemed very honest, not to mention that I had little choice. Refusing a German soldier could prove fatal.

"The loaf tucked firmly under my arm, I looked around. Dozens of corpses lay across the marketplace: Polish soldiers and horses. Numerous wagons and carts were overturned and in flames. The municipal building, the prison, Yoshchick Houses, the Blumenfrucht family's home in the city center – all burning like torches. My grandmother's house was on fire, too. We tried to put the fire out, but the Germans wouldn't let us get close. It was their revenge against people who'd dared to oppose them. Now they simply hung around and stared at the destruction.

"On the other side of the street I noticed a familiar beard and sidelocks: Moshe Ginzberg lay on the ground, shot, blood oozing from him, packages of matzah strewn nearby. He must have been on his way home, bringing food for his children. A few buildings farther away was our synagogue and study hall; it, too, shot tongues of flame upwards. I caught sight of several Torah scrolls ripped and burning.

"In Głowackiego Street, next to Shlomo Blum's house, lay a dead Polish soldier, but his body was on fire. I wanted to drag him away and put the flames out but suddenly I saw a German officer next to me, his gun drawn. 'Leave that pig alone!' he screamed at me. He went over to the body and stamped with sheer cruelty. The corpse broke into two.

"On Kraków Street, several Polish soldiers surrendered. Their weapons were taken and they were led away with their arms raised. Suddenly a German jumped up behind them and shot them, right there in the middle of the street, in broad daylight, in front of everyone. For no reason! I couldn't understand the scenario. How can you shoot captured soldiers? The Germans, it seemed, had no rules. I wondered whether each German sets his own rules. And that's what the town looked like when the Germans took it over — death and destruction everywhere."

Abba paused briefly before continuing. "Terrible, for a boy of 13 to see such brutal scenes!" He paused again, but only for a minute. "What I didn't know then was that the worst was yet to come."

That's how it is when you travel with Abba. You need to be ready to hear and experience the story again, from start to finish, as though you'd never heard it before. And what if you have? Doesn't matter. Hear it again! You can't get out of not hearing it.

Exhaustion began to envelope me. I'd spent long days preparing for this trip. I was nervous and had hardly slept the night before the flight. Closing my eyes, sleep was a blessing.

"Ladies and gentlemen..."

My eyelids fly open. The captain is announcing that "In a few minutes we'll begin our descent into Kraków Airport."

An easy landing, as befits El Al. We disembark. When Abba's feet touch the ground, I chuckle and wish him, "Welcome home, Abba."

His answer carries a serious tone. "What home? This is blighted land, infused with bitter memories and never-ending longing." I know that he means his lost family. I see his eyes following a group of Polish cleaners going aboard to clean the plane.

They stand in a line. El Al's security commander, a young Israeli proud of his country and standing very straight, checks each of them meticulously with the magnetometer before they go on board. Their posture is one of submission, arms raised to allow the device's movement, while the security commander calmly carries out the thorough checking procedure.

His mouth agape, Abba stands there watching, not believing. "Is this the end of days, Arie?" he asks rhetorically. "To see Poles standing like that, getting checked by Jews? Who'd have thought it?"

I draw him away towards the waiting bus as I bend down to whisper in his ear. "Abba, he's Jewish, sure, but more than that, he's Israeli, and without our country, without Israel, we'd never have reached the day that we can watch out for ourselves!"

Meeting the Proszowice Mayor

We're shown in for a preparatory meeting with the mayor of Proszowice. He's young, new in his role, and the first Pole I've encountered who speaks fluent English and is technologically proficient. His room holds a large screen connected to a laptop, and every topic that comes up in our discussion is accompanied by visual content displayed on the screen. It helps keep the conversation moving smoothly along.

In addition to the mayor, Abba, and me, a Proszowice resident is in the office with us: Wiestaw Paluch, a good friend of Abba's, is a pensioner who worked for the municipality in the past, remained politically active, and handles Abba's interests in the town. He's also the man who has the keys to the Jewish cemetery and is called on every time someone wants to visit or pray there.

The mayor seemed to be a well-seasoned politician, pen-minded enough to take on changes. He lets a photojournalist into the meeting to take a quick set of pictures for press releases and social media, including Twitter. The mayor is concerned about what Abba might say in his speech and is interested in the overall message, i.e., that the event is taking place despite the crisis in Poland-Israel affairs around the role of Poles vis-à-vis Jews in the Holocaust.

The conclusion I reach is that the Poles of today are indeed sorry — to some degree or another — that the Jews have been pushed out of their lives, possibly because there's now no one that Poles can blame for any of the Polish government's unsuccessful policies or the Polish people's everyday difficulties. Fascinatingly, wherever you look, indicators of Jewish culture remain highly evident reminders of the impact Jewish life had on the country.

Most of the Poles are quite sympathetic, cultured, show support, and speak with affectionate nostalgia about us, the Jews. The church has also taken on a more placating approach, particularly under the last two popes, one of whom was Polish, which helps drive religious harmony. When I mention this to Abba, his instantaneous response is: "Arie, that's nonsense. It's simply because we now have a strong country."

I watch the meeting progress and think about the symbolic counterpoints: the mayor is young, Polish, Christian, and a politician in body and mind. Everywhere in Poland, Christianity is visible. The wall of the mayor's office is adorned by a large cross, and the Proszowice emblem bears the image of "Jan," as John the Baptist is known here, famous in Christian tradition for having baptized the Jewish Jesus as a Christian. In utter contrast, here's Abba, elderly, Jewish, representing the story of the township's residents, lacking any political mannerism, but equipped with life experiences, smart thinking, vigilance, and, most of all, an amazing degree of flexibility and adaptation to any situation, as the Talmud indeed advises: "One should endeavor to be as flexible as the reed rather than as hard as cedar." Abba is doing all he can to win the mayor's trust; after all, it's the mayor who holds the keys to the local Jewish cemetery's future and the continued perpetuation of the Jewish presence up until 1942.

Mostly, the mayor is worried about what Abba will say. G-d forbid that nothing violate recently passed Polish laws about casting responsibility for the Holocaust on the Poles. Abba, for his part, is thinking about how to promote Poland-Israel relations and their shared interests here in Proszowice. In practical terms, achievements thus far include reciprocal visits, exchanges of viewpoints, educating the youth on the importance of acknowledging and respecting each other, and even the cemetery's clean-up and some level of care and restoration.

That's how Abba is. He recalls the past as he lives and enjoys the present while optimistically working to better the future.

The meeting ends. Abba is pleased. "Did you notice that I can think like they do? I understand what's bothering them, and in the end we all moved forward – us, and the Poles." And then he adds his signature summary, meant not only for others but primarily for himself: "Was it a good meeting?"

And in the question is the answer.

I know Abba well, but the mayor was a refreshing surprise. We, as Jews, always prefer to see the half-full glass and focus on it as we build the future. It's epitomized in the blessing repeated every year throughout the millennia of exile: "Next year in Jerusalem." This meeting is a form of realizing that blessing, and I feel that relative to my own personal angle, I did find what I was seeking.

Proszowice under Nazi Occupation

Meeting the mayor was the opening volley in a series of preparatory actions for the upcoming event. Meanwhile, Abba scored his first achievement: The meeting was considered to be a success.

Leaving city hall, we breathe in the crisp air and the town's atmosphere. The municipal building is part-way down the sloping street leading from the city square, and just minutes away from Abba's destroyed childhood home. We decide to leave the rented car in the municipal parking lot and walk, releasing some of the tension. The more we mingle with people in the street going about their daily routines, unlike us, the more Abba catches the dialect he knew so well. It takes him back to those long-ago times. I glance at him, thinking how ironic it is that the more we advance in time, the more he goes back. I let him be, respecting his silence with my own.

He stops, suddenly, and turns to speak. He begins, not about the meeting we've just had, not about the mayor, but without any introduction, delves into one of his memories.

"You know, Arie, we spoke about this," he says softly, almost as though to himself. Just to be sure, though, he repeats my name. "Arie, from the first moment after the Germans took over the town, the Jews tasted the bitterness of German rule. Jews were snatched up by force for hard labor. The immediate tasks were to bury the dead soldiers and horses and clean the streets of the ashes piled up by the burnt houses."

"The Jews got used to the way we were kidnapped by the Germans. Even if we'd wanted to, we couldn't oppose them. Later, a Jewish community led by Rabbi Getzel Pińczewski was organized. Getzel was head of the new Judenrat, and recruiting Jews for work was carried out in a more systematic fashion. Based on carefully prepared lists, the community provided Jews who swept the streets, cleared snow, cleaned the German offices, did field work, paved roads, and did other jobs in Pietkiewicz, the neighboring town. Dread filled us all. When you left your house in the morning for an assigned job, you never knew if you'd come back. Where might they take you? Where would you eat? What would you need to do? Would you see your Mama and Tateh in the evening? Perhaps something would happen to you along the way."

Abba's return to the town through his stories causes him to relive the agony and sorrow, even though for a long time he has fully understood that in retrospect, there was almost no chance of surviving the harsh reality of those times. Abba realizes that as a child he was exposed to the dangers of death, and as time passed, the cruelty intensified. Every story spins around a death-related axis, recurrently summed up in one of two phrases: "Too bad I didn't die then," or "If I'd died then, I'd have been saved so much pain and suffering."

He tried to explain what he meant, but every story scarred my soul a touch more throughout my childhood without my realizing it back then. How can a child explain to his father that it's great that he didn't die, because otherwise how would he have been born? Doesn't he get that? But in our family, talk of loss, death, and bereavement were woven into our daily lives and mingled with the joys that also came along. That was the standard fare I knew most intimately, and which enabled me to understand, to some limited extent, why my family had only a father, mother, sisters, and one grandmother, but no aunts and uncles or cousins. Where was everyone? Something wasn't normal in the fundamental concept of "family" for us. It defies childhood logic.

How ironic, I thought as Abba and I stood there, thousands of kilometers from home, to be in Proszowice, which catapults us both back to our childhoods: his of the 1940s and mine of the 1960s. We're together, our legs are on the same square of Proszowice sidewalk, but the thoughts in each of our heads are as different as chalk and cheese, distanced by time and place. Abba's thinking about what might happen to him in the future; I'm thinking about what happened to him in the past.

Abba talks as though reliving the moment. "At this point, various decrees were announced concerning the Jews. Every Jew aged ten and up – me among them, of course – must wear white armbands with a blue Star of David. Everyone must hand over their fur coats. None of us can walk on the sidewalks. No one can leave the town. Leaving town without a permit is a crime that is punishable by death. More and more rules, incomprehensible and demeaning, joined the list; their only purpose was to demoralize and undermine Jewish unity.

Jewish refugees from Łódź and Kraków began streaming into Proszowice and the surrounding villages. Before its annihilation, the town's population swelled to more than 5,000 people, of whom about half were Jewish. The town's Jews did what they could to help refugees at least find a roof over their heads. Countless Jews shared their homes with their fellow Jews. Because the community needed to supply daily quotas of hundreds of workers, local wealthy Jews would pay and send the refugees out in their stead. This allowed the locals to work in their professions or trade with the non-Jews from nearby villages. Trading with non-Jewish locals was also extremely risky and conducted under the constant threat of the death if caught.

"Concerned about the incoming refugees, a soup kitchen was set up despite the difficulties experienced by the local Jewish population. But having been educated to do good deeds, to be compassionate to others, to show the solidarity and mutuality that are so fundamental to Judaism, overrode any other consideration. It's how Jewish refugees who'd had no choice but to leave everything they owned behind, even their money and their respect, could nonetheless enjoy a bowl of hot soup and slice of bread every day, thus staving off their hunger.

"Proszowice Jews were a mixed bunch. Begging just didn't take place among them, and even in the harshest of times, Proszowice Jews never took untoward advantage of the soup kitchen set up for refugees. This let the refugees enjoy the town's support, such as it was. It was an act of pure caring, which the non-Jewish neighbors clearly noticed."

"On top of these difficulties, typhus broke out. The Germans warned the Poles to have no contact whatsoever with the Jews. Every day, scores of us fell ill after being infected. Dr. Lepholz, the municipality's Jewish physician, took care of the sick Jewish patients with tremendous dedication, doing all he could under very limited conditions. Then one day our savior came down with the sickness, too, and there was no one to save him. He managed to recover, converted to Christianity, and his Christian neighbors hid him throughout the whole war. When it was over, he returned to being Jewish, emigrated to Israel, and lived in Haifa. A few years later he passed away."

"In 1940 a convoy of Nazi soldiers from Kraków turned up to run a check at the house of Gershon Wolf Grundman, uncle of Yakov Grundman, who survived and became Israel's national soccer team's coach and manager, and a successful businessman as well. They arrested Gershon, confiscated his large truck, and as punishment for doing business with Poles, sent him to Auschwitz. Several months later the family received notice that he'd been murdered there."

"In fact, Gershon was Proszowice's first Jewish murder victim in Auschwitz after the Nazis took over the town."

Occupation's New Routines

We pass the town's main square, which is adjacent to the large church, then turn towards the town school and stop to rest on a bench. I want to take in the town's atmosphere. In his mind Abba continues living the early 1940s. And he continues telling me the tale.

"One Shabbat early in 1942 a Nazi clerk named Gorniak arrived from Kraków, together with Beckman, the Nazi clerk from Michów. They ordered everyone in the community aged 12– 62 to come out for a lineup – both men and women. Dressed in his SS uniform, Beckman set himself up in the community offices. Gorniak wore civilian clothing. They were joined by the community head, Getzel Pińczewski, and the secretary, Ruhama Lichtenstein. Right here was the community center," Abba points to an old two-story building in the town's center.

"The building's street entrance led to an internal courtyard that was overlooked by a balcony on the second floor. Here in the courtyard," Abba's voice drops to a whisper suddenly, and his gaze darts from side to side, as though fearing someone might overhear and understand us before he continues in whispered Yiddish, as he did in Israel, too, when he wanted to say something to me that he didn't want my friends to understand, "here, six innocent Jews were buried."

I shudder. "Right here?" I ask.

"Yes."

Firmly and with concern, I suggest, "So let's make sure we exhume them and bring them to burial in Israel!"

Glancing again to each side to be sure no one's listening in or understands us, Abba continues to whisper. "They've already been removed. I'll tell you about it later. Not here." That shunts my question aside, leaving me feeling defeated. Is he trying to distract me, I wonder. But he reads my mind and knows I won't let the issue slip by, so he reassures me, "When we're back in the hotel, I'll tell you." And again, I'm deflected as he looks for ways to gain time. He ignores my curiosity and continues his story.

"The Jewish men in that age range, 12 to 62, got themselves into alphabetical order and each stated his profession and current occupation. You know," he looks me in the eye, "there's no messing around with the Germans. Time is time!" He pauses, taking a deep breath before continuing. "A few days afterwards, Commander Beckman came to Getzel as head of the Judenrat, and ordered him to assemble all those who'd come late to work over the past few days, together with all the others in the community courtyard."

"At the end of that workday we all marched to the community courtyard as the Germans had instructed. Standing at the entrance was Herr Beckman, carefully counting us to be sure those present were on the list. He ordered someone to bring him a chair. Then he called out names – mine among them – and stood us to the side."

He stops talking to be sure I've caught all the details correctly, which makes me even more curious.

"Beckman screamed at us that by coming late to work, we were sabotaging work at the German "Strauss" factory and he'd teach us a thing or two! As punishment, each of us was to be whipped 20 times with a pliable, and therefore highly painful, rod. Beckman turned to the people there and asked, 'Who volunteers to carry out the whippings?' He was met with a frightening silence. No one was willing to do that to a friend at the Nazi's cruel demand. Not getting what he wanted, he turned to Moshe Leibenberg, a tall, chubby boy standing in the crowd. 'You, the tall fat one, you must have plenty of strength, so whip this boy here,' he said as he pointed to me."

"I went white at the thought of what awaited me," Abba continues. "Big Moshe pleaded with Beckman like a child, his eyes filled with tears. 'Sir,' he wept, trying to stop the tears from falling, 'I can't hit him. He's my neighbor, my friend.' 'Then you get down on your knees too!' the German commander bellowed at Moshe. Then Beckman ordered his German driver to whip us both, which he did – first me, then Moshe, me again, then Moshe again, and so on – 20 times. The sound echoed through the town's alleys where our mothers were gathered. They raised their arms, begging, beseeching, wailing, absorbing every swish of the whip in their souls."

"The community was given permission to make matzah for Passover 1942 and a spark of hope was lit in our hearts: the Proszowicenka Matzah brand was in high demand back then. But right after Pesach," Abba used the Hebrew word for the week-long festival, "urgent dispatches of Jews were sent to the Płaszów and Prokocim forced labor centers near Kraków. But the regular work of the municipality also had to be carried out. The number of workers needed was greater than the number of adults living in Proszowice, and the community couldn't recruit the necessary quota."

"The German employment office put the job of recruiting workers onto the community's shoulders, demanding that all teens aged 14 and up come to what had been the school, right here near the community office," Abba points. "Many of us, including me, didn't respond to the community's request and didn't show up. As punishment, the OD guys showed up; Ordnungspolizei are uniformed Jewish police who arrested the errant kids' parents, which meant that Tateh was also arrested."

Abba's face shows shame. "The crying and wailing in our house broke my heart. My little brothers cried all the way to the community courtyard as they accompanied Tateh. Shmuel Solewicz and blind Mordechai Nigoslavski were already there. The

Germans made it very clear to our parents that if their children don't present themselves, they'll be sent to the concentration camp and there even G-d won't be able to help them."

"Abba," I butt in and ask, "but what about the bodies?" because that issue's really bothering me now. But Dad is focused on chronology, although he does relate to my question in some way.

"Wait. Just be patient. We'll get to that. You need to understand the background and the reason before you get the answer," and he returns to the narrative the way he wants it laid out.

He's so obstinate, I think to myself, but Abba holds the reins here.

"When I saw Tateh being led away in handcuffs, humiliated, through the town's streets, my mind was battling with the idea that I had no right to take my father away from his younger children and leave them orphans. Of course not – so I ran to the school via the marketplace."

"It was a cold, overcast day. A shallow puddle of mud was building up at the school's entrance. My family, standing at the gate, was very surprised to see me come at a run. Dozens of parents were already gathered there. My mother's gaze followed me closely. On the one hand, she preferred that I go to work in Płaszów rather than Tateh, but on the other, it was hard for her to accept that her young, inexperienced son would have to live alone in a strange place. Her cry is etched in my memory. 'Oy! Our children will be lost in that foreign place!' and those are the words that accompanied me up to the building's entrance.

"I was put into the second group of arrested youngsters. The German officer questioned us about why I'd turned up late, adding a liberal number of slaps to our faces, and ordering us to be handcuffed. Several Polish policemen led us through the town's yards to the local prison. Our families trailed behind us, weeping bitterly.

"Two days later we were sent, as planned, to the Płaszów labor camp. The town's Jews gathered at the prison's entrance to hand out food and backpacks and walk alongside us, as encouragement. It was Friday; we called it 'black Friday.' Families said farewell to their sons, people hugged, embraced, wailed, kissed, blessed each other, and spoke words of well-wishing, saying that we'd yet all meet, safe and sound.

"There was a bit of drama a few minutes before getting into the bus that drove us to the labor camp. Prisoners' names were announced according to a list prepared in advance. Motl Freiman was the 50th name. I was the 51st. Behind the scenes, negotiations were taking place with the head of the community. Since I was only 15 and Motl was already 20, the suggestion to release me was raised, especially since I also functioned as a community messenger. The community pressured to have me freed, but the Freiman family paid a bribe to have Motl released, so instead, I was sent to the Płaszów labor camp.

"Mama and Tateh waited for me next to the bus, and so did Grandma Haya. All the generations and their families. Everyone hugged and kissed me. Tateh handed me a backpack with my tefillin bag. 'Son,' he said, 'put your tefillin on every day, no matter what. These are the tefillin that Grandpa Yehezkel, the scribe, sent from Kelcz. He wrote them especially for you. And that was my grandfather's final wish before he passed away. G-d will protect you from all evil if you do this, and bring you back to us safe and sound.' Like a bad dream, the bus drove past the town. On the way I could still hear the cries and moans. That image has stayed with me, unforgettably. We reached Płaszów towards evening.

"See, Arie," Abba suddenly assails me with one of his tales of humiliation, which run through my mind like frames of film. "At 15, instead of going to the scouts camp with my classmates,

I was taken against my will, battered, beaten and humiliated, together with people a lot older than me, to the Nazi camp for hard labor. That was my fate, and that was what I had to contend with."

Reb Getzel Pińczewski, Head of the Proszowice Judenrat: How He Was Chosen, His Role, and His Bitter End

Abba is ready to move on and leave the bench next to the Jewish Community House, but I'm still stuck on those six people buried in its yard. This mystery drives me to urge Abba to tell that tale; I couldn't help wondering if he was trying to blur the details and prevent me from grabbing a shovel and digging right then and there. With obvious reluctance, he sits back down and begins the tale from the beginning. Initially it's amusing, but then changes altogether. In my mind, I remember something that a good friend once said: "It begins with parody, continues on to drama, and ends in tragedy."

And so Abba tells me how Getzel Pińczewski became the Head of the Judenrat and sorrowfully describes how his role ended.

"Right after they entered the town in September 1939, the Germans began snatching Jews and sending them to work. Once the gunshots died down and we left our shelter, a horrible scream was heard from a German soldier. 'You're under arrest! Come here!' At first, I thought it was directed at me, but the soldier clearly meant a black-haired, pot-bellied Jew.

He was clean-shaven, his skin was dark, his nose aquiline, and his black eyes shone. 'Are you Jewish?' the soldier asked. The man paled a little and gazed back. 'What's your name?' the German asked.

"His voice trembling, the man answered, 'Getzel Pińczewski.' 'Stand right here,' the German commanded. Then Rabbi Abba Wachs was brought there, as well as Volf Rotmantsch, and many others familiar from the community. The German had them stand next to the dead horses and soldiers' corpses and asked another German to take a photo of him as he grasped Rabbi Wachs' beard. Then the soldier roared, 'Now, Jews, to work!' as he ordered them to clear the horses, the corpses, and the remains of the violent battle."

"Once they'd finished, the German soldier asked them a question. 'Who is the oldest Jew in town?' What the German meant was who was in charge of the town's affairs. Reb Getzel Pińczewski didn't seem to understand what the German wanted. He heard 'oldest Jew' and thought he meant in years, not in terms of authority, so he raised his hand. 'Are you the elder of the Jews?' the soldier asked again. Getzel glanced at the rabbi and wondered: 'His level of honor is greater than mine, but I am older. So he nodded. Rabbi Wachs' silence also made Getzel think that indeed he'd answered correctly. 'In that case, from now on you're responsible for work getting done in the town,' the soldier told him, so that's how Getzel Pińczewski became the Head of the Proszowice Judenrat."

I'd met Abba's cousin Eliezer Jurista, the only one of the extended family who survived. Older than Abba, he lived in Haifa's Kiryat Eliezer neighborhood. What I hadn't known was that he'd been married with children, and lost his entire family in the Shoah. Even his own children from his second marriage and his rehabilitated life, and with whom I was familiar, didn't know the story.

Eager to confiscate Jewish property, the German showed up one day to run an audit on Eliezer, seeking fur pelts. Every Jew in town fled indoors and watched from their windows in fear. The greatest tragedy imaginable that any Jew could experience was taking place inside the house. The German officer's loaded gun lay on the table. Eliezer stood with his face turned to the wall and his arms raised, his face white, his body engulfed in a cold sweat, certain he was about to faint. His wife, mother-in-law, and children wept bitterly at the humiliation and beating their father was getting while the Gestapo head, Kozak, ripped the leather coverings off the mattresses in order to confiscate them while shouting, "You Jewish pig! Where are your other possessions?"

"Meanwhile, two Polish policemen tried to tempt Eliezer and advised him to jump from the landing. They planned to shoot him as he jumped but instead, he froze where he stood. Only Getzel Pińczewski, who had ties to Kozak, would be able to save Eliezer's life. But where was Getzel? The town's Jews believed that Getzel was in hiding until the German calmed down.

"Reb Getzel suddenly came running in, breathlessly bursting into Eliezer's house. He greeted the German, cleverly sweet-talking him in front of the soldier while indicating to Eliezer to kiss the German's hands. Miserable, Eliezer did as Getzel urged. 'Kiss them more. Give it all you've got. Rip the mattresses one by one. Add money and the commander will have mercy on your life.' Eventually the commander was gratified, took the furs and left, leaving Eliezer to combat his humiliation."

He survived the Shoah, he survived Buchenwald, remarried, moved to Israel and raised a family there. Uncle Eliezer Jurista never spoke about this. When he passed away, Abba told his children about his history.

"And the bodies..." I prompt, leaning back on the bench to show that I won't move until I hear the story. Nonchalantly,

Abba says, "Earlier you were thinking that I'm stubborn, yes? But just know that you're more stubborn than I am!"

His quip takes me by surprise. How could he know what I was thinking? Another proof of the binary communication between us. We don't need to talk in order to communicate, and once again Abba's caught on that in my mind I'm agreeing with him. But the stubborn fellow who is my father picks up the tale from a point of his choosing.

"Getzel had developed a good relationship with the Germans, and especially with Kozak, the Gestapo commander in charge of Jewish property in the Michów District. Every Shabbat the Nazi showed up to eat lunch with them. Several weeks of relative calm later, the Pińczewski family's tragedy occurred.

"A surprise visit to Proszowice was made by Martin Friedrich Breilin, the Michów District Gestapo Commander, whose authority included responsibility for looted Jewish property throughout the district. Of course that included Proszowice. He was accompanied by his driver and David Bialobroda, a Jewish collaborator from Slomniki, activated by the Proszowice Nazis. All three showed up on Shabbat afternoon. They went straight to the community offices and ordered the community head to appear with his five sons. Getzel immediately sensed that something was very wrong. Usually, guests of such importance would come to his house for lunch, but Bialobroda, a good friend of Getzel's, noticed the panic in Getzel's eyes and swore to him on all that was holy that there was no reason to be afraid, since he and Friedrich knew him well and trusted him. Getzel's sons came, one at a time, and once all were there, the horror of a kind only Germans could devise took place.

"Ruhama Lichtenstein, the Judenrat's secretary, told me what she'd seen and heard. Bialobroda went out into the street and pulled the ropes off one of the wagons tied up there. With the help of the Gestapo officer and the driver, the three wound the rope around Getzel's arms and hung the poor man on the window of Fishel Shapira's house, right here next to the community house's second-floor balcony," Abba pointed, "with Getzel's face turned to the former prison."

Friedrich accused Getzel and his sons of exploitation and defrauding the German government because Proszowice Jews left too little silver and gold behind following the deportation. He found the loot unsatisfactory; therefore, in the name of German justice, they deserved to die by shooting. No amount of begging and pleading by Getzel that he was innocent and that the claims were untrue simply because Proszowice Jews were not well off would change Friedrich's stance.

Clearly Getzel had outlived his usefulness. He also knew too much about Friedrich Breilin's and Kozak's personal stashes of booty, and would need to be permanently silenced. That Shabbat afternoon, in late October 1942, as the sun began to set, Getzel's five sons, from oldest to youngest, some of whom were married and had young children, were shot dead in the community courtyard as their father watched. Getzel was taken down from the rope with critical injuries. He could barely move his legs.

"He cried out, 'My children, my children! G-d in heaven, they're all here. Yidl, Berish, Shmerl, Yossl, Leizer,'" Abba recalls their names. "Falling onto the sons, some still taking their last breaths, Getzel cried out, *"Sh'ma Yisrael!"* (Hear O' Israel) He turned to the murderer. 'What are you waiting for? Shoot! Go on, shoot me too. And fast!' The Nazi laughed at Getzel's misery, winked at his driver and his Jewish collaborator, and filled Getzel's body with gunshots. Once he'd calmed down, he put one bullet in the head of each of the six dead men."

Countless residents watched the incident from a nearby hilltop, mourning this tragic end. Friedrich ordered them buried right there where they lay next to the prison building. From the upper floor, Notte Leib Feiner's daughter, her infant in her arms, saw the German kill her beloved husband. Ruhama Lichtenstein, Getzel's brother Kalman, Mordechair Kleiner, Ozer Feigeh, and several other Jews buried the dead, and that's where their bodies remained until 1952.

"Gabriel Grundman's family, hidden throughout the war with Christians, vowed that if they survived, they'd make sure to provide the six deceased Pińczewskis with a proper Jewish burial," Abba explains. "In 1952, before the Grundmans left for Israel, they reburied Getzel and his sons in the Kraków Jewish cemetery. May their souls be granted eternal life."

The Pińczewskis' violent end upsets me deeply. I make a note to check whether their bodies are indeed in the Kraków Cemetery, or whether Abba has altered the story's end so that I don't take some kind of rash, unplanned action. Has he simply prepared the ground for further details later on? Abba is a master tactician and uses his skill to shorten procedures. For example, he wrote his memoirs but for years refused to publish them. He repeatedly said, "When I'm gone, do with the material whatever you want." In our private language, that means he gave me the green light to act the way I think appropriate rather than continue his way. This is the thrust of the insider language that clues me in to his answers without needing to ask the questions.

We go back to our car and drive to Kraków. The scenery reminds Abba of the days when he constantly fled Nazis, the Jewish police, home, the forced labor camp, finding himself taking the same route back and forth like a hunted animal, never finding a place to rest. A few minutes later he takes up the thread again.

Fleeing the Forced Labor Camp for Proszowice

Abba talks about his experiences as though they're taking place in the here and now. His story still piques my curiosity, even though I've heard it countless times. It keeps us busy as we quickly make our way to our hotel in Kraków, a hot shower and a clean bed after a tense, exhausting day. A comforting thought.

"After I turned myself in, we were transferred to the Kraków area due to a need for laborers to lay railroad tracks. The physical work was tough, even without adding the abuse I'd just taken."

I try to interject. He insists on the monologue and continues. "Don't forget that I was only 15," he says, ignoring the fact that I want to speak. "The German experts related to us cruelly. Albert, the expert on setting railway sleepers, would whack me with a metal rod as I worked, add harsh physical punishment, and once even shot a prisoner to death right in front of me in order to prove his cruelty."

"I wrote sad letters home. Longing broke my heart. The letters got through via couriers, mostly youth who'd flee the forced labor camps and would run the Kraków-Proszowice route. Later on I also became a courier. In one of the letters I received from home, my mother asked if the rumor was true that we were beaten and tortured as we worked. With the innocence of a youngster, I answered that anything they heard in town is nothing compared to the reality we face. That sent the town into an uproar. For days afterwards I couldn't forgive myself for writing so blatantly and making my parents and those of my friends so worried and miserable. What did I expect by pouring my heart out? And anyhow, what could our parents have done?"

"As time passed, things got worse. Guards became stricter. Work was accompanied by more beatings. Terrible rumors were leaking from the Kraków Ghetto that a list of Jews aged 55 and over had been made in readiness for a deportation eastward. The words "eastwards" or "east" became synonymous with extermination at the renowned Belzec concentration camp.

"I managed to sneak off to the Jewish cemetery in Kraków's Jerusalimska (Jeruzulimskiej) Street during work hours. I got friendly with the grave digger, Mr. Koza, in June 1942. I was there with him when we watched an 'aktzia' (a deportation), the first one in the Kraków Ghetto. I saw how they deported the Jews. From the distance I could identify Moshe Yeshurun Blumenfeld, my uncle, and the Proszowice cantor. He strode with his head held high and his long beard giving him a regal appearance. From a distance he looked like a spiritual leader, maybe the way we imagine Moses leading the Children of Israel through the wilderness. His wife and daughters walked alongside him, followed by thousands of Jews – really like the exodus from Egypt, except that in reality this was Poland, 1942, and they were being taken eastward to oppression and death.

"From my observation point at the cemetery, I saw how the Germans were moving closed cattle cars that had carried chlorine and lime. They shoved thousands of elderly people, and women and children into them. It was heart- wrenching to see. Entire families, with children, with babies. Any older people who couldn't – or refused to board – were simply shot dead. Each cattle car was stuffed with about 150 people, and the doors slammed shut and locked. I saw a Jewish sanitary worker following Nazi instructions to shove the people on board suddenly see his wife, his own children, inside a cattle car. I heard him beg the German to let him join his family. 'There's no point in my living,' he cried over and over, but the German wouldn't open the door and let him inside. When the man tried forcing his way in, the Nazi just shot him. He fell dead, right there. A tragic, horrific scene. Children and the elderly sobbed and howled. Those sounds rang in my ears for many years afterwards.

"When the train pulled out, we found hundreds of photos and notes. People I didn't know were making their last wishes known, e.g., 'Should anyone find this please give it to their remaining family,' and so on.

"After June's deportation, the German command in the camp where I worked changed and we were treated even more cruelly. The new commander beat us mercilessly. Our food rations were reduced. We wandered around starving, beaten, and demeaned. One day an SS officer showed up: Franz Jozef Miller. That evening he ordered us all to line up while he gave a threat-filled speech: 'From now on you'll lack for nothing in the camp. If you leave without a permit, your punishment will be death. But if you obey my commands you won't lack for anything.' The next day two boys from Stopnica fled. They were caught not far from Kraków and returned to the camp. Franz Jozef shot them in front of us and let their bodies rot near the toilets for a full day. The message was clear: 'Learn a lesson, because this is what happens if you try to escape.'

"Despite, or maybe because of, the terrible scene where the two boys were killed, the next day I decided to flee, too. I took circuitous paths that added more than 40 kilometers until I reached home. I lay in bed for several days in a state of shock and complete exhaustion. My mother, helpless, sat next to me, stroking my face, kissing me over and over. I was pleased with my decision. Very quickly the town found out that I'd escaped, and the Jewish police began hunting for me. They came to the house, disrupted the family, and I had to hide. But I came up with a principle: If I'd eaten somewhere on a certain day I wouldn't stay there to sleep. I never stayed in the same place for two nights in a row. I wandered, sleeping in attics and hay lofts. At home the same question came up repeatedly: Why did I run away? Either way, I have no real peace.

"But that image of the Kraków Jews' roundup, and the knowledge that it'd soon happen in Proszowice, were uppermost in my mind. On the other hand, I'd already gained some experience and didn't say anything to anyone. Only my heart knew what a horrific fate awaited Proszowice – the same as that of Kraków's Jews. That would be the end of us all. My only comfort was the thought that at least I'd be together with my family.

"And on a daily basis, the decrees against Jews got increasingly harsher."

Farewell to the Family Forever

"It was on Friday, August 28, 1942, when Reb Getzel arrived from Michów in a large black car with terrible news: The town was about to be wiped out."

Abba pauses as though hurtling back in time to that moment. His body tenses. It's almost as though he's readying to burst like a shell blasting from a cannon. I see his emotions changing and suggest he take a few sips of water. He takes a long swig, then takes a deep breath as though he's about to dive into deep water, and goes on.

"Getzel Pińczewski immediately convened the Judenrat for an emergency meeting. Lists were drawn up; you know that, Arie," he emphasizes. "The Germans need perfection and order. So, while deportation lists were being drafted, Ruhama, the Judenrat secretary, went down into the yard looking for a quiet spot to digest the news and catch her breath. That was next to

Fishl Shapira's house. She noticed me, called me over, and whispered a secret to me. 'Flee as fast as you can. Tomorrow there's going to be an aktzia. Tell that to everyone you meet along the way, but for heaven's sake don't mention my name.' I was shaken by the fear in her voice, something I'd never heard before, and it made me certain that this was indeed not a false alarm but the truth. I stared hard at her face. Tears filled the eyes of his precious woman.

"I felt my body tense, and my skin became full of goosebumps. I broke into a crazy run home, passing the homes of friends and acquaintances, all of whom I told. Don't forget that for a long time I'd been a community runner, too, transferring messages among the community's families, so I had an excellent path tracked out. First, I told Adela Bick; her son Yossl was the friend I'd flee with later on. She instantly packed some of his things and ordered him to go back to the forced labor camp he'd escaped from several days earlier. Then I told the Nirnberg family, refugees from Kraków, and many others.

"Finally I reached home. 'Mama!' I called out with a rush of emotion as I burst into the house, 'the end, it's the bitter end.' My mother was extremely upset, in a manner untypical of her usual reactions. 'Gevald!' she began repeating, 'Terrible, terrible!' 'Where are all the children? Run, bring them all home. Heshel!' she called out to Tateh, 'come, get some bundles ready. What a hard life...' she broke down crying.

"Just a week earlier my brother and I had collected several sheaves of wheat, and dried and ground them. It's what most of the kids were doing at the time. That Friday, mother woke me early. 'My son, wake up. If you've brought a sack of wheat grains, why not use it? Let's grind them. Zamski's barn has grinding stones.' So we all went, ground the grains, and it took hours. We were talking about the June deportation in the Kraków Ghetto, how they'd made the women and children run, constantly urging them on by raining blows down on their back, and shooting alongside them, then shoving them into the cattle cars that reeked from the smell of chlorine and plaster. I imagined my own family instead of those poor people, and tears began rolling down my cheeks. But I made no sound. My mother, sensing what I was going through, asked me quietly if things were difficult for me. I didn't answer. I tried to behave as though nothing at all had happened.

"We were almost finished when I burst into heaving sobs that I couldn't hold back. 'What's wrong?' Mama asked, 'is there something in your eye?' I just said it's nothing. 'Don't worry,' she said, kissing my eyes. 'You'll see that G-d will let us be, and we'll still see joy from you all. G-d is a merciful Father and helps those in need.' That infused a bit of hope into my deep despair.

"I loaded the sack of freshly ground wheat onto my shoulders and left the barn, my eyes half closed because of the tears. There was a small house next to the barn. Its door was open, and the voices of children learning Torah with their teacher, Yankel Shohat, could be heard. The little ones were so enthusiastic; surely their voices would open the gates of heaven. I opened my eyes, feeling a flush of hope and faith. Among the voices I could identify those of my two youngest brothers.

"I remember thinking, 'Children, if only your sweet happiness isn't quashed. Could it be that our town, just 17 kilometers east of Belzec, where Jews are being exterminated, might be the lucky one? If only these sweet voices will continue to be heard for years to come.' Anyhow, we went back home, and Mama set about baking bread to last several days from the grain we'd just ground, and I went out into the community house's yard where Ruhama would convey her bitter message to me.

"Mama was the first to recover. She immediately packed me a bag of food and bread, added a few shirts, and gave everyone instructions. To me she said, 'My child, get out of here as fast as you can before it's too late. Go back to the work camp you fled.' I refused. How could I leave my family? 'No, Mama,' I said with determination, 'I escaped from there to be with you all at this critical time. I can't go back,' I said firmly. 'Here is where I belong. I don't have a greater right than any of you to stay alive.'"

"Mama, Tateh, and my oldest sister forced me to the door and began to shout and cry. 'Run as fast as you can. Don't play smart. Save your life. We know the truth. We've heard your dreams, we've heard you screaming in your sleep that babies and women are being butchered.' Trying hard to convince me, Mama added, 'I'd join you but we won't leave the little ones behind.' Mama put her delicate hands on my cheeks and begged me, 'You don't even have the beginning of a beard yet. You're still a child, and you're already forced to take your fate into your own hands.' My family all kissed me, from the youngest to the oldest, making their farewells with a great deal of crying. Those sounds have never left me. They ring clearly in my mind, as though it is all happening now."

"Suddenly my brother Moshe'leh burst into the house to say that the Polish police, together with the Germans, were surrounding the town. My family literally pushed me forcefully out of the house, hoping that at least I'd somehow save myself.

"At the last minute, Mama pulled out of her dress some money she'd put aside, gave half of it to me, and ordered me to escape. Later I'd wonder why she gave me half of the money, and left the other half for the needs of many more people. She must've sensed something. 'Stay healthy, take care of yourself, and never forget that you're Jewish' were my parents' last words. 'Flesh always fills out again later,' Mama added, but I didn't hear anything more than that. I needed to get going. That's how the family and I separated, and that's how I became an orphan."

***

I park the rental car in the hotel lot. The hotel is in Kraków's Kazimierza Jewish Quarter. The story Abba just recounted has exhausted his mental energy. Lucky we've reached our destination and he'll have to stop talking about the past and shift back to the present. After getting set up in our rooms and enjoying a long, hot shower, I find a moment of quiet for myself and run through the emotionally heavy day I've just been through. What a weight has come down on me. I need time to digest it all.

Fleeing Home

The events that Abba described that day flesh out the story he told me dozens of years earlier on our first visit to Proszowice together in 1993. We were standing on the slope where his house had been. A large park was bordered by houses, among them Abba's childhood home. Behind the park is actually where the town's boundaries lie and the open rural area begins. Signaling to me, Abba indicated his escape route on the day that the Germans encircled the town as part of their plan to purge the area of its Jews. He described the moments following his farewells from his family.

"Yossl Bick meanwhile came tearing down the street. Yossl would later take the name Światowitz. He was calling out to me, huffing and puffing hard. 'C'mon Shmuel, let's run. It's getting late,' he urged. So we did. We went hurtling down that street. I glanced back for a last look at my family, still crowded at the front door and waving. We raced through the fields and reached the train station. Our town was fully surrounded by Polish police and Nazis. We decided to head for the next town, Nowe Brzesko, about 10 kilometers from here. On the way, some four kilometers of panicked running later, we came across a large village, Zebocin."

"Next to the church at the village entrance," Abba signals with his hand before continuing, "we stopped at a group of houses and asked for water. It was warm that day, and running for so long – as well as our fear – had dried our mouths and made us even thirstier. The farmer was decent and gave us water but as we turned to go, we heard someone shout behind us in German: 'Hey, you! Halt! Where's your Judenpass?' referring to a permit allowing movement. It came from an older German in civilian clothes. We ignored him and pretended we couldn't understand, but he insisted we go back with him to Proszowice."

"Yossl immediately responded in a confident tone. 'Oh, no, sir, we're from Kraków, and from his pocket pulled out a group pass for the brick-making factory he worked at in the Kraków Ghetto. 'That has nothing at all to do with Proszowice,' the German shouted as he took his gun out of a leather holster. He diligently checked us, making sure to keep the gun near as a threat. He found my bread and the 500 zlotys Mama had given me just a short while ago. 'Watches?' he asked, not happy with what he already had. We shook our heads. 'Then you're coming with me to Proszowice,' he repeated.

"Yossl whispered to me with a determined tone. 'No, we're not going. They'll shoot us there and that'll sadden our parents terribly. Better we attack him.' I took on a weepy beseeching tone. 'Our lives are in your honor's hands,' I said, still amazed at Yossl's idea. 'Better that you do whatever you feel is right, here and now,' I added. Yossl was signaling that we should break into a run in two opposite directions and at least one of us might be saved. 'Or we could attack him right now and try to get his pistol.'

"It was getting darker. That would increase our chances of fleeing safely. Initially I thought, 'Okay, two young, healthy boys like us could overpower this much older man,' but I wondered if attacking him wouldn't cause other innocent Jews even greater troubles. The Germans had a system where any harm caused to a German would be avenged with the murder of dozens of Jews.

"So I tried my luck once more. I moved a little closer and tried speaking to his conscience, explaining, begging, that we're young, we just want to get through the village on our way back to our labor camp and having heard that our parents would be deported we came to say farewell."

Then Abba bends down to demonstrate how he kissed that German's boots. I'm overcome with a feeling of helplessness, of deep shame, at the demeaning image. Abba continues to describe the situation, not noticing the anger and disgust I'm experiencing.

"The German lowered his gun and tried again, hoping for a different answer. 'Is that all the money you have? You don't have more?' 'That's all we have, sir,' I answered. He peeled off half the notes, and handed the other half back to us. Did he nonetheless feel a pang of pity? 'Today's your lucky day, boys,' he added, although it was clear that he was thinking about what to do with us. 'Some luck,' I was thinking. A few kilometers from here Jews are being murdered but he thinks we're lucky. 'If only I could die instead of my family,' I remember thinking.

"In the distance, a gaggle of people made their way to, or from: wandering about. The German left us and ran after them, no doubt sure he'd make good money from them, too. We didn't need to think twice; we were off running before he could change his mind. After running a few hundred meters, we saw Polish police hurrying off in vans to provide guarding backup for Proszowice. The focus of military and police activities was now on deporting the town's Jews to the east – our families among them."

Later, Yossl and Abba parted ways, but both survived that hell and remained friends to the end of their lives.

* * *

Years later, during the 2016 March of the Living, Abba was in his regular role of accompanying a group to provide live testimony. This time he headed a delegation of Israel Discount Bank employees when he suddenly noticed a group of Korean Christian tourists holding a sign which, on behalf of all peoples of the world, sought forgiveness from the remaining survivors. Moved by this very unusual gesture, Abba left the delegation and walked over to the Christians to thank them.

One of the Koreans noted the number tattooed on Abba's arm. Realizing he was a survivor, he fell to his knees and wept and begged forgiveness. He kissed Abba's shoes as a quick-thinking photographer snapped the moment and uploaded the image to social media. In no time it went viral. My sister, living in Milan, sent me images of it also being featured on worldwide TV stations covering the delegation. I watched Abba's face, beside himself at the embarrassing incident. As the broadcaster described the details, my thoughts wandered to that day when we stood, the two of us, in Proszowice, where he told me how he'd kissed the boots of a German to save his life. Here was yet another situation that had come full circle.

"If You Want to Know…"

Before 1993 Abba never mentioned the event at Slomniki, nor did he ever say, "The hell of Slomniki." Even though he spoke fairly freely of his Shoah experiences, Slomniki seemed to be just too tough to face.

In the 1993 delegation we joined, we'd planned in advance to set aside one day to tour the town of Abba's birth, and indeed that's what we did. On our way we passed through Slomniki, some 18 kilometers from Proszowice. Slomniki is where all the Jews from the region, including his family, were gathered and, following six days of unbearable waiting, loaded onto trains headed for the Belzec concentration camp.

In a forest clearing adjacent to the Slomniki Railway Station stood a very large crucifix bearing a Polish inscription: "Here thousands of Poles from the region were concentrated and murdered by the Nazis in August 1942." This is where Abba asked the car's driver to stop and let us take a closer look. I thought a brief ceremony would be held, but Abba said silent prayers, spontaneous, unplanned, for the souls of the victims, including his family. I didn't pay too much attention to the place. It looked like dozens of others we'd seen during the past few days. When you travel around Poland, at some point you begin to acclimate to the locations and narratives of horror that are, one by one, too horrific to absorb. And at some point, each horror begins to sound like the one you've just heard – a sort of variation on a theme.

As I busy myself with the large video camera I was lugging everywhere to record the places and events, Abba asks if he can read out something he prepared.

"Of course!" I say, immediately, naturally. "Wait a second. I'll get the camera ready."

Signaling to Abba to begin, I click the button to start filming. He takes a page of math paper out of his pocket. His neat handwriting covers it. He is directing the words to my sister — even though she's not here — and me.

"If you want to know, my dear children, who your family is, it's not to the books and albums that you should go."

That's the opening volley. He continues, without missing a beat.

"Rather, the Slomniki Railway Station is where you must go. Here is where the despicable Nazis dragged Proszowice's Jews and their families, including Mama, Tateh, and my siblings. Here they looted them, tortured them, and murdered them."

In an instant I feel it: Right here is where my family last breathed, the family I've missed all my life. Abba's voice pierces my soul.

"Helpless, we implored, we begged, we cried out to G-d, but he did not save us."

My hair stands on edge. Tears begin to appear behind the lens. Abba's voice continues, metallic, reading from the page. He doesn't see the storm of emotion engulfing me. His words reopen every wound I might have managed to close. I zoom in, onto the yellowed math page in Abba's hand, and realize that it's dated July 19, 1969. Thinking back, I remember it's when Abba's physician told him he had a virulent type of cancer and would have approximately three months to live, at the most. Back then Abba had two young children to whom he had yet to relay the baton of memory. The scars in his heart hadn't yet come anywhere close to healing; the news brought images of his own father bidding farewell to a son much too early in the lives of both. The parallel is seared firmly in his thoughts. Nights made sleepless by such thoughts drove him to sit and write his testimony. I would have been 12, and my sister, 17. "A Will for My Children for the Day After," the paper is titled.

For 24 years, the page will wait in our bookcase, folded, ready to thwart the Angel of Death skulking Abba every minute of every day of his life for years now. But that dark messenger never arrives, and misses him again and again. Abba's mission in this world is far from over, and the square-lined pages will wait in the crate of documents, yellowing until this opportunity, until Abba takes me to the place which he'd thought he'd be sending me to on my own a long time after his death. Reality can so easily override imagination: Abba and his son, his heir, his family's future, stand proudly together at the place that once marked the lowest point the family could ever have been at.

This is the event from which the concept "Shoah" — vis-à-vis Abba — will be imbued with a different meaning in my life and become a formative event. I'm crying like a baby; Abba notices the strong emotions flooding me and suggests we walk some of the way, as our family had done during their deportation — but, he emphasizes, we'll be walking in the opposite direction, from Slomniki to Proszowice, in order to proclaim to all, but most of all to ourselves, that "We're back! And we're stronger than ever!"

In this particular instance our schedules are insufficient, our available time is short, and the group I'm responsible for is waiting for us. We have so much yet to accomplish. We decide to postpone the walk to another occasion, perhaps to our next visit.

I hadn't thought it would really happen. I'd related to it as an objective that would be put aside, one that I'd wanted to achieve but couldn't. Life sometimes throws us the oddest curveballs, though: When we arrived for the 2018 ceremony, which we labeled "The Last Time We Go to Proszowice," I reminded Abba of our promise, and suggested that on the following day we do go to Slomniki and complete the mission we'd been unable to fulfill the previous time, a mere couple of years earlier.

Abba agreed. If we're already in Poland, and dealing with the issue of the Shoah, yes, it was an excellent idea, because the more we talk about those who perished, the better it is. "This is our personal exodus from Egypt," he tells me, underscoring his own view as well as mine.

Slomniki: The Hellhole of the Michów District's Towns

Abba is up early and begins his morning routine. His fixed ritual includes arranging everything he needs to take with him for the day: documents, camera, medicines, and so on. He organizes his bag, then starts to check that he hasn't forgotten anything. The process is repeated until we leave the hotel. Suddenly he stops me. "I forgot a bottle of water," he says. I could be annoyed, but how can anyone complain about a man of 92 who gets up without assistance, washes, brushes his teeth, dresses, and waits for you until you get up and join him, offering you the coffee he's just made? So instead I say to myself, "Please G-d, let him continue to be the way he is."

In the hotel dining room, a full meal is waiting for us, including fruit and vegetables. Self-serve buffet tables are loaded with the best of everything as befits a luxury hotel, which I booked much to Abba's chagrin. My logic was that our days would be filled with highly emotional activities, so at least at night and in the morning we can relax and enjoy the hotel's luxuries. Abba looks around and sighs. "What days I had in this country... Where was I then, and where am I now..." And then – with the kind of innocence he has that makes me smile – he half-asks and half-reminds me, as though by the way, "You remember that today we're going to Slomniki?" Without waiting for an answer, he asks and answers, "That's what you said yesterday," leaving no room for changes of mind.

At breakfast he prepares three sandwiches, one for each of us, including his grandson, my son, "because we might get hungry," he explains to my questioning glance, and continues in an apologetic tone, "Just in case, because what if everything's closed today?" He's imagined a scenario that's definitely possible.

We're on our way to Slomniki and Abba can't hold back. He begins telling one of the stories as soon as the car door closes, as though I've never heard it before. It's about what happened in Slomniki and what my grandfather told my father when they met up in the Kraków labor camp. Now Abba is telling me and my son, who's with us in the car. We're fulfilling the saying in Jewish liturgy, "And you shall tell your son on that day." For us, though, the story isn't about the exodus from Egypt, but rather a situation where G-d remained hidden from his people, and no exodus occurred. Perhaps, though, it depends on the angle you're looking at this catastrophe from, because Abba was saved, and did indeed establish a family.

When the Jews left Proszowice, my grandfather told Abba, the Germans urged them on without rest. Any attempt to halt for a moment was met by a volley of bullets aimed at no one in particular and everyone in general, just for the sake of killing. For 18 kilometers the Jews ran: Proszowice to Slomniki. As they did, people began dropping their bundles, as it was just too difficult to carry heavy loads.

With the last of their strength they reached the grassy clearing and Slomniki's wet fields. There they found some 10,000 Jews from towns of the Michów District crowded into a space that might have been able to hold about 2,000 at the most. The extreme congestion made things even harder.

For six days, the Jews were kept waiting on that wet land near the Slomniki Railway Station, under insufferable conditions. They were kept hungry and thirsty. Labor recruits, including police and SS soldiers, kept guard over them. Hundreds of murders and rapes were carried out by the guards. Despondent parents watched, unable to do anything to protect their starving, dying children.

Later the Nazis shot Yeinkel Krzesiwo in the head and threw his body into a pit filled with manure, along with several people still alive, including the wife of Rabbi Horowice, and Milcah, Yossel Feigeh's wife, who had just recently become blind in both eyes. Fishl Dziewienzce's wife gave birth to a baby boy in the Slomniki fields, as though proving to the Jews that the world keeps turning despite the suffering and the feeling that their end was near. Fishl, the new grandfather, founder of the "Tehillim" company in town, named the newborn "Gott Helf" – May G-d help us.

On their fifth day there, representatives of the German labor office showed up. Herr Gorniak came with an officer named Beckman, who ordered all the men off to the side and to line up in fives. A *selektzia* (selection) was conducted, and men were chosen for forced labor camps and sent to Kraków. Despite the fact that being in a labor camp increased the possibility of surviving, many of those chosen refused to go, and preferred to remain with the families and be sent to their deaths in the east. Many believed that they would soon be rescued, and that the miracle they awaited would occur. Scenes of farewells from women and children were heart-wrenching. Little children howled for their fathers; being separated from them was so difficult.

"My young brothers called out, too: 'Tati? Are you leaving us alone?' My mother shouted, 'Heshel, 22 years we're together. How can you abandon me?' Like so many others, my grandfather refused to go to the labor camp, but the pelting and beating the Germans rained down on him left him no choice. It tore his heart to see little Pinhas, age five, my youngest brother, squirm out of his mother's grip and race to our father, 'Tati, Tati, take my scarf so you won't be cold at work! And come back to us safe and sound!' he screamed hysterically."

Abba was clearly re-experiencing the events as he spoke, and I was focusing on the drive to this abhorrent place, Slomniki, but a cold sweat covered my body. The helplessness my grandfather felt was being conveyed by Abba and now being felt by me, too. I glance up at the heavens, hoping for a happy end to the horrifying scene that I'm now sadly a part of.

But Abba, as usual in tough moments, doesn't stop. His story curls around my soul in a vise-like grip. After the selektzia, the Germans loaded the Jewish men into the cattle cars. From there they watched the Germans load everyone else onto carts and wagons: men, women, the elderly, young kids not selected – including Haim David Shohat, Benzion Feldman, Zweibel Letrowski, and Esther Dziewienzke. Her husband Fishel was a colorful character in town, but at this critical moment he held a book of Tehillim (Psalms) tightly in one hand, his grandson Gott Helf in the other, and whispered to his wife, 'Esther, we have been together for 40 years. We built a Jewish life, a kosher home, we educated our children in the tradition of our forefathers. Esther, I know this wagon will take us on our last journey, and I'm joining you. Wherever you go, I will uphold the verse from Psalm 23: 'Though I walk through the Valley of the Shadow of Death, I will fear no evil, for you are with me; your rod and your staff will comfort me.'"

And Gott Helf did not help. Haim Benzion, standing to the side, was overcome by despair and shouted to the Jews being led to their slaughter, "Where is your divine savior now, who we worshipped faithfully and prayed to all our lives?" Fishl, his wife, and their newborn grandson were all taken on one of the wagons to their death, Fishl nonetheless reading Psalms aloud, psalm after psalm. And why not? It's what he'd done his whole life in Proszowice, and it's what he did until his life ended.

A few hundred meters from the main square of Slomniki, between two hills, on one of which a tall cross adorned with the image of Mary stood, all the elderly people were shot dead, including Abba's grandmother, Haiya Platkowicz. Among the Jews gathered in the square was Shlomo Bardin, who, with a sense of premonition, had wrapped himself in shrouds and his tallit and kept a tight grip on his siddur, the traditional prayer book. When asked by the Nazi officer, surprised at Shlomo's action, "What do you think you're doing?" Shlomo merely answered that his last wish is to die in his shrouds and tallit as is the custom among Jews. "We Jews wrap our dead in shrouds before their burial. Since you're going to kill me, I've come prepared." Taken aback, the German left him alone.

There also in the Slomniki square was Avreimeleh Bonek, the merry beggar of Proszowice. "The day will come, my lovely fellows, when we'll sing again." Those were his last words before dying. "And that's how the well-known characters of Proszowice died," Abba sums up as he sighs deeply, testifying to his mood.

Volf Lehrer, who lives in Israel, told Abba much later that "After the men able to work were taken, only women and children were left. They were pushed into the cattle cars. Slomniki's Jews were also pushed into the cars and deported to an unknown location. And then all that was left were grassy areas steeped in the blood and tears of our ancestors."

Lehrer and others from Proszowice sent a special emissary following the deportation of the area's elderly, women, and children. The messenger returned a few days later with the news that the Ukrainian guards at the Belzec concentration camp murdered some of the Jews with axes and shovels, and the rest with gas, in the most barbaric fashion. The rabbi of Belzec conveyed a brief written message: "They are all righteous."

Pavlowka's daughter managed to arrive later with the terrible news that Belzec's furnaces had swallowed up most of Proszowice's Jewish population, including Abba's mother and siblings.

May their memories be a blessing.

"And me?" Abba asks. "I was left in pain, wondering, 'Was this what G-d did for me by taking me out of Egypt?' according to Exodus 13:8. Where are you, my G-d? I asked repeatedly."

On our 2018 visit, Abba and I fulfill our promise which, due to insufficient time on our previous visit, we couldn't complete. We walked the last few kilometers between Proszowice and Slomniki, but in the opposite direction: from Slomniki to Proszowice, to convey the message that "Look! We are stronger than ever."

We enter the Proszowice gates. In my heart, I shout out a blessing: Blessed are you, Lord, our G-d, King of the Universe, who has granted us life, and sustained us, and brought us to this time." Jews of Proszowice, I scream in my heart, Shmuel Blumenfeld has returned and he is free and happy!

But in Poland of today, Jews don't have too many moments of joy. Everywhere you go, you re-live the memories of sorrow, bereavement, and blood spilled on every inch of space.

After Fleeing Home

We reach Proszowice's main square, and Abba continues to talk.

"Right after I fled and the town was surrounded in August 1942, old Shumienski, who was the municipal town crier, went about calling out that all the Jews would have to gather the next day in the marketplace at 7 a.m., and by midday at the latest, in order to leave the town forever.

"That night, Friday night, the start of Shabbat, things got particularly cruel. Wild shooting at Jews in the streets. Houses being looted. Harsh events breaking the Jews' spirit. My sister dressed as a man and tried escaping town on a truck taking workers to forced labor camps but she was outed as a woman, taken off the truck, and would have been shot to death if not for Getzel Pińczewski who saved her at the last second. By contrast, a few Jews did manage to save themselves by being gutsy, courageous, and/or taking initiative.

"I came across Tateh about a week later, doing forced labor in Kraków. He described what happened after I left. Later that same night no one in the family slept. My little brothers eventually fell asleep from exhaustion and towards morning, mother made the last meal anyone of my family would eat in our house. She put the bedding in the attic and told Wincenty Chmielarski, our Polish neighbor, that he should give anyone of the family who comes back home whatever they request. In the morning, the children put on their good Shabbat clothes and the shoes that our uncle, Eliezer Jurista, had made for them. When Mama tied a satchel of food onto each one's back, they didn't understand what was happening.

Abba sighs in a way that rips my heart.

"And so that's how the family left home, without even locking the door, in the hope that they'd be back soon. Mama and Tateh, with backpacks on their backs, and five little kids. They stood for several long moments at the front door, unable to leave, as though feeling that something was not right with this kind of departure. Then they took hold of each other's hands and gazed at each other. 'Roizeh,' Tateh said to Mama, 'for 22 years, since our marriage, we've lived together in these two small rooms. We worked. We built our little nest. Eight children you gave me. Six boys, one girl, and one child sadly lost as an infant. I don't think we've ever sinned or complained to G-d about our fate. We always blessed and praised everything. We were always satisfied with our lot in life. Our only wish is that at least one of the family members survives so that we aren't all, G-d forbid, wiped out. Let there be someone to remember us.'"

Abba is breathing hard. He rubs his chin, wrinkles his forehead, and is torn over whether to say the next sentence but does, with great sorrow.

"Tateh began to cry," Abba tries to overcome his sobs. I stand next to him quietly, feeling awkward and truly sorry for him. But he doesn't let that take over our conversation. This moment is too important for him to let awkwardness stand between us. "Mama took hold of Tateh in both her hands and whispered, 'Heshel, have pity on the little ones and don't ruin their happiness. They think we're going for a Shabbat stroll.'"

At 11:00 that morning, the Blumenfeld children left their house, nicely dressed, their shoes shining, happy as children on an outing could be, not understanding that this would be the last time they would go anywhere. Walking behind them with bowed heads, Mama and Tateh cried without making a sound. They were not going to ruin the children's excitement.

Meanwhile, the time for all Jews to be gathered in the square for their last journey approached. Gunshots could be heard in the town. Francuski was shot to death as he stepped out of his front door to obey orders. A German citizen who supplied the German military with vegetables lived in town. Although he wasn't directly involved in the activities around the deportation, he noticed Rozenberg wearing his Judenrat member armband, and simply shot him dead. Mordechai Kleiner, another member of the Judenrat and a man of noble character, tried to save several Jews but the Germans noticed, shot him, and left him there where he lay, severely wounded.

On the 17th of Elul, the Jewish calendar date corresponding to August 29, 1942, the Proszowice Jewish residents' hopes faded away. Two weeks before Rosh Hashanah, the Jewish New Year, the Nazis carried out the deportation while simultaneously conducting an extensive massacre. As the church bells rang out, old Shumienski shouted repeatedly that the town's Jews were leaving their homes forever.

Precisely at midday on that sunny Shabbat, heads bowed and tears flowing, the Jews left town. Heading the group like a spiritual shepherd was the community's righteous rabbi, Nahum Ber Horowice, together with his family. Behind him came the community's main philanthropists: Yossel Feigeh, Haim David Shohat, Yirmiyahu Zeifman, Yisrelka Goldkorn, Pinhas Kornfeld, Hirsch Spokoineh, Benzion Feldman, Moshe Shohat, the Shidlowski family, Itcheh Levi, the Liess and Dziewienzce families, and Zeinwel Letrowska.

"Similarities and contrasts among the various groups typical of the Proszowice Jewish population disappeared. Now there was only one unifying element: Jews going to Slomniki. It marked the end of a community's long existence., Everyone else straggled in a long line behind the town's leaders. And of course that included my mother Roizeh, my father Heshel, my older sister, and my five younger brothers. Walking next to them was Adela Bick, whose son Yossel fled together with me. She was such a gentle, decent person. She was helping my mother to keep the children in line and behave nicely. That's how they went to their slaughter."

The Ceremony

The important day – the highlight of our trip – arrives. Abba is very emotional as he prepares himself for the ceremony. Billie Landau, her sisters, and their families have also come to the ceremony. They, too, have a unique story tied to Proszowice, and there is also a non-Jew recognized as a "Righteous Among the Nations" for saving their mother.

We are joined by Hieronim Cęckiewicza, who has come from Berlin. He is the son of the man who owned the house Abba grew up in as a child. Hieronim is an amazing artist with a wonderful personality. He was as pleased to meet us as we were to meet him. A representative of the Kraków Jewish community has also come. Among his tasks is the preservation of local places sacred to Jews, including Poland's Jewish cemeteries, and, of course, that of Proszowice.

A large number of important locals and media people are also there, including some 20 representatives of the municipality, headed by the mayor. Excitement fills the air. There's also tension: What will my father say on this auspicious occasion? There's no turning back now, and every word carries significance not only at the level of local politics but at the national level, too – both here in Poland and back home in Israel.

Abba doesn't usually speak for anyone but himself. He represents no one but himself. This makes it impossible to make any claims against him. He even accepted German reparations for himself but politely refused what might have been paid out for other members of his family. When someone asks his forgiveness for the Holocaust, he answers, "I will forgive you, but I do not have the right to speak on behalf of others."

Symbolically, on that same day, the Polish parliament convenes and confirms the agreement for renewed relations between Poland and Israel, which causes a storm of reactions in Israel, led by the Yad Vashem World Holocaust Remembrance Center. We have no knowledge of this event, being disconnected from the news in Israel.

The events begin. They are festive, moving. The council chairperson presents each of us: "Mr. Shmuel Blumenfeld!" Applause. Abba springs up like a healthy boy of 15 about to flee. He bows to acknowledge the event's importance and the honor bestowed upon him. Only Polish is spoken, but I don't really need a translator; the respect and anticipation can clearly be felt.

The chairperson introduces me. "Mr. Arie Blumenfeld!" Abba smiles to signal that I should stand, as though I haven't understood the weight of the situation. I do, and nod lightly with my head. The chairperson describes me as a historian, since it's hard to find a Polish word for "teacher of current, national and social affairs, and knowledge of Israel."

Then Ashley Blumenfeld is introduced. This time I'm the one signaling; I encourage my son – the primary honoree's grandson – to stand. He does. His posture is powerful, upright, and he smiles politely.

The event's attendees show typically European politeness; they do not chatter among themselves, and there are no interruptions. I scan the room, trying to find the one person whose face shows opposition to the honor being shown us, but I can't see anyone who'd fit that bill. Perhaps there really is across-the-board agreement to honor Abba in the city of his birth; after all, had he not been deported in 1942 because of his religion, he may well have stayed there to this very day, together with the other 2,000 or so Jews, or about half the population, who'd lived in Proszowice at the time.

June 2019: Proszowice Municipal Council ceremony acknowledging Shmuel Blumenfeld's activities towards perpetuating the Proszowice Jewish community following the Holocaust

The mayor offers introductory remarks, then invites Abba to speak. He does, at length, and in fluent Polish, describing the events of his life. He also thanks the mayor, the council, and the city's residents for the honor being shown him 76 years after he fled.

I know Abba's speech inside out even though I don't understand a word of Polish. Council members are listening politely, attentively – some even quite enthusiastically – and in their hearts some of them must surely be at least slightly envious of this 92-year-old man who has the energy of a wound-up spring, who speaks with clarity, and bypasses the political minefield with such elegance and diplomacy. With no effort at all, Abba draws on his wisdom and resourcefulness, the same traits that helped him survive so long ago.

Hearty applause is heard at last. This is a relief to Abba. No doubt the mayor, the city council members, and the audience, are also relieved. Nothing has been said that could cause any drama. Everyone's on their feet in respect as Abba steps down from the dais and walks over to the mayor, who's waiting for him with an array of certificates and badges of honor.

Looking around, I'm deeply moved, and trying to digest the situation. Yesterday we were in Auschwitz-Birkenau, the extermination camp where Abba spent almost two years. Then we visited Jawiszowice, a satellite camp of Auschwitz, and the coal mine where Abba worked like a hunted dog. That was the lowest point of his life. And now, look at us, here, closing a circle of the triumph of good over evil, victory of justice over wickedness, and I'm thrilled that my son and I can witness this historic moment. I thank G-d for giving Abba a long, healthy life, long enough to let him see at least some level of the justice being done this day.

I feel the need to write what I feel towards the Proszowice mayor, this humane, empathic young man who initiated and promoted the event despite some degree of risk to his own political career. This is my letter:

To: The Mayor of Proszowice
Dear Sir,
I wish to thank you, and the Council of Proszowice and the region, for the great honor you showed towards my father, Mr. Shmuel Blumenfeld. My father, and our heritage, educated me to always see the cup as half full, to look ahead with optimism, without forgetting the past, and to objectively examine the present with hope for a much better future.

What I saw at the Proszowice Council meeting on Wednesday, 28 June 2018, strengthened my view that indeed a respectful present creates changes and implants hope for a better future. As a teacher in a school in Israel, the homeland of the Jewish people, I teach my students to examine the reality and judge it according to the truth reflected to them, sounded to them, and understood by their intellect. What I saw, heard, and felt at the Proszowice Council's festive meeting was respectful, cultured, and filled with hope for the future.

I wish to thank you for choosing my father and promoting this honorable event, and look forward to maintaining relations between yourself and the people of Proszowice in the future which are as good as those my father has experienced today, and up until today.

Yours sincerely,
Arie Blumenfeld

And thus, another circle is closed.

The Second Deportation from Proszowice

We set out with the mayor and his entourage of dignitaries for a festive lunch at the only hotel in town. Its style is rustic, clean, and of pleasingly high quality. Attending are people who were at the ceremony. Of them, Hieronim the artist attracts my attention. We chat; he tells me how much he's become attached to Abba and his stories, and that this event is such a joyful one. In his view, Abba definitely deserves the same acknowledgment as other city honorees receive. He shows me his sketches reflecting Abba's experiences as he heard and understood them.

I ask if it's possible to receive scans of those that speak to me the most. Agreeing, he sets a meeting for the next day in Proszowice, and we arrange to go together to Abba's pre-war house. I have a plan. There's a story Abba told me when I was a kid – how on the evening before the deportation, Abba hid the family's treasures in a pit he dug in the yard, "so that someone could begin something," as he explained it. As a kid, I imagined digging up a huge trove of gold coins. Whenever I'd raise the topic, Abba would shrug it away with an array of excuses, such as "Can you imagine what would happen if we start digging there? The locals will show up in hordes!"

Later, when I studied archeology at university, and suggested a clever way of finding the family's possessions, he'd say things like "It's worthless." But I wasn't giving up, nor was Abba. In recent years he'd adopted a new strategy, a different and uncompromising line of defense: He doesn't remember exactly where it was. More recently, he started saying that he vowed never to go into that yard again, unless someone of his family returned there.

Over the many dozens of times that Abba went to Poland with Israeli delegations, he'd get tens, if not hundreds, of visitors together in front of the house but never stepped foot on the property itself, even though the yard and the house built on it had never been renovated and continued to stand, mute and bare, as though cursed with the same annihilation that the Germans, assisted by the Poles, inflicted on the locals — Abba's family among them.

At the hotel, the luncheon has come to a close and I say goodbye to Hieronim with a friendly hug and my assurance that we'd meet the next day. Abba joins us, catching the tail end of our conversation, happy for another opportunity to visit Proszowice. In my mind, I'm playing out my tactics for tomorrow, hoping to access our family treasure. To get my plans up and running, I need to collaborate with two people who are currently blocking my progress. The first is Hieronim himself, who will need to bring me into the house tomorrow as an accomplice, so to speak. The second is Abba, and that requires his agreeing to enter the yard and point out the location, more or less. My son, catching on, shakes his head. "Bored?" he asks. "You're just like Saba!" he tells me, using the Hebrew for grandfather. But to me that sounds like a real compliment: what he means is that my father and I are constantly looking out for something that needs doing.

As we head back to our car in the municipal parking lot, we pass the house where Abba's uncle, Eliezer Jurista, used to live. Abba, still excited about the moving event he's just experienced, gets excited again at what the house means to him. And so he tells us what happened at the time of the second deportation. The story begins as we get into the car and continues all the way to Kraków.

***

After losing contact with his own father in the Kraków Ghetto, Abba returned to Proszowice, hoping to find someone from the family. On November 9, 1942, the second wave of deportations took place. For the third time, Abba was forced to flee the town in his continuing struggle to save his life. His experience thus far had taught him that it was best to be constantly on the move because the Jewish police knew all the possible hiding places in town. A well-oiled and well-rewarded system of informants also operated; Jewish police collaborated with their Polish counterparts and German forces were particularly active and aggressive.

For that reason, Abba chose to go to his Uncle Eliezer, deported in the first round, separated from his wife in the selection process, and taken to work in Kraków. From there he went back to Proszowice to try and find out what happened to his uncle's three children. Eliezer had smuggled them out the night before the deportation to a neighboring town, thinking, mistakenly, that he could save them that way. Eliezer's situation was dreadful, like that of so many of the Proszowice Jews still alive at that stage. His wife had been sent east, then murdered at Belzec. He'd sent his children to his wife's sister who lived in a relatively quiet village, believing that the Germans wouldn't get to the Jews there. In retrospect, that was a fateful error. They were sent east with their aunt. Eliezer made it back to Proszowice and hid, together with another sister-in-law and her daughter, in the sister-in-law's house in the center of town.

"When I reached him that night," Abba says, "I found him there with Aunt Feigeh and Feigeh's daughter Basha. I told them there'd be another deportation the next day and they had to flee immediately. A Polish man living in a neighboring village had promised to hide Uncle Eliezer in return for fair compensation.

Uncle Eliezer and Feigeh very firmly insisted that this time I flee with them and they assured me there was enough room for all of us. At 9 p.m. we left Proszowice via circuitous routes. I carried Feigeh's young daughter on my back the whole night. At this early stage, the town was surrounded mostly by Jewish and Polish police. As we left, light from Meir Goldstein's hand-held lamp beamed right at us. He was with the Jewish police. I knew him well. I know he identified me but pretended not to have seen us sneaking out, which saved our lives. Proszowice had thus become 'Judenrein,' (Jew-free).

"At the end of November 1942, the Gestapo corralled several hundred Jews who'd been hiding and caught in the second deportation in Proszowice. They were brought to Michów. Among them was Aharon Yossef and his family, together with Nehama, the Proszowice Judenrat's secretary. Those Jews were made to run from Michów to the nearby Chodówki Forest, to the sound of insults and blasphemies, and shouts of "Hurrah!" from the local kids. The Jews were simply shot to death, as was Ruhama Lichtenstein, who took the story of Proszowice Jewry's suffering with her upon her death.

"Uncle Eliezer, Feigeh, their little daughter and I walked all night to Karwin. We entered the Polish farmer's house. He was happy to see us. We planned to hide there for several days until things blew over.

"Smiling at Uncle Eliezer, the farmer said, 'See? I promised!' That gave my uncle a lot of hope. 'I told you that if there's trouble, I'll help. Matke!' he called to his wife. 'Get food ready for the Zyds,' he said, using the Polish word for Jews. 'Here, you take my bed,' the farmer offered my uncle with a show of politeness. 'Who's the young man?' he then casually asked. 'My family,' Feigeh answered.

"Rudely, the farmer responded. 'My dear lady, for you I have room, but for him, I don't.' He made it very clear that I was irrelevant and he was unwilling to help me. I looked at them with envy. 'For sure I won't survive the coming days,' I remember thinking, but they will for sure. My uncle did survive the Shoah, but his wife, children, sister-in-law and her daughter, hidden at the non-Jew's house, were murdered by the Nazis.

"Barely pausing for a breath while staring at me, the Christian farmer continued. 'I have a plan. At night my son will be going to Kraków with a delivery of tobacco leaves and can take this young fellow here with him. He can sit on the wagon axle in the back. You don't need to worry, lady,' the farmer reassured my aunt, who looked very concerned at how things were developing."

"At 2 a.m. I got up and went into the yard. I helped the young Pole harness the horses and load the tobacco. I wanted to show him that I know how to ride horses and was also thinking that if I'm holding the reins, in control, I'd feel safer. But from the outset I could feel his hostile attitude and realized I needed to be ready for any eventuality. Before setting out, with feigned warmth the farmer placed his hand on my shoulder and spoke to his son in a joking tone, accompanied by a wink. 'Take the Zyd to Kraków as we decided.' It wasn't hard to detect his dislike of me.

"The son suggested I sit on the back axle. I said that I prefer to go on foot. I asked him to give me a whip because that way I could help him with the journey but he refused, adding a few choice vulgar words. He didn't even try to hide his loathing for me as a Jew. I saw him watching me closely so I went to the wagon's other side. That way he couldn't see me or what I was doing. From my position I could see the path, stay alert to any danger, and simultaneously keep him in my range of vision."

"A few kilometers later we came closer to a group of horse-drawn carts parked on the roadside. The sheigetz," Abba said, using the Yiddish word for non-Jew, "suddenly started shouting that he'd caught a Jew. All the wagoners began to run towards him hysterically. In an instant I'd dived into the snow, crawling on all fours through the field in the direction we'd come until I was under a tree. But the wagon kept rolling forward for another 20 meters or so before it eventually stopped. The wagoners couldn't find me in the wagon and started to hunt for me, racing through the fields like crazed men. But they couldn't find me, so eventually they gave up. They made a lot of fun of the Pole and were sure he was kidding them, making the story up. 'Jak Boga Kochem!' (I swear, as I love the Lord!) he shouted to them over and over.

"Once everyone had gone far enough off and the danger had passed, I was left alone in that dark forest. I burst into tears. I was hunted, I was in despair, and I didn't have a penny to my name. I spoke to G-d. 'Gottenyu!' My G-d! 'Is it really worth fighting so hard to stay alive? Everyone hates me even though I did nothing bad to anyone. I don't have hope. I don't have a solution.' I was in such despair that I decided to go back to the Polish farmer in the village, hand myself over and leave myself in fate's hands.'

"But a few steps later I changed my mind. I was talking to myself, weighing the pros and cons aloud. 'Shmuel, you're living in cruel times. You've got to fight for your life. Mama told you before her death to take good care of your bones, because flesh can fill out again.

"Suddenly I heard the sound of a flatbed wagon approaching. I could see the farmer dozing in the wagon that was bringing canisters of milk. I got up my courage and stood right in the middle of the path, waving my arms. 'Halt! Halt!,' I commanded the farmer with inexplicable confidence. 'Dzien dobri, panya.' Good morning, sir, he addressed me. 'Where do you want to go?' he asked. 'I work at the Kraków dairy,' I answered.

"Immediately I was invited to take my place on the wagon. 'Here, sit next to me,' he politely offered. Concerned for my health, he covered me in a heavy cloth. I asked for the reins. He agreed, sitting next to me, feeling safe, dozing off. 'Panya,' he said, using the polite term, 'there are Zyds around here, wandering about like stray dogs. I don't like Zyds. You've got to be careful,' he added with fatherly concern. I nodded to show my thanks for his advice. And so I got back to Kraków, to the municipal gas factories, leaving Proszowice behind until the next time."

* * *

This story ends with spine-tingling accuracy just as we roll into Kraków 75 years later. It feels like a repeat, except back then Abba was scrawny, frightened, traveling on a wagon, and now he's accompanied by family, feels proud and safe, and is traveling in a rented luxury vehicle.

My Last Visit to My Childhood Home in Proszowice

In 1992 my family – my wife and I and our three children – moved to our new home in Rishon LeZion. It's a one-family house, fairly spacious and comfortable. On the day we held the Khanukat HaBayit, the Jewish term for the housewarming, my wife asked me to affix the mezuzah to the front door's doorpost. I looked at her, surprised, because we are a secular family. But tradition has long-reaching roots. "Why should it bother you?" she challenged. "Even if you don't think it can help, it certainly can't do harm."

With a kippah on my head, I picked up the mezuzah in one hand, the hammer and nails in the other, and my wife, moved, opened the siddur and pointed to the specific blessing I needed to say as she instructed me: "Read it out loud and clear!" She's watching me closely but can't imagine why I've become emotional. "What's all the excitement about? You're just putting the mezuzah up," she remarks. Instantly I'm immersed in my childhood, when Abba told me one of his stories about his last visit to his abandoned house in Proszowice after all the Jews had been deported. By the time this event took place, his mother and siblings had been murdered in the east, his father was trapped in the labor camp, and he was a courier in the service of anyone and everyone, risking his life to help the former community's members on the Kraków- Proszowice line.

On one of his runs to Proszowice, Abba slept in the tiny storage attic belonging to his neighbor, Wincenty Chmielarski. He was still hoping to find a tidbit of information about his siblings and family. Every time he returned to the town, he left disheartened until suddenly the realization hit him: Everyone must be dead. It made his already melancholy mood more desperate, so much so that he had trouble falling asleep. But on that visit, unlike so many previous ones, his longing for his past overcame his caution. He desperately wanted to live, and was innocently hopeful that there was still a possibility of good times ahead.

He described what he went through that night in the attic.

"I was lying there, unable to fall asleep, remembering the past, my parents, my little brothers, thinking about their being dead. I could hear them crying, I could hear my mother wailing, and I couldn't decide if it was my imagination playing games with me or really happening. I decided to open up my family's closed house. The Jewish police, the OD, were checking abandoned Jewish houses and attaching a metal seal to show that the house had been checked and was empty. It was dark, about

1 .am., and the Christian neighbors were asleep. And here I was, a Jewish kid, crawling out of the attic, knocking softly on our neighbor Chmielarski 's door. 'Panya, terrible dreams are disturbing me. I keep dreaming that someone is hiding in our house. Maybe it's one of my little brothers who managed to escape at the last second, or maybe my mother forgot to take him,' I whispered loudly, fearfully.

"He answered, 'Son, I think your mind is playing tricks on you because of recent events. For weeks, your family hasn't been anywhere nearby. They were sent away. How could you possibly think anyone's living in there?' Nonetheless I tried convincing him: 'Sir, you have to come with me. I'll break the metal seal and give you all the tools in return,' I said, tempting him to get up and come out with me in the night."

"His wife, Jadwiga, locked the gate on one side. Wincenty locked it on the other and stood guard to be sure no one unwanted could come while he kept watch over me. Using a metal rod I broke the door's seal. Like a snake, I crawled across the wooden floor between the shoes and socks my family had left scattered there. Plates and pots they hadn't had time to wash were still piled up on the kitchen table. Everything pointed to a family knowingly leaving forever. Household items spoke a mute language: furniture, the items we used on Shabbat, my sister's floral embroidery. The letters stitched in gold on my sister's schoolbag: Sheindeleh Blumenfeld, Grade 7, 1943.

"Everything was covered with a light film of mildew. Mattresses on the beds had been half stripped as though my mother, having hidden the best of our items with her Christian neighbors in the hope of coming back one day, had checked once more just to be sure nothing important had been left behind. Tablecloths and children's holiday clothing were strewn across the beds. Family photos still hung on the walls; in one of them, my parents held me and my sister. In another, everyone stood, six boys and one girl. Next to that, a photo of our Zeideh, our grandfather Shmuel Platkiewice, whose wide beard and regal manner still shone in the house's dank darkness.

"Not far from there hung a photo of the luminary, the Admor Rabbi Haim Shmuel Halevi Horowice of Chęciny, and other rabbis from Kielce. On the windowsill, mother's flowerpots now held withered lifeless plants. They used to bloom in beautiful colors. 'You won't open your petals anymore,' I whispered. How sad, how cold my childhood home was, this home that was once filled with joy. This is where my family lived, happy with what they had, hoping that G-d would one day bring a time of equality between rich and poor.

"Old Wincenty Chmielarski couldn't understand what was keeping me so long. Every so often he whispered: 'Shmulik, why so long? Didn't you find anything?' 'Panya,' I answered, 'everything looks so weird here. It's as though all the things here are talking to me, as though they're speaking quietly with everyone I love.' Suddenly I noticed our Jewish books: Bibles, siddur and other prayer books, Tateh's Gemara. I carried them through the rooms and packed them in a white sheet so that the Nazis wouldn't desecrate them, because it seemed that Jews would no longer live there.

"I missed the house, yet I hated it; with tears rolling down my cheeks, I looked around. Memories of the past. Shadows moved across the silent walls, across the curtains. In the kitchen I came across a dried spot of my mother's blood. I kissed it. Days earlier Mama had been beaten by Gorniak, the Kraków work officer, because her name hadn't appeared on his work list. Someone had been an informer, bringing Gorniak to our house. The instant he'd entered, he asked, 'Have you already registered?' Mama was shaken. She thought he was talking about me. 'No, sir, I'm just making food for the children,' she'd said.

"He began beating her with his cane. 'To hell with your kids! I'll show you who's boss here!' he shouted as blood fell into the pot and onto the floor. She went right then to the registration offices. 'You should be ashamed of yourself,' Mama said to the Jewish informant, 'for bringing him to your relatives!' That day we ate soup with mother's blood in it. We had no choice. There was nothing else. Now I took a last look at the dark crimson stain.

"I left carrying the heavy pack of holy books and closed the door behind me. I noticed the mezuzah hung on the doorpost, the one that Tateh had placed there as his six children watched, in the hope that the Holy One, Blessed be He, would protect us and bless us with a good life. How foolish we were. As a last thought, I took it down. 'There's no need for it here anymore,' I remember thinking. Here we lived until August 29, 1942, until that terrible Shabbat when we were torn from our roots."

"Arie! Arie?" my wife shook me out of my thoughts. "What's the matter with you? Asleep on your feet?"

I shook my head, then whispered. "Blessed are you, G-d, King of the universe...." The tears pent up inside me stayed there. Let no one see! That's what we were taught, how we were raised: Keep it inside. Weeping is a sign of weakness. I sniffle quietly. My wife is so focused on the mezuzah that she doesn't notice what I'm feeling. I make myself continue, loudly, clearly, just as she requested, "...who has commanded us with His commandment to affix the mezuzah."

But inside my heart is screaming to my father. "Abba, because of the Germans you ripped the mezuzah off your house, but from today on, your grandchildren and I will affix more and more mezuzahs in the Land of Israel!" And I reach the end of the second blessing. "...who infuses us with life, and sustains us, and brings us to this time!"

My wife, for whom such ceremonies are natural and normal, looks around, satisfied, and answers, "Amen" to the blessings. "See?" she smiles, her hand on my back, "It's no big deal to attach the mezuzah to the doorpost!"

Another circle has closed.

Wicek Wincenty and His Wife Jadwiga: A Ray of Light in Poland's Darkness

The end of the Six-Day War, on June 10, 1967, led to the termination of diplomatic relations between Poland and Israel. I clearly remember Abba sending packages of clothing and food for years to an elderly woman, Jadwiga, who occasionally hid him in Proszowice when he turned up covertly during the town's Judenrein period. Sheltering a Jew in those days was risky, and could cause the non-Jew a serious penalty, sanctions, or even death. Hiding a Jew put the non-Jew's entire immediate, and even extended, family at dire risk.

My parents didn't have money to spare when I was a kid. Both worked hard from morning to night to support our little family, but from the little they did have to spare, Abba made sure to send packages to various people who'd looked after him during those rough times. Every month Abba and I lugged boxes to the post office, and every month Abba would explain what we're doing, wanting to teach me traits of mutuality, acknowledgment, and recognition of another person's nobility. And so almost every month Abba would tell me the following story as though he'd never told it to me before.

"Wherever I went during the 1940s, I felt the alienation and loathing towards Jews. By contrast, Jadwiga and Wincenty were like a ray of light and hope." Abba would pause. "And life. Hope was the only way to preserve life." Then, with a bashful smile, he'd add: "They also had a plan for me to marry their daughter Elka, which would give me a real chance to assimilate into the local population and save my life."

"On one of the most miserable nights I'd ever known, I reached Proszowice in utter despair. It was completely Judenrein and I showed up almost as though I wanted to be caught and get it all over with. At the time I was operating as a courier between Kraków and Proszowice, taking letters to and from Jews and, especially, collecting money for debts owed by non-Jews to Jews. That helped the Jewish families survive by giving them a chance to buy food and bribe the German guards. It was high-risk and I was more nervous than ever, but I operated according to the rigid principles that I'd set in advance – which saved my life over and over. I never stayed long in the houses of local farmers, for example. If they gave me money or food, I took it, and if they didn't, I'd tell them I'd come back later that night, but of course I didn't.

"One day I was carefully approaching Wincenty's house and put my ear to the door to be sure no one unfamiliar was inside. I learned to trust Wincenty. I knocked and turned my back to the door ready to run if necessary. When I heard Jadwiga's voice as the door opened I turned around. She couldn't believe her eyes. Right away she started crossing herself. 'What courage you have, boy, coming here to town, to a place where they shoot Jews!' she said breathlessly. 'Be careful, Wiacek's here,' she added, warning me about the neighbor's son who didn't like me and made no bones about showing it. 'Wiacek! I think your wife's calling you!' she said loudly to him as she opened the door wide to hide me behind it.

"Without suspecting anything, Wiacek answered, 'Yes, that could very well be,' and was gone in a moment.

"Then she called her own husband. 'Wincenty, look who's here! Shmulik!' 'Not possible,' Wincenty answered. 'Come, look for yourself. He's standing right here!' Jadwiga said. 'So why are you standing there? Give him something to eat!' the old man said. Quickly Jadwiga dished up a bowl of cold noodles and despite my hunger, I almost choked on them.

"I turned to Wincenty, using the polite term for 'sir.' 'Panya, I need to ask you for a few things…' and immediately they gave me what I requested. I stood, ready to go to Pawlowski, a villager on the other side of the town's center, to fulfill the task my uncle had given me: to collect money for him. Concerned, Wincenty told me, 'It's extremely dangerous for you to go there. Give me the letter and I'll fix the matter for you.' In any other situation, that suggestion would be my signal to flee, but I trusted these good neighbors and I was already thoroughly despairing. I gave him the letter and he set off.

"Meanwhile Itche-Meir, a friend who'd come with me and had a separate set of houses to visit, was exposed and forced to flee. That exposed my presence in Proszowice, too. The non-Jew from whom Itche fled immediately went to the local police, telling them that 'Zydzi' (Jews), purposely using the plural, were wandering around town. The rumor spread like proverbial wildfire. Numerous officers right away began patrolling the streets. In those days, people who turned Jews in received 10 kilos of sugar and a bottle of vodka – a very profitable deal for the non-Jew. That's what Jews were worth back then.

"Wincenty also caught a whiff of the rumor and actually saw the police running around hunting carefully. He dashed back home, coming across a Ukrainian policeman on the way who told Wincenty they were on the lookout for Jews. 'Oh yes,' Wincenty said very firmly, 'I'm pretty sure I saw one on Kraków

Street going towards the cemetery.' That got everyone off in the opposite direction. He saved my life because his purposeful misdirection gave me sufficient time to escape.

"He came into his house breathing hard. 'Jadwiga, quick, bring me the park keys!' He was the park's guard; when it snowed in winter, the park was kept locked. 'Here, Shmulik,' he handed me a packet, 'take the money and these things for your uncle. G-d watch over you. Come, I'll open the park and you can get away through there. Take good care of yourself.' Heavy snow covered the paths. Wincenty opened the large wooden gate and I set out across the desolate land, exhausted and dejected, to the spot where Itche-Meir Rottenberg and I had planned to meet.

"Itche did show up eventually, and together we returned to the Kraków labor camp we'd sneaked away from. But on another occasion, Itche got caught at our meeting spot at the Jewish cemetery. He wasn't arrested; he was shot on the spot. May Itche's memory be a blessing."

* * *

Following the renewal of diplomatic relations between Israel and Poland in 1989, Abba flew to Proszowice on the first flight he could get. Wincenty had already passed away, but Jadwiga, a "Righteous Among the Nations" as such people are known in Israel, so much older now, met him. A few months later she also passed away.

My first visit to Proszowice was in 1993, together with Abba. We visited Elka, Jadwiga's daughter. Communism was on its last legs in Poland and new economic changes were taking place. Elka, seated with us in her living room, looked so much older than her age; suffering various chronic illnesses, she poured her heart out to us. She had no money to buy coal and therefore couldn't heat the house. In fact, she didn't even have enough money for the most basic items needed to live on.

Abba chats with Elka in Polish. I can't understand a word, but I do understand Elka's deep sighs. Abba is energetic, busy, self-confident, proud, stands tall. How amazing life is… to think of what he came from and where he is today; how he never lost hope and fought for his life; how good people like Elka's parents kept an eye out for him where they could. Abba slips his hand into his pocket and pulls out a sum of money that will not only cover heating the house for a year but other needs as well. It's his way of acknowledging Elka's parents and their integrity. For him, this is historic justice in theory as well as in practice. That's how Abba is; he doesn't forget any good deed enacted for his sake. He focuses on the good, not the bad. I can't help but think how Abba's generosity hardly even comes close to paying back what Elka's parents did for him. But for Elka, Abba's support is huge. We get ready to leave; Elka is crying tears of joy, and kisses me, too, but mostly grasps Abba's hands and kisses him again and again on the cheek for warming her soul, and her home, this winter.

The door closes behind us. I clap Abba on his shoulder light-heartedly. "Did you really consider marrying her to save your life?"

But Abba answers with all seriousness. "Arie, you have to understand that back then I was worth nothing! What they did for me, and wanted to do for my sake, is incomprehensible in light of the times and gave me so much strength. There weren't very many people like them back then."

The Meeting in Kraków

Our meeting with Elka reminded me of something I'd wanted to ask Abba, but with so many emotions and stories coming up, I'd forgotten about it. As we drive back I think about Abba's Slomniki experience. Clearly Slomniki was his harshest breaking point, so I ask him to tell me a bit more about his father who, for some reason, seems left out of the telling.

"Slomniki?" Abba asks, trying to understand what lies behind my question. The story sets off as though we've been talking about it all day.

"Information kept coming from Slomniki that Jews were still being kept there. Initially, Leibeleh Rottenberg and I thought of bringing food there, but people dissuaded us. Several days later, I heard that Tateh was alive and in the Prokocim camp. I stole a bicycle and rode there as fast as I could. It was a forced labor camp near Kraków, and I knew the path well. I did meet up there with my father. We were both overjoyed."

Abba adds details about that very moving moment.

"Tateh was so surprised to see me that he began to cry. 'You're all that's left of my family!' he muttered, pointing to me and the scarf that my little brother had given him. He slipped that children's scarf off and put it around my neck. Then he added his leather trouser belt 'so you don't forget me,' he said with a bitter smile. I suggested we both flee to the ghetto where we could both work as tailors. Two days later Tateh did flee and we spent Shabbat together at our relative's house. Tateh sang Shabbat songs. Briefly we forgot our troubles and lived the Shabbat fully, as though we were back in Proszowice and Mama and the children were with us. It was the last Shabbat I'd ever have with my father. It was also the last Shabbat I observed for the rest of my life."

"Several days later, Tateh's whereabouts were no longer known, nor were they traceable. A few weeks afterwards, I slipped out of the Kraków Ghetto, removed the white band with its Star of David, and moved around freely like a Polish kid through the city's streets and into 77 Grzegorzecka, adjacent to the Ute Company, where I saw a building under construction. I saw Tateh among the laborers.

"I called out loudly, 'Tateshi!' My father! I drew closer. 'You're alive! Can I bring you something?' I asked, concerned. 'Cigarettes. And food,' he answered, 'but be careful,' he whispered, very worried about me, 'because now we are controlled by the SD.' He was referring to the Sicherheitsdienst, the Nazi secret service. As evening fell I came back with food and cigarettes. A Jewish guard stood at the entrance to the site. 'Don't worry,' he said, taking in my wary gaze. 'Go in, see your father. There won't be any problems,' he reassured.

"It was a very moving moment. We wept, hugged, kissed each other. But I could sense that I'd made a mistake. Without any warning the gate closed behind me. In an instant I had the white armband with its blue Magen David back on,' Abba says, using the Hebrew for Star of David, 'and asked the guard to let me out the way I came in. 'No,' he said firmly, denying his earlier assurance, 'the SD officer's on his way,' he added, pointing to a man arriving on his bicycle.

"The bespectacled officer understood that I didn't belong to the group and immediately asked me in anger, 'What are you doing here?!' I was left speechless. The commander ordered an immediate lineup, fearing that someone else might have slipped away. 'Take that pile of shit from here and keep a tight hold on him,' he said to his subordinate while pointing at me.

"I decided to try my luck. 'Officer, sir,' I said, 'I have a travel permit and I'm asking for permission to return to the ghetto. I work in the municipal gas factory there.' He stared at me. 'Damn your work. Stand off to the side,' he ordered.

"Beating and whipping the laborers, they ran into two gypsy wagons parked on the site. The building was blocked and fenced with barbed wire. The officer ordered the guard at the gate, 'Go get me a shovel and I'll finish this little punk off with one shot! We'll dig a pit here and put him in!' he added.

"He gave all these orders while still holding his bicycle. Having decided he was going to kill me, he started looking for somewhere to lean the bike. I continued begging for my life, seeking his mercy. 'You swine,' he roared at me, 'stand a few meters back from me. You stink!' He was handling the bike, and so fully focused on what he was doing that I carefully searched for an escape route. I noticed that the gate was blocked by barbed wire leaning on two wooden piles crossed like an X. And that's when I made the decision that saved my life. Before the German commander could straighten up, I leapt like a tiger at the barbed wire. In an instant I'd leapt over it, landing one foot on the wooden support. In no time I'd merged into the crowd moving towards the tram, which brought me to the Zatorska, the place where ghetto forced laborers were called together.

"Afraid that the German officer might identify me, I was up at dawn the next morning and fled home to Proszowice. That day two miracles occurred. The first was getting out safely; the second was that during the morning lineup, the guard couldn't identify which prisoner was the father of the kid who escaped the German commander the previous day. I didn't want to endanger Tateh, so I didn't go anywhere near his labor camp. But I had no idea I'd never see him again," Abba says, and that twists my heart into a knot.

May my dear grandfather's soul forever be a blessing.

> He slipped the child's scarf off his neck and placed it around mine. Then he added his leather trouser belt 'so that you don't forget me,' he said with a bitter smile.

The Kraków Ghetto Up Until Its Liquidation

Abba was torn apart by sorrow. The harsh conditions and the Germans' attitudes only made things even harder, forcing him to flee once more from the labor camp in Kraków. Very few options were open to him. Judenrein Proszowice had become a death trap. The only choice was the Kraków Ghetto. Conditions there were extremely severe. On the first floor of the ghetto's main building lived a young woman whose family name was Zilberberg. She had a young son. She called Abba "Blondinker," the blond one.

"I did all kinds of jobs for her," Abba says. "I washed floors, chopped wood, babysat her child. In return I received food and a place to sleep. Later, two of my cousins from the Nathansohn family came from the city of Kazimierza Wielka. They had grown up in wealthy families. Accompanying them was a former officer of the Jewish police, known as OD Guttenberg, also from that city. Guttenberg bragged about coming to buy weapons and that he'd be going back to the forest to join the Partisans. He must have bragged to too many people because the story got leaked, it seems, to the Gestapo's intelligence officers.

"A few days later we were sitting in Mrs. Zilberberg's house. It was evening, and she was busy darning her child's socks. The son was playing with some kind of improvised game while a female refugee from Michów was fast asleep on the bed. I was busy sawing a closet door, planning to make a wooden box to take with me if we were going to be deported.

"Suddenly we heard the sound of military boots running up the stairs. We were scared to death. In seconds, the door burst open and German soldiers, accompanied by the Jewish police, weapons drawn, came in shouting, 'Don't move!' The child began crying hysterically. They went right over to the sleeping woman and shook her violently, screaming, 'Don't pretend you're asleep!' But she was, and she woke, confused, wondering if she was having a nightmare.

"The ghetto commander, Sturmführer Hasse himself, together with several other German commanders, stormed into the room. 'Where are your Judenpassen?' he barked, wanting to see the permits given to Jews. 'Hand them over now!' one of the commanders ordered. My hands rattling with fear, I presented mine, showing that I worked in the Strauss gas factories, and stating my name, Samek Blumenfeld, the Polish-sounding name I adopted from the moment my house was destroyed.

"He went over to the two Nathansohn brothers, who held out their permits. He read them slowly and carefully. 'Commander, sir,' one of the soldiers said, 'the names match. These are the two Nathansohns from Kazimierza Wielka.' Quickly the soldiers searched them and confiscated their money. 'Where are you keeping your weapons?' Hasse roared at us. The German officers locked us in an empty room with a guard. I wanted to use that opportunity to escape through the window but Mrs. Zilberberg begged me, with tears in her eyes, not to – 'for my child's sake' – she added. It was clear that if I'd tried to flee they'd have shot everyone else. So I dropped the idea."

And in so doing, Abba upheld the verse from Proverbs 16:32. "Who is strong? A person who overcomes his inclination." And once again, Abba proved that his instinct for self-preservation could be deferred if the good of others was a consideration. The Nathansohns were taken immediately to the Kraków Montelupich Prison, where they were tortured. Shortly afterwards, the Germans returned to the room we were locked in. On top of a tall closet in the room lay a suitcase. Hasse ordered a rigorous search. He ordered me to toss everything in the closet out onto the floor. The he ordered the mattresses overturned. He found a book in German.

"One side of the cover bore a large swastika; the book was titled *Mein Kampf*. 'Ask him how this got here!' he ordered the OD officer who translated the question. Although I understood German, I pretended not to. That gave me time to think about the best answer. While the OD was translating, I was quickly thinking. 'I don't know,' I said simply. He hit me on the head with the book. Hitler's book causes serious headaches in more ways than one, I remember thinking. Orders were given to arrest us and throw us into the Jewish police prison. Only then the soldiers left.

"A few days later, laborers were needed to unload ammunition in the Rakowice Airport. I was chosen, along with several other prisoners from the holding station, for forced labor, constant beating, and when the work was done we were loaded onto a truck with SS guards watching over us to be sure we went back to prison. On the way we passed the ghetto but didn't go in. We figured we must be heading for the Plaszow concentration camp. Just as we reached the tunnel at the camp's entrance, a train went over on the bridge above us. The truck came to a halt. The noise was terrifying. We were right under the train. Our guard was watching the trains passing. Right then the train sounded its horn and I thought my eardrums would burst. I saw one of the prisoners jump off the truck and flee, and without thinking twice, I did the same. We fled together. Behind us, several shots rang out but we were already far enough off to slip away. Minutes later everyone on the truck was shot to death behind a hill, following advance orders from the Plaszow camp commander Amon Göth. Among the dead were David Feifkofe, and Guttenberg from Kazimierza Wielka. As night fell we returned – beaten and cowed – to the ghetto.

> **I saw a prisoner jump off the truck and flee. Without thinking twice, I did the same. We fled together.**

"A few days later I was hunted yet again in the ghetto. This time I managed to get away by going up onto the roof of a three-story building, going into its chimney, and hanging there on a protruding pipe with the last of my strength. But I wasn't careful enough, and a couple of roof tiles slipped down, giving me away. I was caught. The policeman who made the catch brought me down and beat me cruelly. I was covered in soot, which for some reason made the OD laugh uncontrollably.

"And once again I was brought to the prison, now familiar to me, adjacent to the general soup kitchen, where prisoners were kept as slaves on alert for any needs the Germans may have. When I reached the prison gate accompanied by OD officers, dusk had turned to night. The guard opened the locks as the OD officer said to us, 'Drekkers,' you lot of garbage, 'in you go.' As he was trying to count us, I dropped down on all fours and crawled fast to the house opposite us. I took my shoes off and raced silently up the stairs to the fourth floor, and from there to the roof. I could see the OD officers hunting for me in the building. They knocked on all the doors, asking neighbors if they'd seen anyone.

"Next to the attic's door was a kitchen cabinet. I slipped all the drawers out and turned the opening towards the wall, then slid in, and sort of jiggled the cabinet from inside, to get it flush with the wall. I found an old, ripped, reeking cushion. I took all the feathers out and covered my head with them. Seconds later the Germans made it to the attic. A German soldier slid his hand inside the cabinet. He was so disgusted by how the feathers felt that he instantly jerked his hand out. Minutes later they were gone.

"Curled up inside the cabinet for hours, all I could think about was how bitter my life was, while I simultaneously tried to plan what I'd do next. No matter how hard I tried, I couldn't clean all the feathers off. They stuck because of the soot and their own sticky filth. So I left the house like that, passing the building's guard on the way. He looked at me like I was insane. And back I went to the ghetto."

The Kraków Ghetto's Liquidation

The Kraków Ghetto's last hours were bloody, cruel, and an event Abba will never forget despite the many horrors he'd see later during the Holocaust.

Once again the Germans chose Shabbat for their slaughtering. March 13, 1943. The Kraków Ghetto's Jews read the words, black as Hades, on posters hung on ghetto walls. The next day, Sunday, commemorated the day in the Jewish calendar when Moses passed from this world. On that Sunday the 14th, at 7 a.m., all Jews were to gather in Zgoda Square carrying no more than 10 kilos of belongings each. The younger ones would be taken to the Bliżyn forced labor camp, and the older people would "go east," the code for the Belzec death camps. Those posters are deeply engraved in Abba's memory.

"At the Jeruzulimskiej Street Jewish cemetery, headstones had been destroyed and a new camp built on the ruins. My father Heshel was among the laborers," Abba says, deep sorrow evident in his voice. "On one particular day of extremely hard labor, Göth pointed to my father and ordered him to run with a wheelbarrow loaded with chunks from the desecrated headstones while simultaneously beating him for not obeying orders. My father tried in vain to beg for mercy. This event drove me to leave him for good. I couldn't bear seeing his suffering and helplessness, nor could I help him. I desperately wanted to know the real nature of the eastbound deportations. I was thinking that if my family is no longer alive, what do I need this world for? Meanwhile, I kept hidden between the ghetto walls, which helped save my sanity from the shameful horrors outside.

"As dawn broke on Sunday, I left all the neighbors I'd known in the ghetto. I knocked on old Babtshiya's door and woke her up. 'Who's there not letting me sleep?' she cursed as the door opened. 'Pani, come quickly to Zgoda Square, it's almost 7:00!' 'No!' she said firmly and led me to the bed. 'See? Yesterday I changed all the linens. I'm going back to bed and locking the door. The Germans can kiss my ass. I'll die in a clean bed, not in a gas chamber.' She walked me to the door. 'You're still young. Too young to die' was her parting message to me.

"I took my wooden box and backpack, stuffed a few bread rolls into my shirt, and put the tefillin that my grandfather had made for me into a pocket in my pants. I didn't want to leave those behind. In Zgoda Square many people were already gathered, packages hoisted on their shoulders. Several OD officers were looking for people with professions needed for the labor camps. One job included searching for hidden Jewish belongings, cleaning the streets where the Germans would carry out their bloodbath in a few minutes' time, and other jobs. Getting chosen for a job increased your chances of survival, and people were bribing the OD with cash to get their names listed.

"Thousands of Jews filled the square. Among them I saw Rabbi Wachs and his family; Ittel Weinstein and her daughters Malka, Hannah and Esti; Feigeleh Platkewicz; Beileh Izbicki and her children; Hayeleh Schlesinger; Mechl Kleiner; Kalman Shidlowski; Niebilski; the Pińczewski family; Avraham Wolberg and his family; Avreimeleh Feigeh, and dozens of others from Proszowice whom I knew well.

"Bells from the Maritski Church and others across Kraków clanged loudly, marking 7 a.m., calling Christian believers to Sunday morning mass. That's how it is when the Jewish people get murdered. The world keeps turning. Those bells were the Germans' sign to begin.

"Out of nowhere, dozens of armored vehicles outfitted with machine guns suddenly showed up. The square was surrounded by metal and officers of every type and color: Poles were in dark blue, Ukrainians in black, SS in green. Two Germans and a Pole brandishing axes set to work uprooting the barbed wire lining Lebowska Street to make the exit wider. Truck convoys rolled in to conduct the evacuation. Such despair.

"Next, the orders to line up in fives were barked out as the camp commander, Göth, rolled in together with Sturmführer Hasse. Both wore white gloves, as though they were attending a formal ball. Behind them came the SS, and soldiers armed with machine guns, rifles, and bayonets. One unit broke into the hospital. Shots and shouts and screams: they killed all the patients along with all the doctors and nurses.

"Göth and Hasse, and Nazi officers Rudolph Kerner and Wilhelm Kunde, stood at the square's center giving orders: 'Umbringen!' 'Kill! Exterminate!' they roared. Göth was holding a gun and still looking for people with specific professions. Everyone had their hands raised, surrendering in advance: anything to avoid giving the murderers a chance to murder. The next order was to throw all our packages aside. The SS picked the elderly and children out from the crowds, shoving them all into the corridor of a shelter. Armed with machine guns, the SS murdered them all. The corridor filled with corpses. Blood flooded from the house out into Zgoda Square, which turned into a slaughterhouse for Kraków's Jews.

"An alley blocked by a high concrete wall separated the hospital and the shelter. That wall set the Jewish street apart from the non-Jews and the freedom they enjoyed. Now everyone else was being pushed into the alley – men and women, old and young, mothers with babies... everyone, without any order or logic. Piercing shrieks came from mothers who'd lost hold of their children. Into the heart of heaven the voices rose until they surely must have been heard by Governor Frank. Humans, created in the image of G-d, were slaughtering fellow humans, trampling them under German boots. 'Why do you hide your countenance from us, G-d?' I kept asking. Standing in the square, I kept wondering if it would not be better to die, but even that is a thought that a Jew has no control over. We do not determine who lives or who dies. The atrocities were taking place before my eyes like a nightmare. I call on the words that every Jewish infant suckled on together with its mother's milk: 'Hear O Israel, the Lord our G-d, the Lord is One.' I say it over and over in my mind. I whisper the words again and again but G-d isn't listening."

The Murder of Proszowice's Righteous Rabbi Wachs

"Zgoda Square looked like a one-way battlefield. Volleys of heavy shooting by the Germans killed off the Jewish civilian population. The voices of the dying grew weak and slowly became inaudible. Here and there, I heard a mother's faint sigh or the cry of an infant clinging to its mother's bleeding heart, its little fists slipping back and forth in her blood. The sun's first rays lit the head of a little one that the murderous gunners had missed. The child called out, 'Mama, Mama!' Its cries annoyed the Germans so they hunted it down. It cried in pain. They want to finish what they'd started: 'We'll show you, mongrel that you are!' the German hissed at the tiny tot. 'How did we skip you? I'll finish the job right away.'

"Suddenly a German jumped up. He had a skull emblazoned on his helmet. 'Don't shoot!' he shouted. A flash of hope: I wondered whether this soldier might prove that humanity still exists despite the evil. But the seemingly humane soldier flipped the infant, spattered by its mother's blood, up and caught it by its little feet. The infant must have thought it was being played with and broke into a smile. Swinging the infant back a little, the German slammed its head into the concrete wall. Blood spurted from its head, flowing into the river of blood in the alley.

"An SS unit accompanied by Alsatians spread out across the ghetto in search of Jews. The dogs were trained to be vicious. Anyone found alive was shot. From rooms, from kitchens, from attics and stairwells, blood flowed into the square. The ghetto was red. Innocents breathed their last. Who would save them? The question hung in my thoughts. No one came to save them.

"Commander Göth had chosen the people tasked with looting valuables from the dead. Then came the order to shoot the collectors, leaving no evidence. Among those shot were Yossl and Moshe Lewenberg of Proszowice.

"Now those of us selected earlier were given orders. We were hurried onto trucks, beaten as we went. SS guards in a frenzy of blood shot people at random.

"Shlomo Blum stood behind me. So did Leib Bitter and Loizer Meir Grundman. I saw them disappear through the nearest exit gate. Itche Meisels was shot right next to me. So were Avreimeleh Feigeh, Moshe Bienental and many others I knew. Suddenly I heard a whisper behind me. 'Boy. Don't turn your head around. Hide me.' Someone was trying to survive the horrors by slinking close to me but a round of shots from close range hit him. He crumpled to the ground. Something warm trickled down the side of my palm, drawing my attention. A bullet had grazed my left hand.

"The last trucks were being loaded. We were moving towards them at a run. A chair next to the truck was there to help us get inside. With batons and hoes, two SS officers beat anyone taking too long to climb in.

The final victim of this chilling massacre was our righteous Rabbi Wachs. He passed a group of children from the home, standing together, ready to be killed, as he walked to the waiting truck. Gently he stroked a child's head, filling that child with joy a moment before being murdered. Rabbi Wachs then passed by the corpses piled in the square's center. His eyes opened wide behind his glasses as he identified people he knew well as they took their last breaths. Thousands dead, lying in rivers of blood. Suddenly he realized just how much the Kraków and Proszowice Jews had been deceived. He stood there, a man of G-d, his tallit wrapped around him, and began to pray the mourners' prayer: 'Yisgodol v'Yiskodosh Shemay Rabah.' Glorified and sanctified is G-d's great name. He got no further than those first four words. The German fired several shots at him. Rabbi Wachs fell while sanctifying the dead, his tallit slipping off his shoulders and covering several others along with him.

"The children were next. They looked like little angels scattered with red flowers accompanying the martyred rabbi to heaven. But the rabbi wasn't dead yet; he was in terrible agony for a long time, his body twisting in spasms until his soul left him, and all the while he hoarsely whispered psalms. A light breeze lifted the corner of his tallit. When it fell, it covered his face. As he took his last breath, then moved no more, the cries of and groans and sighs of the Proszowice's dying Jews ceased. It brought to an end the long chain of generations that had lived in Kraków and Proszowice. May their memories be a blessing."

The infant clung to its mother's bleeding heart, smearing its tiny hands in her blood.

Assaf, a student in the 11ᵗʰ grade, was part of the March of the Living delegation to Poland in 1993. Assaf is the kind of kid every mother prays for – smart, clever, sensitive, a marathon runner. A student like that in the reality of the 1990s attracted the attention of others. He drew mine, too, from the moment he decided to join the delegation. As far as I knew, he had no direct link to the Shoah. If I go, okay, that's understandable, I remember thinking, not yet aware just how deeply the Holocaust had affected me. But Assaf? What connection did he have to all that? I made a mental note to check it out later.

The flow of delegations bringing thousands of young Israelis to Poland was starting to make the locals raise an eyebrow mostly around their wonder: How is it that so many youth, many of whom never had families victimized by the Holocaust, were coming more than a generation later to weep and mourn and remember what happened to the pre-war local Jewish population? The impact was powerful and utterly unique, with no equivalent anywhere in modern society. That's our secret, I smile to myself: The Torah commanded us to pass on the story of our people's exodus from Egypt from generation to generation; if we do that vis-à-vis an exodus of some 4,000 years ago, would we not do the same for a far more recent, deeply traumatic event experienced by a huge swath of our population?

As the trip's date approached, Assaf was primarily concerned about two issues. The first was the result of his sister joining a similar trip a year earlier and describing how emotional it was, how they all cried so much, and he is anyhow extremely sensitive. The second was how to maintain his fitness and ensure that he runs the quota of weekly kilometers necessary for an active athlete who participates in competitive marathons. Once we reached our hotel in Kraków, the security commander accompanying our group wouldn't allow Assaf out for a night run. My solution was for me to run with him. The security commander found that satisfactory.

So Assaf and I set out for a run through Kraków's streets. The city is very intertwined with my family's history; as we ran, Abba's stories – about life in the ghetto or images of violent deportations – came to mind. I wasn't familiar with the area where Assaf and I were jogging but every house looked to me like it had had some part in the ghetto events; every plaza and square looked like Zgoda, and even the red taillights of cars were reminiscent of blood streaming through the streets, as Abba so frequently described.

What an unbelievable sight: an Israeli teacher and his student jogging through Kraków, so close to each other, but as the one guarding him, so distant from each other. Assaf is completely engrossed in his jogging technique; I'm completely engrossed in fighting off the images of past horrors that are flooding me. I fight myself, my heavy breathing, the mental journey… another Jew dead, more blood, another brutal act, more cruelty. Assaf, with no idea what's going on inside me, urges me on. "C'mon, teacher, you're falling behind on the pace!"

I don't have a problem jogging. My problem has to do with the heavy load I'm carrying, which is getting tougher. In the end I'm left with no choice. "Keep running in a straight line as far as you need to go, then do 180 degrees and come right back and meet me here." Assaf can be relied on. He's pleased with that. I plop down on a bench, hoping to get my thoughts in some kind of organized order. Here I am, I'm thinking, stepping on this pavement where 50 years earlier, a bloodbath eradicated a huge Jewish population. Did Abba stand right here when bullets flew past him, to his right, to his left, and was he unharmed only by the grace of G-d? Here I am now with my student, a symbol of continuity, of rallied existence. I think of Janusz Korczak and how I am fulfilling his wisdom: "Those concerned with days plant wheat; those concerned with years plant trees; those concerned with generations educate people." What a victory!

And suddenly a thought comes along, and I'm flooded with anxiety. Where's Assaf? What if he gets lost? How could I ever explain that? Who'd even believe me? Worry has my heart pumping faster. "Teacher! Teacher!" Assaf's voice rings out. He's extremely pleased: He's hit the target he set for himself and, without noticing my anxiousness, begins his cool-down exercises.

We set out for the hotel once again. He's pleased with his run, and I'm pleased that he's back safely. I comfort myself for this failure of teacherly duty, repeating to myself that Assaf can always be relied upon. Later, he would go on to become an award-winning soldier for his excellence in the Israel Air Force's "669" rescue unit – running, rappelling, rescuing people hundreds of times. In 2008 he won the Israel Triathlon Championship; today he's a trainer and lecturer, and runs a triathlon training center and "Ironman" competition training program. I'm so proud of him, and of myself for identifying that trait in him, but once back in Kraków at the hotel, moments after I feel that the worry of our getting back safely has dissipated, Assaf suddenly turns to me and asks, "Why did you stop?"

In retrospect, he was already showing his inherent coach characteristics. I try to cover up what I'd experienced. A childish surge of victory fills Assaf; he'll have some juicy news to tell his classmates. He has proved that he can be trusted, and in that closeness created between us, I want to tell him Abba's story about Zgoda Square, and the Kraków Ghetto deportation, and the weighty load I carry inside ever since hearing Abba's descriptions. "Assaf," I begin, but then find myself saying something else altogether, "I don't know what happened to me, but I just couldn't keep up with you. You're a fantastic runner. You beat me hands down!" Assaf is thrilled at his achievement and has just been handed a great reason to beam from ear to ear, whereas I've kept Abba's stories tightly locked up in my heart.

For 25 years there was no contact between my student Assaf and me. He graduated and grew up; I also matured. Then on the evening of the 2018 Yom HaShoah (Holocaust Remembrance Day) he contacted Abba, me, and the members of his 1993 delegation to Poland, inviting us all to a "Zikaron Ba'salon" evening, an informal get-together usually hosted in a private home, at which Holocaust memories were shared by people who had experienced the war and its events, with the invited guests. Assaf suggested we talk about the significance and meaning of that trip for us all. Once again, that evening, I lacked the courage to open up to Assaf and share with him what I'd experienced when we ran together in Kraków.

While preparing for this unique evening, when Abba was slated to recount his life story, I once again wondered about the angle he would take to cram five years of suffering and agony into the two hours allocated for his talk before some 100 people in Assaf's garden. My experiences of coping with this in the future would teach me just how difficult it could be.

Knowing Abba, I knew he'd start talking and wouldn't stop. His Shoah begins around September 1939, when the Germans conquered Proszowice, and ends in May 1945, when the transit camp in Theresienstadt, Czechoslovakia, was liberated. He begins this period as an unsullied 13-year-old, and ends it as an extremely mature 18-year-old adult. Wrong! A bell goes off in my teacher's mind, as though the student hadn't given a precise response. Correct! He starts out at 13, but he never leaves that world. I correct my own error. Abba has remained stuck in the Shoah, in that world of its concepts, in its approach, in the scope of interest he shows in it. I sift through the stories, and try to shape a logical, sequential path in that incomprehensible narrative, sprung into the reality and world of concepts we now live in, in the twenty-first century, as citizens with equal rights in the Jewish State. There's no way to talk about something completely irrational in a rational manner, I conclude. The evening could well end up being one great, long, exhausting monologue, I begin to fear. But Abba is very charismatic, very authentic, very honest, very true to the facts; he doesn't dramatize, he doesn't take credit where it's not his to take. He talks, and if you're willing to listen, he'll talk — describing his experiences, sharing his honest emotions, capturing his listeners' minds.

In the paradox that exemplifies Abba's life, the audiences frequently break into laughter. He has an ability to reflect the past in a very gifted manner. I watch the people there; they often end up moved, curious, and definitely admiring Abba's trajectory in life. It's important for us to carry on, to commemorate for the sake of future generations, to uphold the verse "That you shall remember the day you left Egypt, for your entire life" (Deut. 16:3). And this is our exodus from Egypt! Mine too? Yes, and we fulfill this commandment time and again. Abba's testimony shows me that there is a message here, that there's a moral, a lesson to be learned. I choose to take on the task of continuing to share it.

The Path to Hell on Earth

Abba's plan — and wish — to die didn't work out. A divine hand seemed to be guarding him there in Zgoda Square. The killing died down for a moment. Abba checked himself: Yes, his bones were all there, as his mother hoped for. He was alive! He broke into the mad run of a wounded animal that has escaped from a trap, leaping onto the last truck in the convoy. On his way, he absorbed being beaten by a few Germans, but all he was focused on was getting to the truck on time. At the very last second he leaped inside and the door closed behind him. In fact, he was the last of the Jews deported from the Kraków Ghetto who managed to catch a ride out, as though fulfilling the verse from Jeremiah 48:44: "One who flees fear will surely fall into the pit." But as far as Abba's decision as he fled the Kraków Ghetto, his ride in the convoy truck took him to the pits of the Auschwitz-Birkenau death camps.

"Dozens of trucks loaded with the crushed bodies of Jews moved from the location where the massacre was carried out, off to an unknown destination. At the last second, people still being held in the OD prison in the city were loaded on, too. They included Tateh, and I was hoping they included the Nathanson brothers."

Abba described how the convoy moved off, accompanied by Germans on motorbikes and carrying machine guns. An SS officer sat in the truck, constantly whipping the Jews with a slim rod. Devoid of any human rights, at the peak of a bright, clear day, the Jews left Kraków forever, led like animals to a place only the Germans knew.

Driving slowly from Lebowska Street to Limanowska Street, they passed the ghetto. Adjacent to Wengerska Street, thousands of bundles were piled. They belonged to the Jews, they were marked with their addresses, and they were a silent testimony to the orders handed down by Amon Leopold Göth, the senior Nazi in charge of violently razing the Kraków Ghetto. Their owners had been told that they'd be collected and brought to their new place of residence. Standing like a guard dog next to the pile of belongings was David Goyter, the ghetto's commissar, in OD uniform, a middle-aged man whose face was pale and had typical Jewish features. He trusted no one, and watched over the items to be sure nothing would be taken.

The convoy halted near Knyszyn. The Germans needed their coffee break, accompanied by thin slices of bread. Abba noted how it amazed him to watch these people, with their enlightened education, stuffing the food into their mouths without washing their hands first, even though some had dried Jewish blood on them. Midway through their break, the soldiers, bored with not having killed any Jews for an hour or so, suddenly turned with extreme politeness to the Jews crammed into the trucks. "Anyone want to come out for some fresh air?" Several dozen were allowed outside to relieve themselves. Instantly, before they'd even finished jumping off the truck, the killing started. "Please, feel free. Anyone else?" the Germans goaded. Some of those already shot were gasping and convulsing. Happy with themselves, the Germans simply sat down and resumed their coffee and sandwich break. Nothing put a damper on their appetite. Once they'd finished, they pulled another 10 or so Jews off the truck and shot them for no reason.

"The SS men demanded money from us," Abba says. "Gold, silver, watches. 'You're going to the gas chambers anyhow,' they mocked us. I was sitting in the front of the truck next to the SS officer, who pulled my hair every time he wanted to make an announcement. He ordered me to shout out loud that we Jews must hand over everything we have, immediately, while he beat me with his baton.

"Seated in the truck was a familiar-looking man from town, Yisrael Goldstein. He used to be called 'minister' back in the day, a term to indicate respect for his wisdom, which was also acknowledged by the non-Jewish residents. He was brilliant. And even here in the truck he didn't lose his humanity. 'My dears,' he attempted to buoy our spirits, 'hold on. There's no doubt we're being taken to work. Don't lose your self-confidence, my fellow Jews. You see that G-d's still watching over us.' His words did help me, raising the hope that perhaps G-d would still be looking out for me. In Proszowice, whatever he said always came true, so why not now too? That's what I remember thinking at the time.

"The town of Auschwitz was about 60 kilometers from Kraków. The German soldiers rushed us out of the trucks next to a cemetery, screaming wildly at us, hitting us with all their energy. We discovered that these were "tip trucks"; the cabin area simply began to rise and dump us all out like worthless garbage, driving a short way forward, then reversing, shaking the cabins to make sure everyone was out, while crushing people to death. Groups of SS with their Alsatians began to corral us. We had no idea what they wanted or where they wanted us to go. On either side stood a row of SS soldiers holding machine guns. Another group of commanders selected us: who to life, to the right; who to death, to the left. New tragedies took place here. It was our first taste of them. The soldiers weren't shooting wildly this time. They were separating children from parents, husbands from wives. It was so painful to watch. One small flick of a finger by a German officer determined a person's fate. A finger pointing left sent the person to the gas chambers and furnaces. To the right, to forced labor. No investigation into the person's abilities. Just a matter of luck, or the officer in charge of selection making an assumption about each of us.

"I watched the last of Proszowice's Jews disappear. Among them was my aunt, Feigeleh Platkiewice, and her five-year-old daughter Bashaleh, who I carried the night that we fled. I was sure they'd be saved. But here they were, at the mercy of a momentary decision. Avraham Wolberg and his family joined them. So did Ittel Rosenblum, Beileh Izbicki, Ittel Weinstein with her daughters, and so many more people that I knew from home. I saw David Shidlowski's two youngest children, Shmuel and Greineleh, and Ozer Figeh's two youngest, his five-year-old son Moshe and nine-year-old daughter Blumah, running, their hands chained, distraught, panicked, orphaned, right to the furnaces.

"Not far from there, I could see Yossel Hassid with a blond boy and a girl in his arms. Next to him stood Avraham Schneider and his son Fishel. The German murderer making selections signaled to both men to move to the right, and their children to the left. Both men objected. 'No, we can't leave our children,' they said, clinging to them as though locked together. It was the first time I'd seen a Jew oppose the Nazis – ironically, at the Auschwitz crematoria. The SS soldier was insisting that the men go to the right and the children to the left, to their deaths. 'No,' both men shook their heads very blatantly, 'we will not be separated from them.' SS soldiers attacked the two men, beating them with metal rods. When they fell, the SS trampled them with their boots. Both men moaned and groaned, but did not give in.

"Yossel was well known to everyone in Proszowice. He was of average build, but broad shouldered; he had a full face, ruddy cheeks, and a thick beard. Big blue eyes. A high forehead. A quiet, G-d fearing man of great integrity. His father-in-law, Avraham Figa, his wife and their daughter had just been murdered in front of him in the Kraków ghetto. Only he and his two children made it this far. He knew what the murderers would do to his children. He didn't beg for mercy for himself. With great nobility he chose the same fate that his children would be dealt. Avraham Schneider was tall, olive-skinned, and had sparkling black eyes; he was a quiet, clean-shaven man, who wore what was considered German dress, as the Proszowice Jews called it. Like all of us at the time, he hoped for a better future. He never dreamed there would come a day when he and Yossel would stand, proudly Jewish, battling their German overlords right in front of burning furnaces as the stench of burnt flesh filled the air, flames licked the skies, and smoke belched thick and black around them.

"The sun began to set. It was getting dark very quickly. Yossel and Avraham were still battling the cruel German's boot. They lay on the ground, bones broken, covered in blood, and with the last of their strength dragged themselves to the Birkenau furnaces that swallowed them in cries of pain that marked the end of that miserable March 14, 1943. The night's darkness surrounded the hellhole known as Birkenau. The flames took them all; they had no mercy on any of these people. We were marched into the camp. Our heads were bowed, and a silent entreaty to G-d filled our hearts: 'When will this horror stop? How far can human suffering go? And G-d, where are you?' 'The voice of my brother cries out from the ground.' G-d, we beg you; Save us. G-d, we beg you: Save us. That ran through my mind, over and over."

The Jeruzulimskiej Forced Labor Camp and Heshel Blumenfeld's Bitter End

I never saw Abba cry and we never spoke about tears, but crying was viewed in our family as weakness. It was an unspoken rule infused into our family's code of behavior. When my sister married in 1978 and emigrated to Brazil, in essence leaving her family, Abba was happy for her but found it hard to bid her farewell. It was the only time I saw him overcome an inclination to cry, almost crying. In the end, not a single tear fell. I didn't understand it then but now I think that perhaps I do. My older sister, Shoshana, was named for my father's mother, Rosa. The experience of separating from his daughter brought my father back to the experience of separating from his mother in August 1942 in Proszowice. Abba never saw his mother again. Perhaps he'd suppressed this event subconsciously along with her tragic end, and at his daughter's wedding the memories gushed up. Over time, this tendency to suppress was rooted in me, too. Separation, even for the most joyful of reasons, was seen in our family as a very problematic act.

On one of Abba's trips as a living witness, this time with the Ramot School, and during one of the discussions with students – who usually cried at the stories and sights they were being exposed to each day – a student asked, "Shmuel, how is it that you aren't crying? I've never seen you cry."

Partly sarcastic, partly serious, Abba answered, "I cried so much back then that I seem to have run out of tears."

The conclusion is clear. Tears? No, not in our family. But as life shows us, everything has its time. And tears? Let's see.

The deep pain in the following story left Abba speechless. It seemed that every word he spoke was a pang of pain, but he decided to share this story about his father, Heshel Blumenfeld. This time, though, he opted for a different angle, perhaps due to the emotional difficulty, and authored the story about my late grandfather down. Here's the text.

* * *

After the horrifying news about the Germans' behavior in eradicating the Kraków Ghetto reached the Plaszow camp, and the way Zgoda Square turned into a killing field awash with Jewish blood from the massacre of thousands of ghetto Jews, and especially after watching Avraham Yehoshua Heshel Blumenfeld from the Plaszow hilltop for days, working on the trucks clearing the corpses from the Kraków Ghetto, I understood the scope of the catastrophe. A quorum of 10 Jewish men gathered in Plaszow, men whose families had been killed. My father was among them. Silently they said Kaddish, the mourner's prayer. My father was certain I was among the dead, which would have left him alone in the world.

Over the next few days, my father moved like a living shadow, losing his will to live, losing what gave him a reason to live. Some weeks later, not yet 40 years old, he was murdered by Amon Leopold Göth.

Alone, tortured, forlorn, my father's life ended without knowing that I was still alive, and fighting to stay alive as my mother had wanted. My father never knew that even though he had lost his wife and six young children, as well as several hundred extended family members, I was still there.

Hell on Earth: Day One at Birkenau (Brzezinka)

On Pesach we read the verse from Exodus 13:8. "And you shall tell your offspring on that day, saying: It is because of that which the Lord did for me when I came forth out of Egypt."

It seems that there are moments in our lives we've been destined to encounter. My childhood is a now a long-ago memory and I've seen a few things in life, but I'm always surprised anew by how our lives are infused with meaning and seem to be directed by a supreme power, how everything that happens to us happens for a reason. We may not be aware of it as the moment or event plays out, and we may not be able to understand or accept that moment or event right then, but later on it is clarified. Otherwise, how can I explain the fact that exactly when the weekly Torah portion of Balak (Numbers 22-24), being my Bar Mitzvah reading, came up, it was exactly the week when Abba was invited to his hometown in Poland to be honored 76 years after being expelled?

So, there we were, three generations of the same family, touring the Auschwitz-Birkenau death camp so symbolic of the Shoah, and where Abba's family was murdered. This visit to the site says more than all else: Here we are despite it all – believers, optimists – and stronger than ever.

Poland is, for me, one massive cemetery. Wherever I go, I encounter signs of silenced Jews. Lavishly outfitted synagogues now abandoned. Cemeteries, their silence screaming grief, and speaking to the tremendous influence that Jewish communities had here in the past. A silence that exemplifies Genesis 4:10: "The voice of your brother's blood is crying to me from the ground."

This time, however, unlike on my previous visits to Poland, I also felt that the Poles themselves, who are predominantly devout Christians, were feeling the absence of a Jewish entity among them, and maybe even missing them. They talk with longing and nostalgia of our Jewish culture, of our close connection to learning and intellectual enhancement. When I move around through tourist centers and see restaurants with Jewish names, traditional Jewish foods and so on, I understand that something has changed since the darkness experienced in the 1940s. Abba, on the other hand, is busy closing one open end after another. I look on from the sidelines, watching in wonder, observing the miracle taking place before my eyes. It's unbelievable. It takes time to digest, to understand the significance of what's happening to us in the here and now. It's stunning. It's remarkable.

"Not just me," Abba begins as we enter the Auschwitz-Birkenau concentration camp, "but the greatest of authors, the great talents of the time, cannot put into words the suffering in this terrible hellhole called Birkenau. So many talented writers have tried to express the destruction after they healed, after getting back to themselves as best they could, with hindsight, and yet a thought sneaks into their hearts as they write: 'Are we perhaps exaggerating a little when we describe the horrors? Perhaps some Germans were in fact decent, and only we came into the line of fire of the particularly cruel ones?'"

"What could be worse – or more gruesome – than shooting over 4,000 people dead in one day? Shooting the old and young, men and women, children and babies, all crammed into a space of 100 m^2, with killing that began early that morning, right there in the city center and not even off in some distant town? What could be worse than knowing that this all took place in the center of a respectable city, not some hostile village? That it occurred in a city where Polish kings and governors ruled? Where the governor could hear the wailing and crying of children being shot to death, yet chose to pretend that nothing had happened? In this city every Christian child saw, and could describe, what happened to the Kraków Ghetto on that bitter, cursed day.

"The Germans – the supposedly enlightened nation– known for esthetic sensitivity, known for loving order and discipline, known for scientific breakthroughs, cultural leaders of their time, carried out – with their own hands – the horrific massacre, in a single day, of an entire populace. And by looting the murdered civilians' personal belongings, they simultaneously reduced the monies and valuables coming into the Reich's coffers. Nothing bothered them. Were the Germans not bloodthirsty animals, they could have asked us to board vehicles, taken us quietly to the furnaces, and asked us politely, 'Bitte, please, go in.' And if we'd have disobeyed, well, they could have then claimed in their defense that they were justified in carrying out acts of violence against us.

"To carry out this job, the Germans didn't recruit lowly classes from their society's peripheries, rather their military's elite forces, the same units that were busy crushing Europe at the time. Who among us was so lethal that elite forces were called for? Rabbi Wachs, a pious, spiritual man, a luminary of Jewish study, a righteous person, and his Jewish wife? A baby a few months old who was just learning to point to the sun and name it? What thrust of opposition did the Germans recruit their special units for, armed with automatic weapons, dogs, and other tools of war, when the only thing unarmed Jews could be accused of was being Jewish?

"But the Germans did their work very well, preparing themselves for the day when the order would come to eradicate the ghetto. They knew that Jewish families were very cohesive, that none would willingly destroy the unifying fabric of family and community life; the Germans knew they'd encounter difficulties on their way to their supreme objective. So they readied by slaughtering thousands of families, shooting them wildly simply to break the Jewish spirit. They butchered thousands of good people, heroes like Yossel and Avraham, who fought to cling to the highest ethics of humanity as divinely commanded by our Holy Torah, and on which every Jewish child there was raised from infanthood: 'Thou Shalt Not Kill.' A simply worded commandment, it includes men, women, children, and the helpless. The Germans did not expect to encounter Jews willing to go to their deaths to uphold a principle that the Germans neither comprehended nor believed in: sanctifying G-d's name."

We reach Birkenau's gates. Abba stops, looks around, and continues his story.

"Here, before the concentration camp gates, we were stopped and counted. We numbered 480. 'Stramm stehen!' Hut 10! Stand at attention! Forward! March!' was the German command that was barked at us.

"As we marched into the infamous Auschwitz-Birkenau, the camp's bell was ringing. Prisoners' voices could be heard in the blocks. Horses' hooves rang out somewhere. In we marched, our faces gloomy, our heads hung, our bodies bowed. The sun disappeared. The sky grew dark. A pervasive cold filled the place. And we marched on, through Birkenau, just when prisoners were being counted.

"Hundreds of people were standing next to the block closest to us. Living skeletons. They filled us with fear in the night's darkness. Several corpses, people who had been shot, lay a bit farther off. They were naked; a thick black marker had been used to mark their personal numbers on their chests. Once upon a time they'd been proud, living Jews. I focused on the distorted faces, wondering how they could even get so contorted. I wondered if all the crazy people in the world had been brought here, then what was I doing here? It was a mystery for which I had no answer. Slowly it dawned on me: It's very possible that tomorrow I'll also look like that.

"Our group had been urged into a run by roared commands, kicks, whipping, and clubs coming down on us by the people leading us until we reached an empty block. In the few minutes that the Germans left us alone, each of us looked around for people we knew; maybe we'd catch sight of family or friends. I kept wondering who of all the people I knew survived the brutal Kraków Ghetto massacre and the first round of selections. These are the people I gaped at in the block that Sunday morning, the people who came with me from the Kraków Ghetto. Four-hundred and eighty prisoners. I could easily identify Nathan Adler, Itche-Meir Adler, Avraham Blumenfrucht and his sons Hirsch-Meir and Moisheleh, Yossef Bocket and his father Mordechai Shmuel. I also saw Yisrael Hirsch Goldstein, Victor Gross, Meir (Shlepik) Goldstein; Meir, Avraham, Leib, Kalman and Idel Pińczewski; Beirel, Mendel and Dovidel Feifkofe; Shlomo (Tzvaniak) Kleiner and his brother Yankel, and Avreimeleh Shmuel Kleiner; Kalman Shidlowski; Munik and Yankel Shteiner; Michael Kleiner; David Tannenbaum; Yisrael Weinrob; Hirsch Izbiki; Avraham Michaelowicz; Abba Roznik; Shimon Derdik; Idel Niebielski; Avner Weinrob; Volf Rothmansch; Moshe Wolberg; and many others.

"Most of them didn't survive Auschwitz-Birkenau. They, like so many thousands of others, became no more than a puff in a chimney. May the memories of the murdered innocents be blessed forever."

Auschwitz-Birkenau: Learning the Ropes

"I lay in the Birkenau assimilation block, unable to fall asleep. The day's horrors were running through my mind like a movie. I couldn't decide if it was good or bad that I'd survived so far, but I did realize I had little control over any of it. I had no idea how long I'd been lying there when I woke up because several very clean prisoners, with healthy, ruddy faces and carefully tilted camp caps, entered carrying a long table and bench with them. They were dressed in civilian clothes, with crosses marked on their chests in red oil paint. On the left they wore the camp number with a triangle, and on the right a second triangle in yellow and red. The same markings were on their trousers.

"My eyes opened wide on seeing these healthy faces. A snippet of hope slipped into my soul. We'll be all right here, I was thinking. These thoughts and their accompanying hope confused my senses. I turned to the people entering. 'Sir, where are we?' I asked softly.

"The man I was facing cut me short and glared at me, as though indicating that my life depended on his answer. His eyes were clearly asking who the impudent youngster was, daring to speak to him in this place. 'Son of a bitch, this is Birkenau! And here you don't ask questions. Here you come running in through the gate and leave in torment straight to heaven via the chimney.' He paused. 'And one more word from that filthy throat of yours and you won't make it to midday,' he added.

"Feeling awkward, I lowered my eyes. My mind was still full of sights from the massacre, but there's no time to think or get offended in Birkenau. Here the rule was: You live in the present; there's no past, and there's no future."

"The man shouted at everyone with his booming voice. 'Sons of bitches, get in alphabetical order.' They placed lined cards on the table and took out bottles of black ink and wooden pens with nibs that looked like glass. Each of us approached the table in turn."

Son of a bitch, this is Birkenau! And here you don't ask questions. Here you come running in through the gate and leave in torment straight to heaven via the chimney.

"Behind me in the line stood my Proszowice neighbor, Hirsch-Meir Blumenfrucht, his brother, and their father, a tall man with a pale face. The misery in his eyes was evident as he watched the ruddy man write down the details. 'Surname?' 'Blumenfeld,' I answered. 'Given name?' 'Samek,' I said, offering the new name I'd adopted in a moment of frustration in the Kraków Ghetto. Samek is an abbreviated form of 'smotnik,' meaning forlorn, perfectly matching how I felt – without family, without a home. Later I realized that if someone called me 'Shmuel' it meant we were acquainted from before the war, from a time when we were happy, but if a person called me 'Samek,' I'd know we were acquainted from this hellhole. The questions continued. 'Place of birth?' the man carried on, ignoring the agony clearly showing on my face. 'Occupation?' 'Student,' I answered automatically.

"Hirsch-Meir's father, behind me in the line and listening intently, couldn't stop himself. He bent forward, and very firmly corrected the answer, talking directly to this Jew acting as the devil's emissary. 'Tailor,' he said. Then he turned to me. 'Why would you lie to him?' he rebuked me, 'you're not a student, you're a tailor.' He spoke with firm conviction, and by doing so he saved my life. The clerk, who moments before had reprimanded me and told me to be quiet, was pleased with that response and made the correction: 'Apprentice Tailor.' This was a valid reason to keep me alive. On the card's margins was a column dedicated to the reason for the Jewish prisoner's incarceration. At this point nothing was asked; the clerk simply wrote, 'Jewish political prisoner.'"

"I wanted to scream '*Gevald*!' Shmuel, son of Avraham Yehoshua Heshel, is a political prisoner? What, was he plotting to overthrow the German Reich? Me? Still a school kid, in fact, being tutored by Moshe David, who received my mother's hard-earned meager zlotys to teach me as much Torah as possible. All she wanted was that one day I'd be a great, learned rabbi among the Jewish people, that I'd love G-d, love my fellow Jews, and despise cruelty and violence, revenge and bloodshed. When, as a child, I'd walk to the slaughterer to have a chicken butchered, I'd turn away, unable to watch the animal's blood being drained. But here in Birkenau, in a split second I'd become a political prisoner. Even in a place as inhumane as this, I found the insult hard to swallow.

"Right away, the next ruddy-faced man sprang into action, ordering me to pull up my left sleeve. Forcefully, he stretched my skin tight, and started tattooing the number 108006 on my arm. More than 80 pricks of a heated needle point dipped in ink. My arm swelled a moment later. 'Don't forget your number. From now on that's what you are. A number for the furnaces and chimneys,' was all he said.

"Hirsch-Meir's father smiled at me warmly. 'Shmuel, you'll live!' he said. I stared at him, gripping my arm, my face warped in pain. I couldn't understand why he'd say that. He explained. The numeric value of 108 divided by 006 is 18, and that's '*Chai*' in Hebrew, the word for life. 'See, my son? You're going to live for sure!' he encouraged."

Abba would lose the guidance of his friend Hirsch's father in one of the many selections later on. The older man would not survive Auschwitz-Birkenau, but the hope he infused in Abba's heart would stay with Abba through the hard times to come.

Viktor Frankl, the Austrian psychiatrist who would later earn worldwide fame as founder of the psychological logotherapy theory, himself a prisoner at Auschwitz, studied the behavior of prisoners in the forced labor and extermination camps. His research unequivocally delineated the chances of a prisoner surviving the physical and mental difficulties in those camps as dependent on the prisoner's inherent ability not to lose hope, and to believe that he or she could survive anything, despite the difficulties. Two factors reinforced Abba throughout those harsh years in the forced labor and extermination camps: fulfilling his mother's wish that he guard his bones and remain Jewish, and the uplifting hope that the father of his friend Hirsch had expressed on that first night in Birkenau. Abba continues describing the process of assimilation into Birkenau.

"We were then led to the block where we'd stay. It was almost empty. On one side stood a metal stove; next to it was a very disorderly heap of coals. Two prisoners stood next to the oven, baking potatoes on hot coals for themselves. They appeared completely apathetic and took no interest in anything going on around us. They didn't even talk to us or try to communicate in any way with the new influx of prisoners. They simply followed what was unfolding, their eyes glued to us moment by moment. Then the block commander showed up and arranged us in fives. He announced right away that there'd be a roll call attended by the supervising SS officer, who'd run a check and collect our belongings. 'In this hell here you won't need anything,' he mocked. That sentence was the trigger that set off our misery. As soon as he left, anyone who had gold, silver or gems quickly found ways to hide them. Some put them under the pile of coals, some stuffed them into cracks in the walls, some dug pits alongside the block, and others came up with various ideas.

"Roll call began with the SS officer's arrival. He was accompanied by the Blockältester, as the block's commander was called, and a posse of hefty poodles in the form of monstrous, sadistic men who would torment the prisoners for no reason. The officer gazed at us intently. 'As I see,' he began, 'you're still in your filthy clothes. You need to go and wash and clean yourselves up from lice. I want to draw your attention,' he added in a quiet, even polite tone, 'to the fact that you're in Birkenau, where there's no use for silver, gold, watches, photos, and the like. You are obligated to hand all such items over to the German military for safekeeping. And anyone who doesn't,' he emphasized, pulling his pistol from its holster and waving it about as we watched, to add impact to his words, 'will get a bullet in his head.' With that, he slid the pistol back in its place.

"The big heavy guys held sacks open, and we all rummaged in our pockets and tossed things in. I also walked over to a sack and put whatever I had on me in it. Eventually the only thing left was the tefillin my grandfather had made for me. 'Zeideh,' I spoke to him in my mind, using the Yiddish word for grandfather, as I'd always called him, 'I did as you wished and remained a faithful Jew. I guarded the tefillin, but here we are in hell, at Birkenau. And here they can't help me. Here the law of the jungle rules. Wild animals don't comply with the divine commandment of Thou Shalt Not Kill.' And so I placed them carefully in the sack, saying goodbye to them forever. The only thing I kept was a tiny photo of my mother. I glanced at it and slipped it back into my shirt pocket.

"But the block commander noticed that movement. 'What's in your pocket?' he screeched, pulling my ear, dragging me down the rows, throwing me down at the SS officer's feet to make a good impression, all the while screaming that I'd hidden something in my pocket. He handed the photo, savagely pulled from my pocket to the SS officer. 'Here, this is the guy, and here's what he was hiding,' he declared, pointing at me, pleased with having caught me.

"But the German officer asked me softly, politely, 'Who is this woman in the photo?' 'My mother,' I said, tears welling in my eyes at the sliver of hope that perhaps he would be sympathetic towards the situation. 'Your mother?' the officer repeated, and without waiting for an answer, added, 'She was a whore.' He ripped the photo to shreds. 'Your mother is nothing more than garbage to me. Get out of my sight right away!' Humiliated, deflated, I went back to my place."

As a kid, hearing this description of what the German officer did to Abba made me shift uncomfortably in my seat. On the one hand, I pitied him for having been so humiliated. I identified with his affront, which became mine, too. On the other hand, it was hard for my child-self to accept that what I saw was weakness and lack of a reaction on his part. Mostly, I couldn't understand what I do now: that Abba's, or his acquaintances', lack of response was not dependent on any action of any kind, because the Germans had no problem killing a single Jew, or an entire crowd of Jews. Later I understood that opting for silence and humility was an act of heroism, an act of self-restraint, an act of choosing inaction based on his natural instincts. He was putting into practice the well-known phrase from the anthology of sayings known as Pirkei Avot, the Ethics of the Fathers, 4:1: 'Who is strong? He who can control his desires.' No, as a child I couldn't comprehend the concept, but also chose to stay silent, to store my frustration with Abba in that same place within me where I stored, undigested, so many Shoah stories.

In the late 1960s we visited the ancient city of Tzfat, or Safed as it's known to the rest of the world. Abba worked in the police force at the time and this vacation was subsidized by them, one of the job's benefits. I must have been around 10 years old. A superintendent was in charge of the R&R center. His son, older than me, argued with me during a game we were playing. "Your mother's a whore!" he threw at me in the heat of things.

And the devil came out of that internal place: I reacted the way I thought Abba should have in Birkenau! All my strength went into the kick I landed on his face. Taken by surprise, the boy – older and bigger than me by quite a bit – had to be taken to the hospital to have the deep cut stitched. His father was furious with Abba, who apologized in the diplomatic way he has, the way he learned at Birkenau. And me? I was really pleased with myself. No one was going to call my mother a whore and get away with it, even if he was bigger than me, and a higher-ranking police officer's son!

Every time Abba talks about this incident, the story of his assimilation at Auschwitz-Birkenau comes up along with the dialogue between Abba and the Nazi officer who shredded Abba's photo of his mother. But at the preparatory simulation in advance of the "Memories in the Living Room" event to be held at Assaf's house commemorating 25 years since the March of the Living trip to Poland, when my father retells, yet again, the chain of events, he places more emphasis this time on the aspect of throwing his tefillin into the sack. And this is what he says when he notices that my interest has been piqued:

"It was an act that marked the end of being a human and becoming a number, a nothing," Abba says simply, plainly, unaware that the statement draws my attention to an aspect I'd never noticed until now: Abba's home in Poland was religiously observant, and very deeply so. His parents were among the Chęciny Hassidic sect; his whole existence was steeped in learning how to fulfill the Torah commandments, to doing good deeds, to being as careful with commandments that are easy to perform as those that are more complex. Yet I never saw any of this as I was growing up. He didn't attend synagogue ever; he didn't wear tzitziot, the fringed garment religiously observant Jewish men wear pretty much round the clock, nor did he ever put on tefillin. Had Abba lost his faith during the Shoah? It hurt me to recall how the little children of Proszowice, his siblings among them, and despite the winds of war already blowing clearly through the region, dressed some hours before the forthcoming deportation's announcement, and went to kheider to learn about the coming Shabbat's Torah reading. His mother's wish as they separated, "Never forget that you are a Jew," also rings clearly in my mind.

Taking advantage of Abba and me being in something of an open conversation about what to say, and when, for this "Memories in the Salon" event, I ask: "Where did your faith disappear to?" In his special way, he answered, "When my time comes and I ascend to meet the Sovereign of the Universe, or Gottenyu, as we called G-d at home..." Abba pauses. I wonder if that's to let me share in the pain he feels, before continuing. "I'll ask Him several questions that have bothered me all these years." And he refused to detail anything more.

I pressure him a bit. "Wouldn't you like to put tefillin on again?" I ask, smiling forgivingly, continuing with a thread of the conversation he'd begun just moments earlier. "Tefillin?" Abba asks, trying to buy time to find an answer that would close the subject. "Tefillin?" he repeats, before answering with honest simplicity. "But I don't have any. I gave them to the Nazi beasts in hell." My heart recoils in sorrow. It recoils not because Abba doesn't have tefillin but because I'm annoyed with myself: How is it that I never noticed that until now? Arie, what a faux pas! I reprimand myself in the same tone Abba had just used when talking to me.

"I don't have any tefillin. I handed them over to the Nazi beasts in the Auschwitz-Birkenau hell."

Fifty years would pass between putting his tefillin in the Nazi loot-sack in Auschwitz, and his trip with the Ramot School's delegation to Poland. Another 25 would pass until members of that delegation would invite him and me to the Memories in the Living Room evening hosted by Assaf and his wife. It took me 25 years to reach the point where I could find a solution for what had been bothering me for so long.

When the very emotional evening draws to a close, I ask to say a few words of summary, thank our hosts, thank Shelley (who was in the delegation and helped prepare content), thank the members of the 1993 delegation present at this event, colleagues, teachers currently accompanying delegations and were part of that trip so long ago, and other guests who've joined us. Then I turn to speak to my father. "Abba, I truly love you." But thinking about it, I see that I always loved him and it was so obvious to me that I never said so. I felt relief.

And then I bring a package out of a bag I'd prepared in advance. These are my own personal tefillin, purchased by my wife as a gift to me for our wedding day. "Abba, you were forced to hand your tefillin over in that hell, and today I'm handing mine over to you, so that you can fulfill the commandment each Jewish man should fulfill, and simultaneously fulfill your mother's last wish in Proszowice, Poland."

* * *

I think about how that evening at Assaf's is a link to the story Abba is telling me now.

"We left the block and were led to the showering room. Before entering, we were ordered to strip completely. They let me keep only the belt that Tateh had given me. Here in the concentration camp, there was no need for humane coverings. A light snow fell on our naked bodies, giving our skin goosebumps.

"A more veteran group of prisoners took our old clothes away. Our kapo got us running by hitting us. Kapos were also Nazi prisoners but assigned to ensure each block's proper functioning and as such, enjoyed certain privileges, and often took advantage of their position to inflict misery on others. Naked, we reached the large plaza where several long tables were set up and the outfitting process began. First, the barber, who shaved us head to toe. His crude work caused bits of skin and flesh to be pulled out together with my body hair. It also pained me to see my blond curls disappearing into a sack along with all the other hair swept up there.

"After the barber, we were hurried to the tables. On the way we passed through cold showers. Remember, it was winter and icy outside. Anyone refusing to go through the cold shower was mercilessly whipped like an animal. From there we were sent running, urged on by whipping, down a corridor where another long table was set up, alongside of which stood several veteran camp prisoners. Outside, an SS officer was on guard, supervising. We walked down the length of the table, each of us collecting whatever items of clothing were tossed at us: a pair of pants from the first stand, a jacket from the next, shoes from the third. Often we were given a bag containing children's clothes, a woman's robe, or a pair of shoes where one was a woman's and the other a man's. Ask to exchange something and down came the stick on your naked body. We hadn't even said a word and we were already bleeding.

"After this brutal outfitting procedure, we were made to run back to the block. Despite the deep sorrow and shame, chuckles began to spread among us as we started really looking at one another. It was hard to identify people. We didn't look anything like we had! And despite the physical pain from being beaten and the psychological pain of humiliation, I burst out laughing. Tall Yisrael-Hirsch Goldstein stood in pants barely reaching his knees, and a silky woman's blouse. On one foot, a woman's shoe; on the other, a boot. But my laughter stopped suddenly and a deep cry came from my throat; my heart was torn to shreds as I thought about who this man had been just weeks earlier.

"Now we, the prisoners, ashamed of how we looked, were ready to collect the gold and items of value we'd hidden earlier, but it was a waste of time because the pile of coal had been thoroughly overturned and everything looted by the silent pack of prisoners who'd been there earlier. Welcome to Birkenau – Hell on Earth! Night blanketed the camp.

"Our second day in Auschwitz-Birkenau began, without anything to eat. No one dared ask about food. Again, we were lined up in fives. Exercises in maintaining order were carried out endlessly. At attention! Remove caps! Caps on heads! We were fed up with life by the time the caps-on-caps-off commands came to an end.

"The block commander bellowed at us. 'Listen up! The SS commander is coming. At attention! Caps off!' Deathly silence spread among the standing men as the block officer entered in his Nazi uniform with its polished boots and white gloves. He was immediately handed a stool and all the lights went on. He stood on the stool to look at us. A long, lead-tipped whip was in his hand, covered in quality leather and folded in half. Hanging from his belt was a small pistol in a highly polished black leather holster.

"The SS commander scanned all the faces. His vicious eyes glanced at the whip. He looked up again and began to talk with the usual German quiet pseudo-politeness. 'Sirs, as you know, you are in the Birkenau camp. Near Auschwitz,' he added in a mocking tone. 'No one leaves alive. Here there's no chance for your deceit and swindling. Here you work. Whoever can't adapt to the work here…' he straightened the whip, 'goes straight to God.' At that he pointed to the chimneys that we could see through the doorway. 'You're now being transferred to Block 19 for quarantine until we find suitable work for you.' He glanced again at the whip.

"A voice came from somewhere in the middle of our group, surprising everyone and electrifying the air, leaving us all gape-mouthed. 'Hey,' the man called out, likely having lost his mind. 'You, Hitler, you're a strong fellow. Let's check for ourselves who's stronger, me or you. Let's have a contest over morals and human knowledge. Put the pistol down, take off your SS uniform. Just be your regular human self, just the way God created you and me, and then let's battle it out.' The man was overwhelmed by emotion, clearly having lost control. But then he went on. 'Mr. Officer! You're barbarians, swallowing up fellow humans, murdering babies and mothers in gas chambers!' he accused the German officer.

"Taken by surprise, the SS officer pointed to the fellow. 'Come here. Who are you, with such guts?' 'Me,' he answered, his voice already hysterical, 'Avraham Eisenberg of Kraków, former trader in old metals, of 5 Tragowa Street.'

"The SS officer straightened the whip, then snapped it shut again, clearly aggravated, clearly indicating his next move. Eisenberg stepped out from among the rows and began walking towards the officer. Two hefty prisoners who'd sat until this point next to the stove, heavy clubs in their hands, instantly moved in. They dragged him roughly outside, threw him face down, placed a baton on his neck, and stood, one on each side of the protruding baton, seesawing back and forth until the man's soul returned to its Maker. They left him there next to the door so that the other SS could see how they, the Sibiryaks, had done their job faithfully. They reentered with broad grins plastered on their faces. The officer talked on as though nothing had happened. 'As far as I'm concerned, you're all the same garbage. Time's on my side. Carry on.'

"Next came the Block 19 commander and his four division heads. I noticed that all five were Jewish but that didn't make me any happier. I'd already learned that in this place everyone was cruel. They warned us to behave correctly, not to yell, not to dirty anything up, and not to steal. The block commander goaded us, 'You're all bastards, you're...' he halted, drawing in a deep breath of clean air to pollute with filthy words, 'shit. The last batch barely lived a few months. Your lot probably won't last more than several weeks.' That was our camp welcome.

"We were ordered to stand outside on the falling snow. For the first time I marched across the camp known as Birkenau. It was abhorrent: no nature, no godliness. Diseases, dysentery everywhere. If anything, nature was on the Germans' side, helping them achieve their work of large-scale murder. We were brought in to Block 19 adjacent to the electrified barbed wire fence. Before the war, the area held the Polish mounted forces' stables, which had now been turned into the Jewish prisoners' barracks.

"Block 19 was split into four areas: two on the right and two on the left. Down the central aisle was a table with several mugs and a small metal oven. Sleeping was in three-level bunks. A place that should have been for no more than six men was stuffed with double that – 12 of us. In total, 479 men were crammed inside. At the entrance, each of us received two blankets.

"As I lay in my bunk I remembered my teacher Hersh-Volf, who was also my uncle. One Thursday I couldn't remember the name of the upcoming Shabbat's Torah portion. My uncle sat down, put me over his knees, and smacked my bottom really hard. Then he pulled out a book and read to me: Because I was so ignorant and didn't want to learn Torah, I'd be punished in the world to come, I'd be declared an evil-doer, and I'd be sentenced to hell. There, in hell, angels of terror would roast me in a fire. They'd beat me with metal whips and my soul would find no rest. Had I never been in the horrors of Block 19, I'd have thought of all those descriptions were no more than a bad dream as I slept in my mother's fresh linen in Proszowice.

"The first roll call in Birkenau took place at 4 a.m. We stood outside in a large space next to our block. The rules and daily routines hadn't changed since the camp's inception; the only thing that changed was the victims of Nazi sadism and the Nazi machines of human destruction. Usually, people lasted an average of several weeks, and most prisoners were released from their torment by way of the chimneys. It was our third day there and we'd yet to see any food.

"Our block commander's voice was as raspy as an old dog's bark. He showed up for roll call with his four Jewish division heads, people of the most disgusting kind. If you wanted to live in this place, you were forced to take other people's bread and soup, which would cause starvation to deprive them of their lives. This daily fight to exist kept everyone busy even when they slept; it was our only recourse to reprieve, because in a dream you could eat as much as you wanted.

"The division heads blew hard on their whistles and screeched at us. 'Line up in fives!' and immediately began beating us with their heavy sticks. 'Bastards! Why aren't you in order yet?' they roared, blows hailing down on us, our "slowness" being their justification to beat us.

"Not for a second did the snow stop falling. It was intolerably icy, a cold that penetrated your bones. And hunger gnawed at us. We Jewish prisoners sort of bounced up and down to try and warm ourselves a little. We were organized into groups of 100. And then the usual inane stuff: 'Caps on.' A pause. 'Caps off.' Over and over, hundreds of times, until we got sick of the little bit of life we still had left in ourselves. For hours we did these 'practice sessions.' We did them in pouring rain, in howling thunder, in flashes of lightning storms, in falling snow, in frost and hail. And they were persistent, those division heads. Caps-on-caps-off was like a holy ritual that couldn't be changed. Only at 7 a.m., after three hours in bone-chilling cold, the camp commander turned up. We stood at attention. The block commander led the way, flattering the camp commander. The block commander was scared to death. The order came: 'Stand at attention! Caps off!' and then: 'Camp Commander, Sir. I hereby humbly advise of the presence of precisely 478 prisoners.'

"The camp commander looked towards the block's entrance, seeking corpses from the night. The procedure was to include the night's dead in the morning roll call and bring the bodies out to the block's doorway, so if anyone thought they'd try to slip away, we'd understand what would happen to them. When the camp commander realized that no one had died that night, he looked exceptionally displeased. 'Were his subordinates too soft-bellied?' he must have been wondering. It's so hard to comprehend the lowly status we Jews had reached."

* * *

When I did my own military service, our training base was like a catharsis. The officers' course cadets completed their training and received their ranks. The Chief of Staff was the event's guest of honor.

The roll call officer gives the order to his soldiers: "Forward, march!"

I carry the unit's flag, a role of honor given to soldiers who display excellence and have contributed meaningfully to the new officers' progress. Next to me, two soldiers bear weapons. Behind me, three soldiers each carry the flag of Israel, marching to the anthem played by the IDF orchestra. This is a statement of power. It is extremely moving to be part of this, with a large crowd of parents and family members looking on.

We march with our heads held high, in well-pressed uniforms and high military boots polished to a shine, our berets on our heads, proudly leading the officers who've just qualified. We stand in formation, facing the dais of honor; the IDF band plays the salute, and three rounds of trumpet calls end with the flags and weapons held in marching position.

Emotionally charged – for the young officers, for our parents, and for me – every such ceremony infuses me yet again with pride for our symbols, for our flag and anthem, for the IDF, for the Chief of Staff, and for our young officers. None of this can be taken for granted – just ask Abba. I remember his stories of the humiliating roll calls he underwent and think, 'What a miracle. Just a few decades later and the son of my humiliated father stands at the head of a roll call that speaks of uplifted spirits, acknowledgment, power, and the ability to defend ourselves: The Israel Defense Forces."

And Abba's story continues rolling around in my thoughts.

* * *

"After line-up we went back inside the block. A wall cupboard stood next to my bed. The loaves of bread to be divvied up in the afternoon were stored there. I pushed my nose up against it, taking a deep whiff, wanting to satisfy some of my hunger at least with the smell. Someone slammed the cupboard door against my head. My nose was hit so hard that it started bleeding. 'Dog! What are you sniffing at, you shit-bag? Get out of here before we drag you out!' one of the kapos yelled.

"Toilets. We were allowed out in groups of 10, at fixed times. Not when we needed to, or wanted to. Only when they let us. Every so often someone would slip on the mud kept sticky by the heavy, incessant rains. At the entrance to the toilet block a hulking prisoner with a heavy club stood on guard. No one could talk to him. He was a boot-licker type. He'd already forgotten the spirit of socialist revolution and its slogans: liberty, fraternity, equality. He knew that his job at Birkenau gave him the chance to stay alive. If you were in Birkenau and wanted to live, you needed to kill others. In this cruel place, a very simple equation set the tone: The more you further the deaths of others, the more you distance yourself from death. The toilet block was the camp's beating heart. That's where you met up with acquaintances. That's where business was conducted. It was the home of the camp's black market: soap, cigarettes, food. If you wanted to get out of working, you hid there. But it didn't always work.

"The line was long. Many men were standing outside. If the kapo in charge found anyone dawdling or trying to sneak out of work, he'd be shot on the spot. Sometimes he'd punish a prisoner by throwing him right into the pit of feces. The worst of it was that we didn't have anything to wipe ourselves with. There wasn't any toilet paper around. So what did prisoners do? Tear bits of cloth from their shirt. Each day the shirt got smaller and smaller, just like the prisoners being slowly but surely starved.

"Food was handed out at night. Each duo of prisoners shared a single two-liter bowl of soup and a slice of bread weighing 120 grams. And no spoons. So each duo tried to get hold of something like a spoon that they'd made for themselves. First we'd take turns slurping the liquid at the top, which had nothing in it. The thicker part was down at the bottom and we divided it equally between us. One spoonful for you, one spoonful for me. We'd look at the slice of bread with pity: one small bite each was what it amounted to. Most nights I went to sleep hungry and 'filled up' in my dreams. You'd be surprised, but it actually works. In the morning I'd wake up and discover that I was still hungry, but at least that exercise in imagination earned me several hours of sleep.

"One night I dreamed that I was in a dining room at a small table with a German officer. At some point in the conversation, I asked him, 'Do you like the food?' Before he answered, I woke in a panic at my impudence. Even in dreams you're scared to death of being insolent to the Nazi officer. Who am I to ask him such a thing? The next day I was worried the entire time, wondering if I'd muttered something in my sleep and whether anyone had overheard me talking to the SS officer.

"But the wondrous ways of life gave me yet another glimpse at how up and down it could be. In the 1960s, as a warden in the Israel Prison Service, I was to be among the guards of that ultra-Nazi, Adolf Eichmann, held in Israel's Ramle Prison. I would eat soup with him as part of the security routine carried out by his wardens, and I would ask him if he liked the soup, or wanted more. And so my Auschwitz-Birkenau dream would come to fruition. Whatever moral there is to this story, I leave to you and others to extrapolate.

"I'd been in the camp for no more than a few days but already understood that if I wanted to survive and conserve my strength, I'd need to make as many visits to the camp clinic and toilet as possible. But that also held a risk: They might think you're sick and put you at the top of the list for the furnaces. So, like with everything in life, I needed to do the toilets and clinic visits as much as possible but not to the point of exaggeration. In the mornings they listed everyone wanting the clinic. I jumped at the opportunity; after all, my hand had been injured during the Kraków Ghetto deportation and I really did need medical attention. A number of doctors and staff worked at the clinic. Outside, a line of patients was straggling along, most of them suffering from boils on their heads and legs, often with open, pus-filled sores. Don't forget that every day, and in every part of the camp, selections took place: who for life, who for the furnaces. All those with open, oozing sores were sent straight to the gas chambers; nonetheless, scabies was still the most common disease in the camp.

"Wanting to be pleasant, I smiled as I approached the doctor. He wiped that smile off my face right away. 'You still new here?' and without waiting for me to say anything, added, 'Boy, you won't be laughing much longer at Birkenau.' That quickly put me in my place. He examined the wound, nodded at the severity, but reassured me in a whisper, 'You'll keep on living.' Directing his gaze at the chimneys, he added, 'For now.' He sprinkled antibiotic powder on the wound, much like is done at circumcisions, and bandaged my hand, which had begun healing on the outside but was starting to rot on the inside. I left feeling much better than when I'd entered. I stuffed my hand into my pocket because I'd already realized that even a bandage could make a Nazi want to send you to the furnaces.

"I wandered around a bit, curious about the camp, when all of sudden the camp kapo, a Jewish man with a gruff visage, was heading towards me. He could change his features fast. Initially, i.e., before I understood the camp's rules, those faces didn't mean anything to me. 'Come here, boy,' he signaled with his finger. I did. I smiled, removed my cap, and stood at attention, my wounded hand still in my pocket. He landed his stick on me only once, but so hard that I flew across the sticky mud.

"Know why I caressed you?" the kapo goaded.

"No," I said, with honest innocence.

"He grabbed my shirt lapel, shook me harshly, his feet on mine to be sure I wouldn't fall again, and slapped me. Right. Left. Right. Left. Four ringing slaps. 'Know why now?' he asked. 'Yes,' I said, although I honestly didn't have a clue about what was going on.

"From now on,' he spat at me, 'you filthy bastards, you'll know not to put your filthy hands in your pockets.' And as punishment he dragged me off to the women's camp to haul sacks of potatoes.

"Going into the women's camp, deep fear filled me. To one side were Jewish women, skinny, pale, their heads shaven. They wore long coats, inside out. Here in Birkenau everything's inside out and upside down, I remember thinking. I couldn't understand why they'd do that. When I saw them I completely forgot my own suffering. On the other side, plump Russian and Polish women were working. Their bottoms were large, their breasts heavy. When I brought a sack in, a Russian woman came over, shoved me aside, clapped her hand on the sack, and said, 'Hey, you bastard. If you run away, I'll make sure you're circumcised again.' 'What was going on here?' I wondered. 'Everyone's slapping me about. Is there something wrong with me?'

"The workload done, I was sent back to my block. It was the hour when prisoners were being led back in groups from their work. I was aggravated. My heart pounded, especially since I was new and still believed that I was a human. I couldn't accept the fact that I'd been earmarked for death and that my days were numbered.

Camp Routine

"As groups of prisoners organized in rows set out for work before sunrise, the camp orchestra played marches. It also played when the groups returned – always fewer in number – at sunset. Bruised, bleeding, each returning group was also forced to bring back the dead. The corpses would be laid down in a pile next to the block to ensure they were included in the night or morning roll call, and only the next day they were taken to the crematoria.

"What a miserable sight it was – a group of 100 men staggering through the camp gates, carrying their dead, to the sounds of a march. The prisoners still alive looked like walking dead, with corpses slung over their shoulders. The marchers walked on swollen, bleeding feet with the last of their strength, and the orchestra played. So discordant to reality. Prisoners tried as hard as they could to keep their legs moving but some flopped down, heavy as lead. Behind the rows of men came the kapos, lips ruddy, thick clubs in hand.

"Day after day, this march to the orchestra's playing went on as the crematoria burned, looking for all the world like a huge *Ner Tamid*, the eternal flame kept alight in the Biblical Temples. The tall chimney spouted thick gray clouds of smoke that sputtered from so much human fat and spewed the stench of freshly burned human flesh everywhere, as though it were some kind of sausage factory. Later the furnaces would shoot tongues of flame high into the sky, as though the fire was trying to waken G-d. Or so it seemed to me. On behalf of the dead, the flames screamed to the heavens: 'Wake up! This is no time to be asleep!'

"The men returning from work readied for evening roll call. Once again we stood for hours in the icy cold, bobbing up and down to keep warm. But the kapos slammed so hard into anyone moving that prisoners quickly died. Every few minutes, more and more corpses were splayed on the ground. This time the roll call officer was pleased at the sight of the large pile of dead at the block's entrance.

"In the middle of the night, several others and I were taken out of the block for work. We were led to Block 7-8, where people with severe diarrhea caused by dysentery were kept. The Nazi in charge ordered us to drag the dead and dying off the bunks and outside. I couldn't believe the sight. On one bunk lay a red-headed man whose eyes protruded horribly. His skin was covered in swollen boils. Nonetheless I could identify him, mostly because of his golden front tooth. He was a revisionist nicknamed 'Jabotinsky of Proszowice' in our town. 'Yankel Benach, is that you?' I asked hesitantly, still not completely sure it was really him lying in a twisted heap. 'Yes,' he answered, opening his eyes. 'I got caught in Kraków and brought to the Montelupich Prison.

David Shidlowski and Volf Kłapek were with me. It's all down the drain, kid. From here no one gets out alive,' Yankel muttered with the last of his strength. 'Four crematoria, four gas chambers, and several selections each month. That's Birkenau, kid. We're all lost.' And with that he breathed his last.

"I started saying the Kaddish. 'Yisgadal veYiskadash…' as a sign of respect. Meanwhile the kapo and the SS officer wanted us to work faster. '…d'khol beis Yisroel…' I continued silently, in my mind. I joined the others in loading corpses onto a truck as I reached the end of Kaddish: 'Hu ya'aseh shalom aleinu v'al kol Yisroel, v'imru Amen.' My whispers were heard. 'Amen,' responded the fellow next to me quietly. He'd noticed that I was saying Kaddish. We took the bodies to the crematoria.

"The crematoria were built in a sparse oak forest. Next to them were massive floodlights on tall electrical pylons. Narrow, barred apertures were located between the chimneys' thick walls. Now, at night, we could hear terrible sounds – screams that reached the heavens, of Jews freshly brought from Thessaloniki in Greece. They were still unaware of what was going on. Everything looked horrifying, nightmarish. I wanted to die on the spot.

"At last, a few days later, Russian military coats were distributed. I managed to get hold of one. I was so happy, because to me it was a sign that at least there's a smidgen of humanity in this place of alienation. The coat wearers were immediately ordered to the camp's central square, where a large sewer outlet was positioned. Prisoners were given hoes and told to drag the stinky water in one direction, while others were told to draw it in the opposite direction. This was one of the purposeless jobs meant to demean and humiliate, to erase any bit of strength or spirit we had left.

"Then the kapo ordered all coat-wearers to line up in a single row and go to the sewer. We were told to put our coats on back to front, with the buttons at our backs. Then we were ordered to approach and hold the coat out in front of us like a pouch. Several handfuls of sludge were loaded onto the coat. The filthy water filtered down and onto our pants. We were then told to take this past Block 7-8, where the people with diarrhea were lying, and throw the sludge into an empty space. Hours of this hard work later, we were ordered to bring the sludge back.

"Passing Block 7, I remembered how, just days earlier, I'd dragged the dead and dying out of there. The people inside were suffering from typhus, scabies, pneumonia, infected abscesses. I passed the blocks' open windows with this stinky sludge in my coat and yet the stench of rotting, infected flesh hit my nostrils. I saw people slowly rotting away in great pain. Inside, I saw the block doctor and his assistant running checks and follow-ups of experiments they'd been conducting on these terminally ill patients who had no recourse to help.

"Over time I became more closely acquainted with all the areas of Birkenau. I operated like a workhorse. One job I had was driving the camp's garbage wagon, which let me move freely around the camp. I passed the storage space where there were piles of the thousands of shoes and items of clothing that had belonged to people already sent to the furnaces. I came across Itche Eisenberg there, too, familiar from Michów. His job was to collect the clothes of people murdered in the gas chambers and bring them to the storage block. He was lucky in that he'd been doing this same job for over a year. 'Kid,' he said to me from his experience in the camp, 'Flee as soon as you can. Do everything just to find a way out, because there are selections here every few days and your end will be the gas chamber.'

"Initially, I still thought about my family and dreamt about my home, but as I grew weaker, I thought about nothing other than food. I felt so bad, so embittered, and didn't know what to do with myself. I wanted to curse my ethnicity but couldn't

– after all, my parents had wanted only the best for me. If only I could've been born a horse, or a cow... Why not? I tossed the question around in my mind. One day I saw a mouse scuttling around the piles of clothing in the storage block. Even being a mouse would be better than who I am now, I thought. I was so jealous of that mouse. It was scrabbling about freely, eating what it wanted, when it wanted. If only I could turn into a bird and fly away from this hell. And so, I'd imagine various scenarios to help pass the time, such as which animal would be the best option – as though I could do something about it!

"But the more I was tormented, the more I wanted to live, to struggle for the sake of a greater purpose to life. The desecrated corpses next to every block, the humiliation meant to turn us bestial – all these reinforced my will to live. Now I know the truth. Why didn't we take up our axes and shovels and rise up against the German enemy? Why didn't we burn what they had there? With hindsight, I know what we should have done, but it is too late.

"A deathly silence suddenly filled the block. Camp Commander Schwartz and Camp Physician Josef Mengele had arrived. We were organized in fives and marched to the showers. At the entrance we were told to strip naked and shoved into the shower block. We were told that as we exited we'd be given our clothes back. We'd learned the rules of selection. There was no need to tell us that some of us wouldn't make it back out. I wondered about what was better – to die in this selection, or continue fighting to stay alive. But I also knew that in this despicable place, nothing depended on your preferences.

"I passed Commander Schwartz and Dr. Mengele. They stood, legs spread, watching me naked and humiliated, and ordered me to turn around. With a finger one indicated I should turn to face right. That meant that several others from my group disappeared from my line of sight. After Mengele directed me to the right, I went into the shower block, with no idea where the path led. About 100 people had gone in before me, but I couldn't see any of them. Where were they? Gone. My logic told me that I was stepping closer to my death. That was certainly how it looked to me. I started saying my farewells to life, yet it surprised me that I wasn't afraid to die. This kind of life isn't for me, I kept thinking. Maybe it really is better to die.

"Next to me sat another boy, naked, like me. He looked at my body. 'What do you think?' he asked me. 'Is it the end for us now?' I stared hard at him. 'If I look as scrawny as you do, I guess that yes, it's the end.' Those minutes were so hard to bear. My month at Birkenau made me feel incredibly old. Chronologically, I was still young, but my woes were those of an old, exhausted man."

* * *

Each time Abba retells this story, I'm reminded of the parable I tell my students: "The Angel of Death from Tehran." This is how it goes:

A Persian prince was walking in the garden one day with his servant, who was deeply disturbed and upset. When the prince asked why, the servant explained that the Angel of Death had crossed paths with him and threatened him. The servant begged the prince to give him his fastest horse, letting him escape and reaching Tehran that same night. In this way he would take the initiative over his life and save himself. The prince, having pity on his servant, gladly gave him the fastest horse in his stable, and the servant set off in a great rush. Back in his palace, the prince encountered the Angel of Death. "Why did you frighten my servant? Why did you threaten him? What exactly transpired?" The Angel of Death answered, "I didn't pose any threat.

I just expressed how amazed I was to find him still in your palace, because I'd decided to meet him tonight in Tehran, and wondered how he'd manage to get there on time."

And the only conclusion we can reach is that sometimes taking no action and leaving things to the heavens is the most appropriate action.

***

Later Abba was hurried out and received the striped prisoners' uniform. He and other prisoners in similar uniforms were ordered onto a truck. The camp commander stood there counting the men himself, indicating the importance of this shipment of people. Abba stared at the men with him: they all looked so old. We must be going to the gas chambers, Abba was thinking. As they rode in the truck, he could see that they were getting closer to the crematoria. He was amazed when the truck didn't stop there but drove on. Abba looked around; suddenly the crematoria seemed to be farther and farther in the distance. Today, or so it seemed, they wouldn't be cremated, at least not there in Birkenau.

A miracle: The gates of Birkenau swung open and they drove to the town of Auschwitz. The prisoners had left hell and suddenly saw Polish citizens. Their eyes almost popped out of their sockets; they couldn't believe it. Less than an hour later they'd reached the Jawiszowice forced labor camp, an Auschwitz satellite camp where the coal mines were located.

The Jawiszowice Coal Mining Camp: Auschwitz's Hellish Satellite

Twelve kilometers from Auschwitz, at the junction for Beilsko and Pless Castle in Pszczyna, in a large green park that hides the site's horrific past, is the Jawiszowice camp. Today only a lone shack is left, a far cry from reflecting the location's 1940s history. Adjacent to the shack is a memorial that was set up after the war, and next to that are two statues sculpted by a French Jewish sculptor and prisoner at the camp during WWII. One statue is of a coal miner, the other of a worker from the support team. Both statues were produced while the camp was operating as a forced labor camp, and part of the factory was geared to the Nazis' Final Solution to the Jewish Question. This camp's appearance is impressive compared to that of Auschwitz-Birkenau.

Abba continues talking, picking up the previous narrative's chain.

"On the day we arrived in that wintry March 1943, there were 14 shacks holding 1,200 prisoners. A spark of hope lit in us: We noticed very quickly that there were no crematoria here. We didn't yet know that the Nazi monster had yet other, smarter methods of cruelty.

"In the camp's vicinity, beyond the barbed wire fencing, lived Polish citizens and German members of the SS. Some worked in the coal mines. The camp commander and his family also lived nearby. At first glance, the camp made a good impression on everyone. Upon a closer look, we were able to see that behind the German architecture was the murder machine. Thousands of Jewish prisoners lost their lives here. Cruelly, sneakily, the

Nazis sucked out the very marrow of our bones. Week after week, new shipments of Jews arrived – from Germany, France, Poland, Belgium, The Netherlands, Greece, Hungary, and Italy. Even though so many Jews died here every day, the number of prisoners remained fixed at 1,200. The human brain cannot comprehend the massive scope of horror through forced slavery at Jawiszowice.

"Two concrete pillars with two solid doors painted black stood at the camp's entrance. This is where we entered. Following a month next to Birkenau's crematoria – where we lost any sense of hope for even the tiniest bit of freedom – those black gates nonetheless looked a whole lot friendlier, and our reception was much less aggressive. We even felt less threatened. It seems we'd also acclimated to the horrors, unfortunately. The region, and the atmosphere, made us believe that this time the Nazis wanted to work us hard, but not kill us off. The same SS officers who'd spoken so harshly to us an hour or so earlier modulated their tone of voice now.

"Waiting for us at the gate was the camp commander, Unterscharführer SS Wilhelm Kowl himself. Tall, with the appearance of a glutton, his mannerism filled us with fear. 'To work!' he roared as soon as he noticed us. Right away we heard the hoarse, barking voice of Fritz, our block commander from Birkenau: 'Stand at attention. Now at a run. Go, you lazy dogs.'

"So we ran, like animals, with the last of our strength, across the camp. Wet snow stuck to our feet. Prisoners slipped and broke hands and legs. It didn't bother any of those in charge. 'Lie down! Get up! Lie down and roll!' they ordered without cessation. That lasted for at least an hour. Almost all of us were covered in mud and blood from our wounds.

"Suddenly, a new order: 'Attention!' Deathly silence fell. Not even a groan was heard. Fritz checked each of us over. He went in and out of the rows and kicked Yisrael Goldstein, in the row behind me. 'Oy, oy, oy!' Yisrael yelped. Biele, Gensenheimer, and his loyal, cruel assistants, helped him with the beating. The usual 'caps' hazing began: on, off, on, off, hundreds of times. 'Left, turn! Forward, march!' he led us to the registration office. Here he raised his voice: 'March in place! Attention! Right, turn!' Fritz stepped into the office looking very pleased with himself. A few minutes later he was outside, screaming at us, 'Everyone, hats off!' Kowol, the camp commander, stepped out, as did his deputy, Dreshner, our block führer as he was known, and the registration officer, Karl Griemer.

"They stood there evaluating the new slave-shipment. 'Yes,' they agreed with each other. 'These are definitely Polish Jews.' The camp commander gave a sign to Fritz, who shouted at us, 'Caps on!' We were led to Block 7 for lice- checking. Doctors were ready inside. The camp commander personally supervised the process. We stripped down naked outside the block, in the snow, the biting cold, and each of us went inside, one at a time. The cold made us bounce up and down on our heels to try and stay warm. 'Let me help you!' Fritz roared, annoyed by our movement. 'Begin! Run! Lie down. Roll! Up! Dogs that you all are. Cold, now? I'll help you warm up.' And so he continued to torture us until the camp commander had had enough and signaled to him to stop.

"The medical examination: Each of us held out our underpants. The doctors checked them thoroughly for lice. Anyone with lice in their underwear was signaled to one side for a punishing treatment of ice-cold showering. Paul Skeuritzky, a German criminal, short and potbellied, arrived and stood on a step stool brought for him. He took his place and gave us his welcoming speech. 'Dear gentlemen, as you know, you are at Jawiszowice, an Auschwitz sub-camp. This is a labor camp for coal miners. You have no doubt noticed the words adorning the black gate: "Work Sets You Free." Here people eat properly, and order is the guiding principle. But you? You lazy Polish Jews, you aren't used to working and you don't want to work. Therefore, this is the end of your white gloves and hands. Here you will invest yourselves in hard work; otherwise, you will die.' On and on the speech went, but no one really took any of it in. Hunger gnawed at us, and when it was over, we were left for the night to lie on the floor with no blankets. And that's how we slept.

"The next day we were awakened early and ordered again to undress near the showers. It was the end of March 1943. Snow still covered the ground and people shivered. Block commander Fritz toyed with us as much as he wanted.

"We were sent to the cold showers. From there we ran naked to the medical examinations held in the coal miners' dining hall. The camp doctors waited impatiently for the camp commander's arrival and the signal to begin the medical tests to evaluate our ability to work. Next to a small table covered in a white cloth sat a white-robed doctor, his stethoscope hung around his neck. Doctors sorted the prisoners: the stronger ones would become coal miners; the weaker ones would belong to the 'shecht' unit, working in the mines' toilet blocks.

"The medical exam included overall health, muscle mass, and state of our teeth. I was among Fritz's laborers. We were allocated to the mine in Area 2. Before going back inside the block, Fritz accosted us with another speech: 'From today on, I'm your boss. I can kill whoever I want, hang you, break your bones. In my block, there'll be perfect order. Beds must look identical, like boxes of matches. One for all, all for one. One bed not made properly will bring my retraining upon you all. Make sure you wash, get up on time, and look after your eating utensils and German property. I will beat you to death if you break these rules. On the other hand, if anyone else but me tries to harm you, that person will incur my wrath. As of tomorrow at 5 a.m., you will rise and march to work at the Brzeszcze mine, about four kilometers from here. And now: Get out!'

"We went into the block to get our bed allocation, our straw mattresses, and three blankets. We tried to fulfill Fritz's rules, made our beds according to his instructions, and he actually showed that he was pleased with the results. As the time for sleep approached, I went outside to catch a breath of air and sniff around the camp a bit, even though I was thoroughly exhausted. I met another local prisoner. We chatted; he was from Warsaw, was in Jawiszowice for two months, and had lost all his friends. 'You can't last here longer than two, maybe three, months. In the end, we'll all die here,' he said firmly, adding that the worst place was the Area 2 mine 'where no one lasts at all.'"

Abba halts his story and a somber silence fills the air.

"So where were you slotted?" I ask.

"Unfortunately for me," Abba answers, with a sad smile on his face, "I was sent to Area 2."

The Brzeszcze Area 2 Coal Mine

"We were up the next day at 5 a.m. Breakfast included a small bowl of tea and two thin slices of bread weighing 50 grams each. We hadn't had time to finish the tea when a whistle was blown sharply, followed by the order: 'Organize for the exit roll call!' Minutes later we were on our way. 'Brzeszcze group, 100 men … Forward… March!' came from Fritz, with his squeaky bark. On the first day we were accompanied by the camp commander with his threatening

Alsatian, trained to rip us to shreds. It was dark, and cold. A few pairs of prisoners carried heavy mine lamps to light our way.

"At the coal mine's entrance I handed over my token, numbered 36, and received a mine lamp with the same number. We were taken by the mine cart, which climbed the hill and then sharply descended into the mine's depths. There, deep in the earth, far beyond the end of the world – so it felt to us – we reached Area 2. We couldn't believe our eyes. Here, deep underground, was a massive maze of cement tunnels, busy movement of loaded wagons and carts carrying coal, and workers going from place to place; in other words, an entire city with its main streets lit by countless torches. Semi-blinded, solidly built horses pulled wagons loaded with coal from place to place. A frightening thought came to mind: Would I ever see the light of day again? Bistron, Area 2's Polish head manager, would call out our names with something of an ironic tone. He sent me to work under the supervision of a German from Silesia who showed very little humaneness towards us Jews.

"Survival probability in this place was a maximum of three months under optimal conditions, and no small amount of good fortune, such as where you were when an accident occurred or when the ground beneath you collapsed. Even your death depended on luck, it seemed, and I had none of that, either. For 22 months I trudged, winter and summer, in driving rain and harsh winds, in snow and frost, with shoes and without shoes, with a swollen leg and an injured hand. I mined down on my knees; my stomach and head were hit by falling coals. I worked for days, for weeks, under the annoyingly constant trickle of underground aquifers, and stubbornly fought to stay alive."

"You know, Arie," Abba emphasizes, "for 22 months I didn't see the light of day, because we left early in the morning while it was still dark, and we worked way beyond normal hours to fill the Germans' unfathomable quotas. My prison mates changed, got sick, died. I kept fighting to stay alive. A daily war. Over time, I turned into a skilled veteran miner, a real professional. I was already familiar with the rocks, their movements, and I knew what to expect if I did this or that. Even the horses were already familiar with me and would open their mouths in recognition," Abba says, thinking about them.

"On the other hand, the human 'horses' – our managers – attacked me endlessly. I didn't fit the German statistics. As far as they were concerned, I should've long since been a corpse. SS camouflaged as citizens would eavesdrop on prisoners' conversations. Polish civilians also worked there, some of whom were very decent, and would encourage us, support us, give us a good word here and there, but they were few and far between."

"During one of my early days there, a nice Polish fellow came up to me and let me know who the local experts were, which of them was nice, which to be wary of, and who I could talk to if I was feeling low, because the Germans had Polish-speakers planted all over the place who encouraged prisoners to share their political views simply to catch them out. One day a man with the Polish name Vitek showed up. He spoke Polish fluently, but I could sense that he was German. He came over and tried to befriend me, asking me whether I was satisfied here. Then he held out a piece of bread. 'You don't need to make such an effort. The Germans will lose the war anyhow,' he said. He asked me what I thought about that, and wanted to know how I found out what was going on. He also asked if it was true that women and children were cremated in Auschwitz.

"I didn't answer any of his questions. A big mistake, so to punish me, he set me working for two months under the drizzle of water in the earth's bowels. This was the most wretched spot in an already wretched mine. You just work and work, and water black from coal drips on you from natural underground aquifers. Later he moved me to the seam of coal in the most dangerous place. One knock on the wrong place could cause a slide of stones that would bury you alive beneath them.

"The Poles wore reinforced helmets, but we worked bare-headed and were also forced to remove our shirts while working. There must have been a divine force haloing us like helmets, protecting us," Abba smiles. "Our lives were bitter, gloomy, despondent. We marched there and back every day, leaving in darkness at 5 a.m., returning late at night after an exhausting day. We were also required to carry chunks of coal back with us for the camp's needs, or bricks for some new structure going up in the camp.

"As we re-entered the camp, we were meticulously searched to make sure we hadn't smuggled anything for our own use. Fritz loved waiting for us at the gate and would find various excuses for pestering us. One time, the beds weren't uniformly made; another time, some eating utensils seemed to have gotten lost; and so, as we reached the camp, he'd start his 'sport' of running, rolling, dropping down, until prisoners simply fainted. When at last he was pleased with what he saw, he'd have us go to the showers at a run. Always at a run. Each prisoner received a piece of soap. Fritz beat our shrunken bodies with their warts and infected boils from the filth, the lack of proper nutrition, and mostly, the constant beatings opening our skin. So he'd beat us if he didn't think we were showering properly. Then Fritz would lead us all to the dining hall. It was best to try and be the last one in, because the thick part of their soup would be down at the bottom and the last in got that ladled into their bowl."

* * *

Anything having to do with food is a major issue in Holocaust survivor families. It comes from the simple, quickly learned rule: Never throw any food away. We didn't have any, the Shoah survivors repeated to us, so we appreciate the importance of even the tiniest morsel, whether it's half-rotten, tasteless, old, or carries any other trait that would void it in the modern world and send it to the garbage tin. But families of Shoah survivors never throw food away; it goes into your stomach.

On one of my visits to my maternal grandmother in Haifa, she wanted to treat me to biscuits she'd bought specially for us…a month earlier, for our previous visit. On that earlier occasion, I hadn't finished everything she'd put out, so she'd kept them in a plastic jar. She undid the lid and offered me biscuits but I was so disappointed: they were covered in light, moldy fuzz. I remember glancing at Abba, disgusted that he was eating them, ignoring their greenish-blue tinge. Glancing back at me, he understands why I'm not taking any. That's when he lays out the Holocaust survivor's principle vis-à-vis food: "Eat quickly and you won't feel it," then adds the clincher. "In the Shoah this would have been a true delicacy!" So I ate a biscuit.

When I was a child, my mother ran a grocery store. Abba would take over when he'd finish his shifts in the prison services. They would bring home only products that couldn't be sold for a variety of reasons — beyond the expiry date, or the salami's scrunched-up end, or packs of cheese, packets and canned items that had fallen and didn't look appetizing to the consumer. The common denominator was that everything brought home was something no one else would buy. Specialty items like pineapple, mango, pomegranates, and other "luxuries" never entered our house. The first time I tasted any of them was when I met my wife.

My wife's family were wholesalers dealing in fresh fruit and vegetables. I joined my brother-in-law one workday and was surprised by the vast difference in attitude: the best box of mango and kiwi fruit went home, and the biggest watermelon was put aside to take home. I learned that things can be done in other ways. I don't have any complaints against my parents: How can one accuse people who, for three years, managed to live on a bowl of liquid with barely anything in it (yet called "soup"), two slices of bread a day, and one mug of tea most days? How can one blame a person who was so hungry for those three years that when the war was over, he weighed 33 kilos at age 19?

Abba continues to describe the reasons behind Holocaust survivors' food traumas.

"At the dining hall's entrance, a huge sign greeted us: 'Eat to satisfaction, add fat, and keep your mouth shut about politics.' The cook had a very odd custom: If you looked good, relatively healthy, he'd dish out a nice thick portion, but if you looked terrible, wasted, and close to death, you got the meager liquid with nothing in it, accompanied by a smack on the head with his baton. That's how it is in hell: Everything is back to front.

"One day we came back from work," Abba's monologue continues, "and Fritz had invented a new, cruel game. He took us to clean the ditch where we washed our plates and cutlery after eating. Several spoons had fallen in over time so he ordered us to fish them out and place them in the lineup area. Then he told all the non-Jewish prisoners to equip themselves with sticks. We Jews were ordered to flee while the non-Jews gave chase and beat us mercilessly. Fleeing prisoners accidentally tripped each other up trying to avoid the batons raining down on them, but ending up trampling each other. This sick game ended with several dead Jews – but who gave a damn? Jews didn't count there unless they were dead. For instance,

Camp Commander Kowol loved music and would force us to sing German folk songs every time we marched somewhere. If you didn't sing the words, you paid with your life."

* * *

In 2018 we – Abba, my son, and I – visited the site. The only thing left of this miserable story is one renovated shack surrounded by a lovely garden, a statue, and a sign in Polish: "Man is stronger than stone." The impressive statement utterly conceals one of humanity's most horrific crimes.

The Camp Work Routine

"Eight months of work in the coal mines, with a hand still wounded from the Kraków Ghetto eradication," Abba suddenly brings my thoughts back to Jawiszowice of 1943, "I was still battling the infection. My arm was swelling up and I couldn't move it. As December 1943 drew to a close, I went to the clinic. I begged Dr. Robert, the Jewish doctor from France, to refer me to the SS physician. That meant putting yourself in line faster for selection: It would redeem me from my torment, from the horrors and pain I was suffering. 'Please send me to the gas chambers. I can't work anymore,' I begged the doctor, showing him my bloated hand. Dr. Robert had me lie down immediately on the surgery table; he dug out the infection, operated on my hand in two places, inserted a tube to drain the abscess, and thereby breathed new life into me.

"I was hospitalized for recovery in the camp hospital where hundreds of ill patients lay. Next to me were Nathan Adler and

Itche Federman, both from Proszowice. The next day Itche was gone. May his soul be a blessing. The ward held people sick with intestinal diseases, infected abscesses, typhus, and broken arms and legs.

"It was around then that Jews from Italy began to arrive in Jawiszowice. They couldn't withstand the harsh weather and the tough living conditions. Dozens died every day. I decided that despite functioning with only one hand, I'd help with various service jobs. When a patient screamed in pain I went over and tried to make it easier for him. When someone asked for a urine bottle to relieve himself and no one responded, I raced over and took care of him. The Angel of Death worked overtime in that place, taking one victim after another. Such pitiful patients. One of them hospitalized there was a rabbi and ritual slaughterer from Italy. Named Fottocci, this noble man would get down from his bed each time a patient passed away and say Kaddish once the body was removed from the block. Sadly, he was kept very busy.

"Yankel Miller was one of the Jewish leaders at the hospital. He assisted the clinic manager and noticed me and what I was doing to help patients. A good relationship developed between us. He was a sort of father to me, which I so lacked in those tough times, and I was a kind of son instead of the boy he'd lost to one of the selections. He spread his wings over me, so to speak, and they were very broad wings indeed. One day, Camp Commander Kowol gave the order to split the block into two clinics: one for patients whose recovery was worth investing in because they had a chance of making it, and the other for 'the trash,' as he called the patients with no chance of survival. He ordered that the trash stop receiving food, and anyone daring to ignore his rule and give them food would be shot on the spot.

"Miller put me in charge of the 'trash.' He dried pieces of bread and told me to feed them on the sly. In this way, Miller saved dozens of Jews from certain death. Over a three-day period, dozens of patients did die, but around half of them – considered to be lacking any chance – managed to overcome the stringencies. A few days later, a special department was set up for those survivors, which ensured that some of them continued to live.

"A month after I was hospitalized, I was sent back to the mines. Once again I stopped seeing the light of day, this time for months. One day I got trapped under a rockslide together with several Poles who supervised our work. Despite their efforts, the rescue team could only reach us the next day. That whole time I just lay there quietly waiting for death to come – or rescue –, whichever came first. But the Poles lying next to me whimpered, cried, begged, prayed, and made various vows. 'What kind of person are you?' they complained to me. 'Don't you care about your life at all?' 'Sir,' I answered, politely, apologetically, 'I'm doomed to die either way, so what does it matter what kind of death it will be?'

"That rockslide broke my miner's flashlight. I was given a replacement. A few weeks later my name was called out at the roll call before entering the mine. Camp Commander Kowol ordered me to step out of the line. 'Where is your original miner's light?' My voice trembling, I answered, fearful of what would come next. 'Sir, it's being repaired.' 'And do you have a document that it's in repair?' he asked. 'Sir, the store man and Manager Bistron refused to give a Jew that document,' I said, my heart racing.

"The commander nodded and made a signal that meant 'Just you wait. My reaction is yet to come.' The next day, during roll call, a sharp whistle was sounded, meant to bring us all to standing at attention. 'Prisoner 108006. Where is he?' the commander shouted. So I ran over to him. He was looking at me like I was worthless. 'Block Commander Fritz, bring this sack of shit to the registration office,' he ordered, and left.

"The camp commander was already waiting for me in the office, together with his deputy, Dr. Stepan Budjaczek. He ordered the camp registrar to enter all the details using the typewriter. Herr Kowol accused me of intentional damage, of having thrown the flashlight purposely, to damage German Reich property. He raised his voice and rebuked me, 'You, bastard that you are, for a month you enjoyed what we gave you free of charge, not to mention the lighting and clothes. One lamp costs 16.5 Deutschmarks.'"

"In my heart I cursed them: 'May their names all be erased forever' for the two slices of bread and watery soup that I was given. I work 16 hours a day underground and walk two hours to and from the mine each day, so something in the Germans' calculations were askew. But instead of complaining or getting conflictual, I found myself saying, aloud, in a trembling voice, 'Herr Lager Führer, I'm not guilty. The lamp broke in the last rockslide and I gave it in for repair after I was rescued along with the others. It happens sometimes that citizens working in the mines remove the number on the lamp they have during their work hours, and take the lamp for themselves. I'm a veteran prisoner, I'm a good worker, I'm asking forgiveness from the Lager Führer. I've been here for 18 months.' In vain I tried to convince the German commander. I was so afraid and insulted that I was sure my heart would simply stop beating. I choked back what I would have liked to have said, but I really couldn't say a word more. And there it was: the fight to survive. Would I live to see the next day?

"I muttered a few more incomprehensible words until the commander blew up in anger. 'Shut your mouth, smart aleck. How old is this sack of shit?'

"Eighteen," someone else answered.

"With mind-numbing ease, the commander gave his verdict. 'So let him be whipped double 18 times.' Bill Hans, the block commander, brought a special chair used for whipping prisoners. They bent me over the chair. Bill twisted my arms down and shoved my head between his legs. I could feel the clammy cold of death spreading through my body. 'Whip him!' came the command.

"My only consolation at that moment was Mama's words: The whipping would be cruel and painful, but my bones would remain whole."

Fritz and Drezcne, two pieces of scum, picked up lead rods wrapped in leather. Kowol told me to count. Initially I did feel the pain but slowly I felt nothing. I was as faint as a person about to die. After the 36th stroke, I couldn't stand on my legs. Fritz dragged me to the corridor and threw me onto the paved path like a worthless piece of trash. Eventually he threw a bucket of water over me and I rallied a little. The next day I crawled on all fours to the coal mine.

"Month after month, my being alive drew the attention of Nazi officers visiting the site. They would make things tougher for me because I disrupted their extermination statistics, which presumed two months of existence under camp conditions. Try to think, Arie, how long a person can live on two pieces of bread totaling 50 grams, with a cup of tea in the morning, and at night a bowl of something they called soup, and constantly being harassed? Eventually my weight dropped to 33 kilos.

"One day a Gestapo expert showed up at the mine. Watching me pick up small lumps of coal that fell from the conveyor, he came over, furious, his face conveying that 'Wait until you see what I'm going to do to you' look. Remembering the whippings and sadistic punishments common in the camp, I already knew what awaited. I stood there, helpless, defenseless, praying to Mama in heaven to watch over me. I often did that in the mines, during the harshest of times, or when I was exhausted but had to carry on. I begged her: 'Mama dearest, you're so close to *Gottenyu*, our G-d. Please talk to him, ask him to make a rock fall off and crush me, bury me beneath it, deliver me from this horrific suffering...' and before I could think any more words for my plea, a massive piece of coal suddenly came loose, causing a slide, lumps of coal dirt rolling down, burying the shocked Gestapo officer up to his waist. Quickly I patted myself down, amazed that I was whole. Fearful, I went over to help the Gestapo officer, whose face was contorted in pain. Other miners joined me as we tried to free the groaning man. Very unexpectedly he began to roar in pain, shooing me away, as though he knew it was because of me. But I gained several hours of peace. The next day I walked straight-backed to the mine, knowing in my heart that Mama had indeed helped save me even when I was down in the depths of the earth.

I begged her: 'Mama dearest, you're so close to Gottenyu, our G-d. Please talk to him, ask him to make a rock fall off and crush me, bury me beneath it, deliver me from this horrific suffering...'

"Throughout, I set myself a rule which I very stringently clung to: Never get up in the middle of the night to go to the toilets. Doing that meant going out of the block, and leaving your bunk could mean that you'd lose it permanently, your things might get stolen, and more than all that, you attracted the kind of attention that would generally produce severe punishment. But one night my stomach was in deep disarray and it was so painful that I couldn't sleep at all despite my fatigue. I dozed lightly and in my dream, saw Mama listening to me intently, convincing me to go out, to the toilet block. 'Go, my child... Go,' she urged me. So I overrode my own rule and quietly, carefully, slipped out of our block. While still busy at the toilets in the complete dark I heard a ruckus outside. Peeking out cautiously through the cracks, I saw a particularly violent selection being conducted in our block! Dozens were picked, loaded onto trucks, and taken for extermination. I kept hidden in the toilet block for a long time. I might have even dozed off there, because suddenly it was morning when I headed back to my bunk. Once again Mama had saved my life."

***

At the entrance to the groomed park currently located on the site, which was once a forced labor camp in name, but an extermination camp in actuality, I stop Abba for a moment. He's gone back to being that 20-year-old, shifting about like a deer trying to evade its hunters. We're standing next to the commemorative statue. Excitedly Abba talks, completely disconnected from the place's current appearance.

"These two statues were made by the French Jewish sculptor. They stood at the camp's entrance. One is working the coal mine, and the other is a 'shecht' worker, the weaker Jews slotted into administrative units."

I try to stop him for a moment, wanting to clarify something, but he's deep into his story now.

"The statues were placed here by survivors after the war. Look what it says here in Polish: 'Man is stronger than stone.'

He pauses, looking around for an additional object clearly erased from the ground in this place that still lives in his mind exactly as it had 70 years ago.

Eventually I do manage to butt in and try to show him the half-full glass in this episode, as he'd always taught me to do. "But Abba, you were saved! You built a home, your life carried on, and most importantly, you produced a family, continuity." For a moment I don the attitude of a divine angel and suggest a deal meant to prove to him that despite the evil, there's a good ending. "Abba, if you were a heavenly angel and I'd suggest that you live your life again, knowing in advance this time what a ripe old age you'd reach in good health, that you'd raise a family, have grandchildren, and even great-grandchildren, would you be willing to return to your 16-year-old self and re-experience it all?"

Abba's staring at me, puzzled: What am I looking for? What am I trying to get at? His face clearly shows how ridiculous it is. But his well-honed instincts, the same ones that helped him survive and regain his life, rise to the occasion. They don't let him enter an unclear deal, even if it's clear to us both that it's nothing but hypothetical.

"I don't understand," he answers to gain time. "You're no angel!" he says, evading the question.

So I respond, "IF, Abba. Only IF I were one."

He's opting for avoidance, wanting to get a better grasp of what I'm trying to say. "Without the Shoah events?" he levels at me.

"The whole package," I answer, "Proszowice, Kraków, Birkenau, Jawiszowice , Buchenwald, Ramsdorf, Theresienstadt." With each camp I name Abba seems to shrink a little, until he sits down. "And in the end, you raise a family, and live a good, long life," I tempt him.

"Impossible!" comes his emphatic response. "What you're suggesting is a nightmare, Arie. There are no words in the human lexicon to describe what we went through. You're suggesting I swap the half-full cup for the completely empty cup." And with that he ends our conversation. That's how my father is: purpose-driven. Either we tour, discuss the Shoah and progress, or let's not waste our time.

"Let's get back to the car and drive to Kraków. Maybe we'll catch a bit of shut-eye along the way." He's done with the fictitious and is back to the real time and practical.

The First Death March: Jawiszowice, Buchenwald, Ramsdorf

"On Thursday, January 18, 1945, a different mood spread through the Jawiszowice forced labor camp. The Russians were advancing quickly. The Germans were feeling hopeless and helpless. Rumors had it that in Auschwitz the gas chambers and crematoria had been destroyed. People began dreaming again, believing that perhaps they'd see their much-longed-for release. Behind the barbed wire fences of Auschwitz and its satellite camps, over 8,000 Jewish slaves and several thousand Christians languished.

"That day we didn't go to work. There was a palpable sense of the Germans' end fast approaching. But what would happen to us? The unanswered question fluttered in the air. No one knew what to say. Gloom filled the camp. The order was for all prisoners to leave the camp, other than the sick ones in the hospital, under the care of a single duty doctor.

"I could have stayed in the hospital," Abba says, "but I knew the Germans would blow it up together with everyone inside.

The person in charge of the hospital convened all the doctors. Miller and I were there too, as members of the medical staff. We loaded up a cart of suitcases containing medicines and equipment for the guards accompanying the SS. There was also a large quantity of bread and margarine. We were among the last out of Jawiszowice. The clinic manager harnessed Miller and me to the cart's hitching bar, and like workhorses we pulled it through the deep snow. We did that for kilometers. No one had a clue where we were headed. The main thing was to distance ourselves as far as possible and as quickly as possible from the border near Jawiszowice.

"The path we were led along was strewn with thousands of dead prisoners. A terrible sight. Revolting. Cruel. Full of people who'd lasted for five years through this dreadful war and had managed to leave on their own two feet from the Auschwitz-Birkenau death camps only to find their deaths an hour after leaving through the camp gates. What a bitter fate. We trod the same path that Auschwitz prisoners had taken a day earlier. Next to the corpses lay whole loaves of bread; they'd taken food in the hope that it would help them reach their destination. But the murdering SS had other plans, shooting at the innocent prisoners for fun.

"On the way, we came across several SS officers. Mounted on motorbikes, they looked panicked and distressed. With pistols drawn, they threatened to shoot us together with our German guard. 'I order you,' the pressured commander screeched, 'to reach the train station within 30 minutes, ready for the train that is about to leave. If you do not board it, I'll be back to shoot you all!' So we ran. We raced ahead as quickly as possible with that cart between us, and at the last second managed to catch the train, part of the retreat activities. There was so much urgency that we simply abandoned the cart and the food as we boarded.

"It took over a week for the train to crawl to Buchenwald. When we arrived, the carriage doors were opened. Only a few people actually struggled down with the last of their strength. Thousands of dead were piled in those carriages, the last of the obstinate fighters who did all they could to outlast Auschwitz and its sub-camps. Their dreams of surviving to see freedom never came to fruition. Blood from shattered, bullet-ridden bodies spilled into the fields between Auschwitz and Jawiszowice, between Leslau and Buchenwald. The edges of those paths hold the innocent blood and bones of thousands of Jews buried where they fell, their names unmarked and no one to mourn or remember them. They fertilize the weeds growing there. With their last breaths they cursed those who caused the loss of their innocent blood. May they rest in peace forever and may the names of the fallen always be remembered.

"From the 20 carriages pulling in at the Buchenwald train station, the survivors of that journey barely filled one block. First we were made to run to the showers. From there we were brought to another bathing procedure containing disinfectant, and each of us was forced to get into that bath. Then we each received one coat, one shirt. and one pair of shoes, but at Buchenwald no one was giving us underpants. After that we were registered and given a new personal number. Mine was 119652. 'Jew or Pole?' I was asked at this stage. 'Jew,' I said with the little pride I could still muster. Right up to the last minute I refused to be anything but Jewish. That's what my mother had willed: Never forget that you're Jewish. How could I forget her last words to me, and so I chose to remain Jewish and, if necessary, die for it. The arrival process over, we were taken for quarantine in Block 56.

"Here in Buchenwald, there was yet another mood. The camp was administered by political prisoners, and no one beat you here. But we arrived in extremely poor physical condition.

At the lineup, we looked like scraggly chickens on the verge of keeling over, working hard to stand straight as the slaughterer's knife hovered near, and not doing it very well. We stood around, helpless, hazy, like people waiting for the final mercy of being killed. I remembered a lesson I'd learned as a child in the kheider: the rabbi was teaching us Chapter 37, Verse 3, in the Book of Ezekiel. It was about the vision of dry bones: *And he said to me: Son of man, can these bones live?* So I answered, "Of course they can't! No, of course not! I repeated my response: Can't you see they're long since dead? I screamed at G-d. And then I remembered the rest of that verse: *'And I answered: Lord G-d, only You know.'* Really? Doubt seeped slowly into my mind. A sliver of hope began to form.

"Several days later we were ordered to line up at the doctor's clinic. He looked us over, not even checking much, and set my fate. I was given the okay that I was fine, without any medical examination. It was Ezekiel's vision of Verse 5 coming true: *'So says the Lord G-d to these bones: Behold, I will cause breath to enter into you, and you shall live.'* That thought made the corners of my mouth curl faintly upwards.

"The assimilation process over, we were sent to the Ramsdorf Camp. More than 800 Jews were crammed into the carriages of the Buchenwald to Ramsdorf train. On arriving there, we were met by wild screams. We were made to run from the platform into Block 2 for quarantine, where we saw wooden bunks without mattresses. Each of us was handed two blankets. The camp already held several thousand Hungarian Jews sent there by Adolf Eichmann to work in the Erdöl Rafinerie Trzebinia GmbH, the oil refinery. Jewish prisoners described Eichmann to me: an SS officer who personally supervised the annihilation of Hungarian Jewry while implementing horrific acts. How can a person behave that way to other humans? From the stories I heard from Hungarian Jews, I imagined him to be some kind of monstrous-looking thing. I was also told that that he was personally responsible for orchestrating Polish Jewry's Final Solution at Auschwitz-Birkenau.

"I couldn't perceive who such an evil person could be and what drove him to hate me so completely, simply for being Jewish, when I'd done nothing bad to him. Some 16 years later I'd sit face to face with Eichmann in a small room, acting as his personal guard following the Israeli court's verdict: the death sentence. I would spend hours talking to him yet never receive an unequivocal answer to my question of what drove him and his colleagues to hate me to the point that they murdered my parents, siblings, extended family, townsfolk, and countless other good, simple Jews.

"The Allied Forces' bombing sorties gave neither the Germans nor us any peace, and severely damaged the camp's infrastructures. Water stopped flowing in the pipes, spattered with holes. For months we couldn't wash, change underwear or shave. Only the tops of our heads were shaved to prevent lice; in the camp, this haircut was called 'LäuseStrasse,'– Lice Street. These are the subhuman conditions that Hungarian Jews were living in when we arrived. The entire camp was muddy. Next to every block, ditches were dug to provide protection from aerial attacks but none of us bothered to use them. We actually all prayed to G-d to send more and more bombs to disrupt the camp. Some even prayed for bombs to fall on them and release them from their suffering.

"Our block's residents were tormented and in pain. Ramsdorf prisoners couldn't wash, and there was no real discipline there. This meant plenty of emaciated, listless prisoners were free to roam: the living-dead Jews. One of the deportations from Częstochowa included my uncle, Eliezer Jurista, whom I hadn't seen since the farmer in Karwin sent me away. I was thrilled to see a familiar face; it filled me with hope that perhaps others had survived, and filled me with a will to keep fighting for my life.

"A speech given by the camp commander, a Roma gypsy prisoner, midway through February 1945, was conciliatory and breathed renewed hope into our hearts. 'Gentlemen, I see that you Polish Jews have suffered terribly. I would like to inform you that as camp commander, you have come here to work and not to be exterminated.' He raised both arms so that we could all see them. 'With these hands I will personally open the gates to freedom for you all.' Next to him stood an SS officer, who also raised his hand as a sign of agreement.

"As one, we all looked up at the heavens. Was this an angel speaking through the Roma, or perhaps just another misleading show? We stood silently, not knowing whether to rejoice or tear off our lice-infested clothes. Our thoughts went back two or more years to when an SS officer spoke to us at the entrance to Auschwitz-Birkenau, making it clear that although we'd come in through the gate, we'd only leave through the chimney.

"Initially I was slotted into work clearing unexploded Allied Forces bombs. Each weighed one ton. I was filled with dread when I saw them. A bomb like that could burrow some 10 meters down into the earth. First I needed to dig around it, remove the dirt hiding the fuse head, and then the sapper would come and defuse it. It was extremely dangerous, intense work, and we'd be running around the camp at all hours of the day. During the many air raid sirens, we'd quickly crawl into the ditches vacated by the unexploded bombs. Thousands of prisoners were kept busy with this work.

"We'd be brought to the area under the guard of three SS officers. We could barely drag our legs along. On the way we'd meet Polish farmers working for the local Germans. One day I noticed a field where a pit was filled with garbage. I asked permission to use the toilets and quickly went to the pit, hunting for scraps of food. I found a real treasure: rotting beets and potatoes. The SS officers didn't initially catch on to why I was always asking to relieve myself in the same place until one followed and noticed I was filling my pockets with the rotting vegetables. He forced me to empty my pockets and gave me a stinging slap for each item that I dropped. From then on he treated me with blatant loathing and forced me to come for my daily slap. 'So you don't forget,' he'd add."

The Second Death March: Ramsdorf to Theresienstadt

On April 22, 1945, news came that the Ramsdorf Camp would be eradicated. The fate of some 2,500 prisoners was set: They would all be killed. Dreams of freedom evaporated. The Roma guard indeed opened the gates as he'd promised, but not to freedom – rather, to further oppression. Since the creation of mankind, it is doubtful that humanity has known such hardship and suffering as Ramsdorf's prisoners experienced. At the camp, which had no facilities for mass extermination, it was decided to transport the prisoners to Theresienstadt.

"Get that, Arie?" Abba says, getting my attention by using my name. "Not only were we physically and mentally 'walking dead,' but now we needed to make a special effort to haul our own bones to the death furnaces – not just a few blocks or streets away – but to Theresienstadt, in Czechoslovakia, a distance of 300 kilometers. But who in that kind of a place asks you whether you want to go there or not?"

"The scenery around the camp was the polar opposite of what we'd felt inside the camp. It was almost spring; forests and wild fields were becoming green and flowering, and birds flew about busying with nests – the complete opposite, if we consider that the news landed on the prisoners at the start of spring. Inside and outside the barbed-wire fences there was nothing but gloom, doom, cold, and darkness. At 5 p.m. a quarantine was announced. Then the order came through to get organized the following day at 4 a.m. in the roll call square for 'transport,' as deportations were called.

"The term that was bandied about was 'liquidation.' Fear of the upcoming deportation spread. We remembered the images of horror we'd been subjected to so far, such as the liquidations and massacres at Kraków and then Jawiszowice. I remember how some 80,000 of us set out from Auschwitz as the Nazi murderers shot at us like animals, killing several thousand, both Christians and Jews, and several thousand more froze to death in the open train carriages taking us to Buchenwald, or died from starvation or dehydration. Of a full trainload of Jews, where each of 20 carriages held far more than 100 prisoners when we left Jawiszowice , barely 900 survived. Death ambushed us every step of the way. Death marches. Is it little wonder that's how they came to be known?

"There's no comparing the liquidation of Auschwitz to that of Ramsdorf," Abba notes. "When we walked away from Auschwitz, we were relatively healthy, the ill having been cremated. The death march from Auschwitz saw people walking out with hope and energy. By Ramsdorf, we were exhausted 'Musselmen,' as prisoners suffering from severe malnutrition and poor mental health were known. A camp of the walking dead. That evening before the camp's liquidation, I lay on my bunk and talked to myself. I studied every move I'd made. In the Kraków Ghetto liquidation, I prayed and was sent to Auschwitz. Then to the hell of Birkenau. Leaving Jawiszowice, I prayed again, and was sent to Ramsdorf – a 'living' cemetery. And now, what should I be doing? I lay there lost in thought when my friend Zemel in the bunk above me questioned me. 'Why think so much? We're only going to die once.'

"I sighed. 'You're right, Zemel. We die once, but why die now? Five years, you hear? Five years I've been fighting to stay alive, from age 14 until now. I'm hoping, with G-d's help, that I'll celebrate my 19th birthday back in my hometown with my family.' Zemel started laughing. 'Oy, how silly. Sure, you've grown up some, but you've still got the brain of a 14-year-old.' I remember answering him in a serious tone. 'Zemel, my Mama's last words were: Look after your bones because the flesh will fill out again.' 'What a sense of humor!' he interrupted. 'You're still a kid. Look here, open your eyes and look, seriously! Lost, we're all lost. So stop being a fool,' he said, and fell asleep.

"The next morning at 4 a.m. the camp's bell rang. For the last time. There's nothing like German order and organization. We had to get up and leave Ramsdorf forever."

* * *

In 2006 Abba visited Ramsdorf. The passage of time had done its work, leaving the place very changed. But there, in what had once been the guard's house at the camp's entrance, which meanwhile had become a German family's home, he suddenly recognized the camp bell hung from the wall. It looked old, neglected, but still rang as loudly as it had, especially on the morning of the day that marked the start of the Ramsdorf camp's death march. It's a day Abba will never forget, ringing as clearly as a bell, slicing as sharp as a razor's edge. Abba stands there for a minute, recalling those 4,340 Jewish prisoners who set out on the impossible trek. Of them, only about 500 reached their destination, having endured abuse by the local population, the Nazi guards, and the constant sorties of the Allied Forces.

And that's when he makes a decision. Abba goes over to the home's owner, asking if he could buy the bell still hung shamefully on its hook. The man sold it to Abba, who brought it back home, waiting for an opportunity to transfer it to the Yad Vashem World Holocaust Remembrance Center in Jerusalem, where it could be rung to awaken all who have forgotten that the Shoah could yet repeat itself, and that what our grandparents and parents have built should never be taken for granted. It is our obligation, as the continuing generations, to remember and to preserve. If we forget, let the Ramsdorf bell that Abba purchased ring out loud and clear as a reminder.

* * *

Abba continues his story.

"Voices could be heard from all the blocks. 'Up, up! Line up!' So we made our way off the lice-ridden bunks where we slept, in the same lice-ridden clothes. It sounds a bit funny but I bid farewell to the lice left behind on the slats; they were almost like old school pals. At roll call, the camp commander informed us that we needed to get onto the transport; anyone staying in the camp or trying to flee would be shot on the spot. The Roma man opened the gates, and several thousand Jews, looking like skeletons, along with several hundred Poles and Ukrainians, left the camp behind.

"The German villagers gathered outside the camp. Over the past year they'd apathetically watched Jews being murdered, ignoring the events. Never let it be said that the Germans as a people had no idea what was happening. They saw. They saw it all but pretended not to understand, afraid that if we were set free, we'd avenge ourselves. Now, with liberation closer than ever, they wanted to get rid of us as fast as possible. Shrieking at us, they had us run to the train station where more than 20 open carriages waited, each able to carry approximately 10 tons. We were brutally shoved in, about 200 of us to a carriage. The crowding in our carriage was so severe that we couldn't move a finger. Two SS murderers accompanied each carriage. The Ramsdorf forced labor camp was closed.

"I have no idea why I always had a feeling that I must survive that bitter period. Somehow I just accepted the constant evil I experienced with equanimity. My goal was to bring my bones to liberty, as my mother had wanted. That's what I'd promised her, in now far-away Proszowice. So I found myself encouraging and consoling others, assuring them that things would get better, that we'd yet meet on joyful occasions. Experience had taught me that in train carriages it was always best to sit on the same side as the guard because prisoners, fearing being beaten, did their best to distance themselves from him, which meant a little more room closer to him. Yankel Miller, Zemel and I therefore sat near the guard, with a bottle of water and a container of bran soup we'd stashed away in our pockets ahead of time. In the darkness, we ate slowly and carefully, using our fingertips. We swallowed bits silently, because if any of our neighbors had known that we had food, they might have strangled us just to get their own hands on it.

"At last the train began to move. Then it halted suddenly, and this went on throughout a very unrestful night until the sun's first rays began to show and warm us up a bit. The train ride so far had been relatively easy, and to our great surprise we discovered that a few hours of stops and starts later we were still in the same place. The camp was empty. Desolate. Even the platforms had been abandoned by all signs of the oncoming spring. We couldn't see any women or children or elderly, nor did we see any of the German civilians who'd always wandered around outside the fence. The place looked as though no Jewish slaves had ever set foot in it.

"People in the train asked the guards for some water. Instead, they got beaten and shot. 'That's the only thing you Jews understand,' the guard growled as his club came down repeatedly. A whistle blew. The train left the Ramsdorf death camp yet again. Thick black clouds blew up from the engine car's chimney, concealing the blue sky and making the camp disappear from view forever. We passed cities and villages. Groans of death were silenced gently by good people trying to encourage the weak and dying to hold on. 'It won't be much longer,' they'd say. The train's wheels spun faster; the monotonous clickety-clack quickly put many of the elderly and children to sleep. Most never woke. Tortured, bitter, angry … so many of those Jews breathed their last on this journey.

"Two days of traveling later, the Germans finally opened the carriage doors for the first time, letting us out. SS forced us to dig deep pits. We didn't know who they were meant for: the dead inside the carriages, or us. But it made no difference to us; either way, other than the fear of death itself, we felt nothing anymore. Walking dead is what we were. That's how human nature is: When you're extremely hungry and have lost your strength, you stop worrying about your fate.

"Later we had to drag out the several hundred corpses of people who'd died over those two days. No eulogies, no tears. The earth covered bodies that were as innocent as the day they were born. Suddenly, without warning, a brave Jew from Hungary straightened up and began to recite the Kaddish. He was as emaciated as a skeleton. Nothing but skin and bones. 'We did all we could as respectfully as we could,' he said, adding the request for forgiveness from the dead for possibly mishandling them in accidental disrespect. "Therefore, speak well of us before our Father in Hea….' He never finished the verse. Mid-word, he was shot dead by an SS officer. He fell into the mass grave as his blood spread like a bright red rose on his prison clothes. He was the final victim – a nameless Jew praying for the souls of fellow nameless Jews somewhere on wretched Nazi soil. I covered his body and continued the ritual words: 'May you, brave anonymous kind Jew, speak well of us in Heaven,' my heart silently intoned.

"Back into the carriages we went. The train began moving again. Hundreds of planes suddenly appeared in the sky above us, bombing the city of Kamenice not far away. The planes also attacked the train with bombs and machine guns. Chaos erupted. The engine was blown off the tracks, as were several carriages. SS guards fled into the forest, fearing the bombs. We just stayed where we were, lying nearby, watching this new situation: scared Germans. Scared, running, scattering, disordered. We walked as best we could, following their tracks into the forest. An armed German farmer and a German police officer caught us and rounded us up, leading us to the local police station.

"The policeman turned to me. 'Why did you run off?' With the last of my strength, I answered. 'I wanted to die in an open space like a free man.' Then I added, 'Sir, my only crime in this world is that my mother was Jewish.' The German farmer, the first decent German I ever met, handed me a glass of water, and gave each of us a carrot. He turned to the German officer and spoke very resolutely. 'This village is not interested in any vile behavior or backlash.' With that he saved our lives, admittedly, but also had us turned away from the village.

"A rumor spread through the village that dangerous political prisoners had fled the train. Farmers left their homes and ran into the fields armed with hoes and other work tools, intending to kill as many of us as possible. Slowly we were all caught and brought to the train station. Not far away were several carriages filled with corpses. It turned out that when the bombing sortie had passed, the guards called everyone who fled into the forest to come out. Everyone who responded right away was organized into a group and walked to the station. Anyone who hesitated before making an appearance was met by a line of machine guns and shot dead on the spot. The dead were tossed onto the carriages which had meanwhile been pushed back onto the tracks. So the Allied Forces had unwittingly helped the Germans in their efforts to eradicate us because their bombing killed hundreds of Jews on their way to freedom.

"Our march to Czechoslovakia continued. We passed through towns and cities. We ate grass. We drank brackish water. We were shot at mercilessly along the way. German civilians watched these repulsive victims of crimes against humanity without batting an eyelid. A few days later we'd reached the Czech border. I just couldn't put one foot in front of the other anymore. I thought that removing items of clothing would help, would lighten the load. First I let my shoes go. Then my coat. Then, at last, my whole body. Because I'd eaten grass and drunk sewage water my mouth swelled and boils covered my lips like fish scales. Over the 10 days of this death march, I turned into a barely moving bag of bones. We all looked like that, barely hauling ourselves forward. But my mother's words surfaced repeatedly in my thoughts and drove me on, as they had from the day we left Proszowice: 'Son, guard your bones. The flesh will always grow back.' If only that were true, Mama, if only, I encouraged myself, one step at a time.

> Over the ten days of this death march, I turned into a barely moving bag of bones. We all looked like that.

"I looked up at where our Father in Heaven should have been, using the term we'd always used at home. 'Gottenyu, look down and see what I've suffered since leaving my city of birth. Look at the life-endangering events I've survived. With your help, I'm still alive. First, Brzeszcze. Then Kraków, where I met with my father. Then the Kazimierza train station again, and the Płaszów bridge where Itche-Meir was shot dead when we fled the truck... Oy, Gottenyu,' I burst into tears, 'then you led me to one hellhole after another: Birkenau, Jawiszowice, Buchenwald, Ramsdorf, and now the forests of Kamenice, and now we've been caught by German citizens and SS and taken to the station.' And while I was muttering and hallucinating, Yankel Miller grabbed me and yanked me hard. 'Stop that! Look what it says here: 1 km to Czechia! We're going to survive this war, you'll see!' His reality check jolted me sharply, encouraged me, filled me with new hope. The SS murderer was there with us the whole way, randomly shooting people down, but one step, two more, and we'll be in Czechia. I owed it to my mother to hang on."

***

Jerusalem Day is a festive celebration held on the Hebrew calendar's 28th of the month of Iyar, which generally corresponds to somewhere around mid-May. It marks the day that Jerusalem was reunited following the 1967 Six-Day War. This day of joy not only signals the reunification of Jerusalem's two areas 2,000 years after the exile of Jews from the Land of Israel, but primarily the unification felt in the hearts of Jews worldwide, Israeli and Diaspora-born, secular and Orthodox. It is particularly celebrated by Israel's students, and especially those in the General Federation Of Working And Studying Youth movement. It's hard to find a topic across Israeli society that carries such a strong national consensus as Jerusalem. In the framework of our Social Studies classes, we join the colorful parade that marches through Jerusalem's streets, urged on by Jerusalem's own residents.

At the end of the 1990s as we marched through the city, received with love and waving flags by the locals, celebrating life, I was filled with emotion as I recalled one of my father's stories describing how the march of death came to an end as he and his fellow prisoners, heads bowed, humiliated, crossed the German-Czech border. And how surprised he was, to see the Czech people receiving them with warmth, with affection! It gave him another tiny spark of hope that perhaps, indeed, he would be saved.

At that moment, Abba never imagined that less than a half a century later, his own son would be leading students through the streets of a unified Jerusalem, capital of Israel and of the Jewish people, on the day that the city celebrates its resurgence to the voices of thousands filling the city with song. This is the city that Abba and his family, and all the Jews whose lives were taken in the Holocaust, prayed for and dreamed of year after year when they recited the well-known slogan: *"Next year in rebuilt Jerusalem!"*

* * *

My thoughts swing back to the moment that Abba described how a straggling line of dead-living death march survivors entered Czechoslovakia, accompanied by the murdering Germans.

"Only around 600 of us reached the border. That's all that was left of the thousands of prisoners who left Ramsdorf together. It was the first time we'd ever met Czech citizens. A noble people. Everywhere – in cities, villages – the Czechs tossed food items at us, not like the Poles and Germans. Some came up to the Germans with food-filled baskets and asked them to distribute it among us. Czech farmers brought out sacks of sliced bread and set them up all along the roadside, just to be sure the prisoners would have food. In the town of Blaszowice, the Czechs closed their businesses on the day we passed through just to stand there and hand food out through their windows.

For a week we marched, our SS guards randomly killing us, but slowly they, too, began to tire. They looked neglected, exhausted; they were unshaven, and had no clue what to do with us. They were starting to behave like us. And they were also hungry. Sometimes prisoners would snatch food from the civilians along the roadside but the guards didn't react! It got to a point where prisoners even hit back at the SS guards, taking food from the guards' mouths. And even then they didn't react!

Eventually we reached the Theresienstadt Ghetto, our final destination.

Release, and Returning Home. Or Not

"Our entry into the Theresienstadt Ghetto looked like a cemetery-load of skeletons had risen and were walking. Rumors of our arrival came with severe warnings that we were contaminated with lice and typhus, and therefore everyone should keep their distance from us. The Germans still controlled Theresienstadt, and the German officer counted us meticulously, because order had to be maintained even if defeat was more imminent than ever. We were sent to a basement and given a piece of bread which was immediately stolen by the heftier bullies among the prisoners. We were sick, apathetic, and withered.

"The next day we were taken to be washed. Two women held me up under the shower and scrubbed my skin. It was my first wash since January 15th, 1945. Five months. I was 19, and weighed 33 kilos. Bones, nothing but bones, but they were all there, as I'd promised Mama. The washing done, the women shaved my hair and dressed me in civilian clothes with a yellow Magen David patch sewn on. Then we were taken to a barracks in the Hamburger military camp.

"A few days later a typhus epidemic broke out in the camp and soon the entire barracks stank. The growing numbers of dead were placed in the corridor near the door. I remember thinking how unfair it was to have suffered all those years, to be so close to freedom – and then die. I was deeply pained by the thought of all these lives lost at the last second.

"May 8, 1945, was when we heard the first shots. Clearly the front lines were nearby. Our signal was the gate guard. At this point, a Czech guard manned the gate alongside a German. That night the first Red Army tanks broke through the front line and approached the camp. In those last hours before liberation, we sat facing the open window of our room in the barracks, breathing in the fresh air of spring's last days.

"A Jewish boy named Katzkeh from Warsaw stood next to the window. In one hand he held a long stick; in the other, a red pillowcase covering a feather pillow. 'When Russian tanks come rolling into the ghetto,' he announced in a lively tone, 'I'll raise this red flag as a sign of victory and then we will break through the gate on our way to freedom!' There we were, some 40 prisoners, lying around on bunks three levels high, although we could only reach the lowest level. We were barely alive. Some of us were in various stages of dying. Only the faintest hope that we'd hear the bells of freedom ringing kept us breathing. If we were to die here, let us at least die as free men, we thought. At that stage, we still had no knowledge that the extermination machine in Theresienstadt had ceased operating a few days earlier, and that we were only about 100 meters from the camp's now-silent crematoria. We were to have been its last job. That's how it was: life and death in such close proximity that a single second could differentiate between them, the lifting of a finger by a German could signal your end, and a facial gesture could keep you alive or send you to your death.

"As the morning sky began to lighten, Katzkeh gave the signal. He tied the pillowcase to the stick and waved it proudly. It was the closest anyone could get to a red flag. The feathers fluttered around, looking for all the world like snowflakes. A Russian tank stopped at the barracks. The German sentinel had disappeared. The Czech guard was told to open the camp gates. Thousands of us poured out into the open space. A cemetery come alive! Skeletons rose from the bunks! Hidden stores of energy fired up! Russian tanks rolled in, liberating it, but the looks on their faces, the horror in their eyes, reflected the scene's incomprehensibility: living-dead roaring and dancing for joy.

"A unit of German soldiers taken as POWs passed us. Our anger was tremendous. Revenge was in our minds. I'd always wondered whether, once liberated, we'd slice the Germans up with axes and knives. It didn't happen because it's not in our nature. G-d would avenge us for the horrors enacted on us, I remember thinking, and off I went to join the other dancing skeletons. May G-d avenge the blood of all the innocents.

"It was a few days later, I was recovering well, and getting ready to return home. Yankel Miller, hearing my plans, was amazed. 'Where are you going?' 'Back to Proszowice,' I said, and on seeing the look on his face, added, 'Yes, to my home, in Proszowice.' I said it emphatically, mostly to keep myself focused on some kind of plan and not be tempted to go off with him somewhere. It was very clear to me that I had to get home and join the rest of my family. Miller, smart fellow that he was, looked at me. 'Samek, there is no home. It's over. There's nothing to go to,' he said, shaking his head.

"But I wasn't willing to believe him and we parted ways. He emigrated to America. I set off for home, covering the 600 kilometers between Theresienstadt and Proszowice in a number of days which seemed like an eternity. I kept imagining how it would feel to meet up with my family again. I imagined embracing my sister, my little brothers, and how we'd make up for all the time lost. With optimism fueled by freedom, I never considered that my family was no more. I passed Kraków on the way and visited the Jewish ghetto. In an instant, the violent scenes of deportation flashed through my mind, but I continued to be encouraged by the thought that I'd soon be reunited with my family and it'd all be behind us.

"In Kraków I came across several old-time acquaintances, each of whom told of the dark years they'd experienced. Slowly

I began to understand the scope of brutality we'd been through, and with that understanding new thoughts began to gnaw at me: Had anyone else of my family survived? Scared of facing the truth, I lingered in Kraków for a few days, only to hear more and more stories of horror. Fear, and primarily my inability to cope with the bitter truth, kept me in Kraków, living with uncertainty. I made it a daily routine to come to the Jewish Community Center where a large notice board held constantly updated lists of people arriving in the city on their way to here or there. I'd see parents and siblings and family members reunite, but not a single name from my family was on the list except my own. In fact, as the days passed, I began to realize that those scenes were the exception, not the norm, and the scope of our loss began to take shape in my mind.

"One morning the name Sheindeleh Blumenfeld, of Proszowice, was on the notice board list. My heart skipped a beat: my sister! Alive! Saved! I held onto that spark of hope, that shred of the past with my wonderful family. I decided to head immediately for Proszowice where I felt sure my sister would go. I imagined our meeting, how we'd hug and kiss each other, how we'd cry over our lost youth, our exterminated family. Perhaps we could rebuild what had been destroyed. Later I'd find out that Sheindeleh was actually my cousin with the same name. I was consoled by the fact that at least their shared name would continue into the future.

"In any event, despite the bitter reality sinking in fast, I decided to head for Proszowice and catch up with Wincenty and Jadwiga, the wonderful non-Jewish neighbors who'd saved me. I figured that if there was even a shred of information about my family, they'd surely know. I raced to the tram station on Kraków's outskirts. While waiting I noticed Marian Kagan, the son of Proszowice's postman, passing on his bike. Marian, my age, was not Jewish and had helped numerous Jews. We'd been fast friends before the war. Even during the war he'd continued helping Jews, including no small number with whom he was unfamiliar. He saved Billy Laniado's mother; Billy established and was chairman of the "Next Generation" Association working on Holocaust-related issues. Billy's mother had been swept up in the second selection, but Marian hid her in his house for several days. For a non-Jew to do such things was extremely risky; if caught, it was certain death for the entire family in whose house the Jewish person had hid.

"I ran out, calling 'Marian, Marian!' He stopped, amazed at hearing his name, and so happy to see me. I was also pleased to meet him again. It gave me a feeling of getting closer to home and continuing life from where it had been halted. I slipped my hand into my pocket and pulled out a pack of shaving blades, handing them to Marian and asking him to take me on his bike to Proszowice.

"He looked at me, stunned. 'But... where do you want to go?' he asked. 'Home, to our town,' I answered, not understanding why the look on his face had altered so much, or why he'd become so serious. What he said next hit me like a ton of bricks and threw me into an abyss, the likes of which I'd never felt before. And there it was: the harsh reality. 'Shmuel,' he began, then hesitated, taking a deep breath. 'There is no home! They're all dead...' Marian suddenly looked very frightened. He looked left, right, reminding me of the days I worked as a courier on the Kraków Proszowice route, feeling hunted all the time. 'The few people who've returned are haunted and hunted, and in danger of dying. There's not a single Jew in the town,' he said.

"Heavy-hearted, I said goodbye and wished him well. Where would I go now? What would I do? Why had G-d left me alive, then? Hadn't I suffered enough? Images of my lost family ran through my thoughts, reminding me of the Jewish holidays, the way we'd greet each other and wish each other: *Next year in rebuilt Jerusalem!* And a flash of hope lit up in my heart. I'd go on the journey of my life. I'd go to the Land of Israel.

* * *

"In 1948 I made aliyah to Israel, after having been involved in the Escapee Organization in Europe for three years. It organized hundreds of thousands of now homeless Jewish Europeans for aliyah to the newly established State of Israel. I'd been searching for fellow Jews as though all were my family. I managed to smuggle thousands across the borders of Europe, which was slowly getting back to routine and having trouble handling the flood of Jewish refugees. I tried rehabilitating my own life, but the rawness of having lost my family was too hard to bear. I couldn't overcome their absence. As the years passed, I learned to simply live with the pain. Meanwhile, as my mother had predicted, my bones slowly filled out with flesh and I started to look more and more like a normal human being. I enlisted to work in the prison services in Israel, and proudly wore my uniform, which gave me a sense of belonging but, most of all, symbolized the Jewish people's and the State of Israel's independence.

"Year after year went by. Outwardly, it seemed that my wounds were healing; inwardly, they continued to bubble up and never fully healed. My vow to remember the victims never let me rest.

Eichmann: The SS Officer I Dream About in Birkenau

A dramatic announcement

In 1960 – 15 years and three days after Abba was liberated from the Theresienstadt transit camp in Czechoslovakia, and certain that the prisoners' liberation marked the end of the Holocaust – he was on his way to Jerusalem to see the film "Exodus." On the drive there he could see fir trees planted by the Jewish National Fund reaching for the sky. Slowly the car made the ascent up the steep mountain, its motor working hard, a wonderful breeze coming through the window, mussing his now regrown blond curls – in short, a day that made the past seem so distant.

Abba is thinking about the millions of trees in Europe, especially those lining the railroad tracks. For him they are grave markers to the Jewish people's innocent dead. The car radio's music suddenly halts and the voice of the Kol Yisrael newscaster comes on, excitedly stating that "Prime Minister David Ben-Gurion will convey an important message within the next few minutes." We tense up. In our young country, we're accustomed to announcements of this kind relating to the drama around a terror attack, a military operation, or some other activity against us by our enemies. Soon we hear Ben-Gurion. "Adolf Eichmann, the greatest tyrant and murderer the Jewish people has ever known, has been captured and is in our hands."

Abba freezes. Eichmann, responsible for the extermination of Hungarian Jewry, Polish Jewry, and that of many other European countries, whose name he heard from so many of the murderer's victims in the extermination camps in Auschwitz-Birkenau, Buchenwald and others, has been caught by the Mossad. He'll be brought to Israel? Abba describes how he felt upon hearing this.

"In a flash, the colossal Jewish tragedy directly linked to Adolf Eichmann passed through my mind. The man who drove the wheels of death at Auschwitz-Birkenau. The man who eradicated Hungarian Jewry in one fell swoop. The man responsible for the cruel, callous murders of millions of Jews, including those with me in Jawiszowice , in Buchenwald, and in Ramsdorf. The man whose name I heard from miserable victims of experiments that could only come from a sick, warped mind. The man whose name was equated with Satan's, back on that other planet that I thought I'd left behind."

At that moment, climbing the mountain on our way to Jerusalem, Abba never imagined that in several months' time he'd be required to meet this top-echelon Nazi face to face, breathe the same air he breathed, smell the cigarette he smoked, eat meals with him, and have conversations in the tyrant's language with him. On hearing our Prime Minister's announcement, he slunk down in his seat, and seemed to collapse, going back some 15 years to those dark, dark days.

On the day that Eichmann was convicted of operating the cruelest hell on earth – known as Auschwitz – a certain citizen, a former Auschwitz prisoner, number 108006, known as Samek Blumenfeld, watched from his seat in the courtroom. Abba watched the Nazi officer closely. May his name and progeny be forever obliterated, Abba thought, as his verdict was read out in the Israeli court of law. On tenterhooks, he listened to the detailed descriptions of life in Auschwitz under Eichmann's command, to testimonies from former extermination camp prisoners who worked in the registration offices and described being commanded by Eichmann to be meticulous when noting which illness caused the death of each and every patient.

Even though Abba personally experienced these horrors a good number of years earlier, he felt as though old wounds were bursting open, that he'd never free himself of Auschwitz-Birkenau, that he was still buried in those darkest of days. Abba could hardly believe how the murderer seated there in his bulletproof glass enclosure placidly watched the court, with evident boredom, publicly displayed by fingertips tapping on his knee or scratching his head. Where was the respect befitting a court of law?

Every so often the accused would glance, without turning his head, at the courtroom attendees. When the prosecutor, Attorney Gideon Hausner, announced that he would be showing a documentary on the Auschwitz and ghetto horrors, and that only persons with specially designated permits could remain in the hall, Abba left and returned home, his heart broken all over again by the memories. For many nights afterwards he suffered terrible nightmares that tore his soul to shreds. When all court matters were over, the court announced that Nazi murderer Adolf Eichmann was guilty and sentenced to death. Eichmann! The very same, the Nazi from Budapest, would be put to death – in Israel!

Eichmann: Abba's Nightmare

Twelve years prior to the court case, Abba was hired for a position with the State of Israel Prison Services. Throughout his years in the service, he'd always tried not to work with the prisoners themselves, since it reminded him that he had once been limited in his freedom. Abba tried never to be tough on people whose freedom had been annulled, even though he knew that most prisoners had definitely deserved their sentences. Nonetheless, he preferred the roles of desk sergeant or storeroom supervisor. When various opportunities opened up for him as his years in the service grew, he was pleased to participate in an accounting course run by the prison services and join the office staff in the Tel Aviv HQ, far from the actual prisons themselves and well away from their freedom-erasing walls.

A few days before the verdict was announced, a senior Prison Services officer came to Abba's office and delivered surprising orders: to come on a certain date to the Prison Service's Special Committee. "Your attendance is mandatory, healthy or ill. You must appear." Laconically stated. Unexplained.

What I'm about to describe has never before been related in full, and Abba never even told me. We never spoke about Eichmann at home other than a rare snippet of something that was generally public knowledge anyhow. Initially, nothing at all could be shared due to unequivocal confidentiality orders. Wardens assigned to the task signed a non-disclosure agreement that included the most stringent terms, and permission had never been granted to describe what actually happened behind the prison walls or inside the important prisoner's special cell.

Over the course of long shifts, day and night, guarding Eichmann, Abba sat and wrote his feelings and experiences down on slips of paper. It provided some level of consolation to his tortured soul. About seven years after Eichmann was hanged, Abba was diagnosed with cancer and told he had just three months to live. I was a kid of 12; my sister was 17. We were so young. How would he hand the torch of remembrance over to us? How would he convey to us what guarding Eichmann made him feel? We were still happy, young, innocent.

And so he did two things: First, he collected his notes documenting his time spent guarding Eichmann in the Ramle prison cell. He titled this written text "Me and Him" and lodged it with Yad Vashem, receiving a commitment from them that it would not be published without the author's written consent.

Secondly, four days later, he wrote a will for his children, which he titled "Should You Wish to Know." In it he describes the expulsion of his family from Proszowice to Slomniki and from there to their deaths. Only when years had passed and the conditions were ripe, Abba agreed to disclose the story to me.

In December 1961, Eichmann's verdict – the death sentence – was handed down by the court to massive media coverage. Captured in Argentina by the Mossad, the SS officer was brought to Israel and handed over to the Israel Prison Services for safekeeping. The greatest fear was that he would commit suicide once the verdict was known, or that someone would understandably try to eliminate him. This led to the Service's establishing a top-secret, special unit titled "A1" expressly for the purpose of guarding the prisoner and ensuring "the important prisoner's good health until the sentencing was carried out."

From among the candidates, all of whom were wardens working in the Prison Services, my father was chosen to be among the prisoner's personal guards. On every shift, three guards provided round-the-clock oversight, with one of them, often my father on his shift, being the one to sit in the cell with him, a mere meter away. This level of thorough supervision also continued when the prisoner slept. One guard sat behind the barred door watching the guard inside, and the third manned the observation room. The third guard was the shift officer, supervising both of the other guards.

Procedures were strict and precisely documented in the daily log. Food brought from a central kitchen was packaged and sealed and tasted first by the warden, reflecting another fear concerning the prisoner's safety: that someone would try to poison him. On one occasion, my father raised the point that if the food was indeed contaminated, all the wardens would die, leaving Eichmann unattended and alive. The commanding officer answered that he has plenty of wardens and will find replacements, but there's only one Eichmann. The team of wardens and other staff involved went out of their way to ensure that the goal would be carried out: to accompany the prisoner to his death, healthy and whole, while walking steadily on his own two legs.

"On the day that the committee convened," Abba explains, "heaven decreed that I'd show up with a post-surgery bandaged leg. Several other wardens I didn't know were also there. We were invited to enter, and an officer explained that in the next few days Eichmann would be handed over to the Prison Services for safeguarding. 'Your children and grandchildren can be proud of you for being chosen for this privilege of guarding the Jewish people's biggest murderer.' The speaker emphasized the historic aspect of the role we were about to take on."

Abba described what he felt at that moment. "My heart pounded. My knees were about to buckle. My mind couldn't believe it. Was this truly happening? How could I reopen those wounds yet again? After a brief personal interview, we were asked to leave the room and consider our immediate answer. We were given to understand, quite simply, that we were being asked to volunteer for this task of national importance.

"I was invited for an additional personal conversation and was asked where was I from, which camps had I been in, who I'd lost in the Shoah, if I was present at Eichmann's trial, and what impression he made on me. I was getting increasingly tense. I refused to dig down into the bleeding wounds that had only healed for appearance's sake. I knew there was a bubbling morass inside just looking for a way to burst through. I was terrified of this moment. With every grain of cunning I had, I tried to evade the job — claiming that I was ill, tended to bouts of anger, recognized as an invalid and a survivor of extermination camps. But no matter what reason I came up with to show the committee how unsuited I was, it made no difference. My rationales were elegantly dispensed with.

"I was asked very private questions. I answered them matter-of-factly. The psychiatrist seated in the room and listening to the interview suddenly asked me how I'd behave when I'd be required to serve Mr. Life or Death. He used an example: Let's say you're required to serve him his food, or light a cigarette if he asks to smoke? I could have said I'd strangle him, but I answered what I thought was the truth. 'I wear a uniform and swore allegiance to the State of Israel – but not a vow of allegiance such as Eichmann's and that of his Nazi officers who swore to eradicate the oldest nation on earth.' I paused and then added, 'I'm disturbed thinking about how I'll cope at the moment of truth with the party responsible for the deaths of so many of my family.'

Dr. Rozner, the psychiatrist, answered that he understands my suffering and wounds, but from the professional perspective, guarding Eichmann would be to my benefit and help my healing process because, he explained, calling on a psychological rationale, everyone aspires to vengeance. That's natural, and clear. But by sitting with Eichmann in his cell, knowing that he murdered my mother, father, siblings, relatives, and even my own soul, the act of guarding him will release me from my suffering, my nightmares will fade, and slowly I'll reach gratification. That was the psychiatrist's professional view."

Inside, I smile. I know Abba and how he'd react to the psychiatrist's explanation: He may be knowledgeable, but he doesn't understand what the job actually requires of the wardens. Abba has a small gesture: His hand moves ever so slightly in a wave of dismissal, usually hidden from everyone's sight. Mostly only his fingers move; occasionally his palm does, too. He adds a tiny movement of his head, which leans fractionally to the left. These two movements together are a sign that he does not hold with what you're saying, especially when he thinks you haven't a clue what you're talking about. It means he's agreeing with you only for appearance's sake, simply because he doesn't want to argue with you. But you haven't persuaded him, even though you're certain he's agreeing with you.

On a certain occasion Abba explained his ideology behind apparent capitulation to others who don't really know what they're talking about. "I don't argue about my experiences," Abba explained, "because those who were there in the Shoah, in the extermination camps, don't need explanations to understand what I'm talking about. And those who weren't there will anyhow never understand what we felt, and how we continue to feel now. So why waste energy?"

But Abba nonetheless leaves the topic open, because from our perspective it's an extremely important one, and so he responds to the psychiatrist many years later and in retrospect. "Dear psychiatrist, a person who has had his fill of suffering, who is broken, shattered from earliest adolescence, deprived of all freedom, a person such as I, has great difficulty healing. What gratification countering the feeling of revenge will I derive from guarding the murderer or seeing the 56-year-old hang, compared to my father, shot dead at 41, my mother choking to death in the gas chambers at age 40, my siblings aged 6 to 20 murdered? By contrast, as far as I'm concerned, the murderer is of zero value. What difference would it make to me if he was shot, hung, or deported back to Germany? But I vowed in my heart, just as I vowed to my mother when she gave me her parting kisses, that I would guard my life to my dying breath and not give in willingly, because that was her parting wish. And I made the same kind of vow to the State of Israel, in honor of the Jewish people, and in honor of extermination camp survivors, to guard Eichmann until his dying breath, so that neither he, nor any other unauthorized person, could take his life until that specific moment when the legendary, demonic individual's life would be terminated."

> I vowed to the State of Israel, in honor of the Jewish people, and in honor of extermination camp survivors, to guard Eichmann until his dying breath.

The Oppressor in Prison

In the middle of the night (when all the other Ramle Prison inmates were asleep, and most of the guards knew nothing of what was about to happen), a black limousine quietly rolled into the prison yard. Inside were several people in civilian clothing, including one who wore glasses, a black suit, and tie. Nothing like this had ever happened before in Israel's main prison, i.e., a vehicle entering without being checked. But a command is a command, and it was clear. The guard at the gate simply asked what to register in the log, and didn't receive a very clear answer. The escorts, all dressed in civilian clothing, quickly locked the bespectacled man in his designated cell.

Waiting inside were the prison commander and the special A1 secret guard team. It was difficult to differentiate between officers and sergeants since all purposely wore uniforms without visible ranks. The only thing that unit members knew was that matters were to be conducted according to the unit commander's direct orders.

Following the extremely brief intake process, Eichmann was taken to his cell. The Nazi oppressor walked, led by escorting staff, and appeared pale and panicked. "Mr. Life or Death," who orchestrated the existence or termination of "the Jewish scum," as Nazis called Jews in Auschwitz, was from this point on under the meticulous control of precisely those who, just a few brief years earlier, were scum to him. One can only imagine the insult, the humiliation, that imprisonment by that same "Jewish scum" in Israel would cause the prisoner!

Yet in his own mind, the prisoner was convinced that he was innocent. In his mind, throughout the trial, he claimed that he was "merely" carrying out the Führer's orders. He was nothing but a simple soldier. He admitted that Jews were put to death in Auschwitz in gas chambers, but he didn't actually do that; his deputy, Rolf Günther, did, and without his knowledge. Nor did he do this out of any evil, but out of mercy. Was it not better to die in the gas chambers than to live and be tormented by terrible suffering? One could only wonder if he'd request a medal of honor for being so merciful towards Europe's Jews.

The cell's metal door swung open, the creaking hinge sounding like an exclamation of amazement at the prisoner who would enter in a moment. The shift commander spoke politely to Eichmann. "Bitte, kommen Sie rein." Please come in. Eichmann glanced left, right, clearly puzzled. In a low, frightened voice he answered, "Ja Wohl, Herr Kommandant. Danke." Yes, Sir Commander. Thank you.

Approaching Eichmann's cell, the shift commander took a good, long look at the prisoner, who was incredibly surprised by his surroundings. Knowing what he knew of imprisonment, he could never have imagined he'd be allocated such a large room, similar to his old-time office in Budapest when he acted as the omnipotent manager of the German death industry. A metal bed frame, pushed up against one wall, was outfitted with two snow-white sheets, three new blankets, and a pillow in a white pillowcase. A new rug was nearby. Not far away was a new desk and a chair with a tall back. Next to the desk were a small mat, a bowl for washing, a cup, and a closed bucket for urination. The desk held an ashtray, a sure sign that he would be allowed cigarettes. Folded on the bed was a red prison uniform and a set of red pajamas, the color signaling that he had been earmarked for death.

The instant he stepped inside, Eichmann froze. His gaze fell on the guard standing at the door. Watching him, the police officer wondered how this miserable, little man wielded the power to massacre millions of Jews? The officer walked over to the unit commander; both entered the cell.

Eichmann slowly removed his clothes, looked at the officers for a moment, then set his trousers aside after meticulously shaking them into their folds, and held them out to the warden. He straightened as though commanding himself "Achtung!" At attention!

"Is there anything you would like?" the commander asked, wanting to make his acclimatization smoother.

"Ja Wohl," he answered. "I would like, if I am allowed, to lie down on the bed. I am extremely tired."

"Ja Wohl," the commander replied. Eichmann went to sleep, amazed at the courtesy he was receiving, and the unit commander marked off the first mental green tick. The initial acclimatization had passed without any provocation on the death row inmate's part.

Tough Days

Abba's first few days in the newly established unit were tough. Particularly difficult was the mind-switch from having been a demeaned Birkenau prisoner whose number was etched into his skin, to a personal guard of the Jewish people's greatest living enemy. His mind found this adaptation virtually incomprehensible, his emotions fluctuating between suffering and satisfaction. Disappointment joined the mix when the shift commander did not slot Abba into the circle of guards closest to Eichmann. "You'll guard outside with the Uzi and secure the yard," he was told.

Didn't the commander trust him, Abba wondered, as the feeling of inferiority typical of Diaspora Jews flooded him. Why wasn't he considered trustworthy? Because he himself had been a prisoner in Auschwitz and the special unit feared he might want to take revenge against the despicable Nazi? Abba patrolled the closed courtyard leading to Eichmann's cell, back and forth, pondering, remembering, reconstructing how he'd been a demeaned slave in the extermination camps, going to and from Jawiszowice's coal mines on swollen, blistered, bleeding feet. He remembered lugging the heavy mine lamp one dark night, its beam the only thing lighting their path during those black days, and all under the SS officers' watchful gaze.

He remembered, too, the sudden slamming of a rifle butt against his head. "To Palestine with you, Bolshevik, Christ-killer!" the SS officer had yelled at him, each part of the phrase accompanied by another blow to his head. At the time, he'd thought, "If only! From your filthy mouth to G-d's ears!" Now here the German officer was, on Israeli soil, but this time Abba was the one holding the submachine gun, and Eichmann was the one barricaded behind bars, unable to change his fate. Abba found this reality inconceivable.

A key's creaking in the metal gate cut Abba's thoughts short; the gate swung open. "Give me the Uzi and go on up to eat," the warden taking over from Abba said. Abba was filled with mixed feelings — relief, yet concern. He moved closer to his fellow guard.

"Tell me, have you seen him yet?" Abba asked.

"No, not up close. He constantly sits in the corner, doesn't look up at all, and is completely withdrawn."

Going inside, Abba locked the door behind him and raced up the few steps, worry and confusion flooding him. He turned back and checked once again that the door was locked, not quite trusting himself. Up the stairs he ran again, as though floating on a cloud. Curiosity urged him on. He was almost at the cell's door. Any moment now and he'd get to see the murderer. Uncertainty gnawed at his gut. What impression would this encounter leave? How would he react? Would he get through this experience easily or, G-d forbid, fail?

Abba knocked on the door with the tip of the key. Seconds later the porthole slid open and a pair of dark eyes looked through. "C'mon, open up already," Abba muttered to himself. The guard moved away a fraction. Then a set of bright white teeth filled the porthole area as the guard quietly spoke in a Yemenite accent. "Pass the key through the slit and I'll open for you." Abba did what he was asked. The heavy iron door swung open. Abba entered; the guard secured the door again with several locks and checked to make sure that they were all properly fastened. Then he burst into laughter at Abba's curiosity. Abba was totally focused on peering through the large, barred door into Eichmann's cell.

"Ah, my friend," the Yemenite guard said, "he's hard to see. He sits in the corner like a robot the entire time."

Several meters away sat another warden guarding Eichmann. Closely he watched even the slightest movement the prisoner made. A meter from the seated guard was a broad barred door that led to the cell's corridor, where yet another guard sat, taking note of anything that the first guard might have missed. In terms of security, both filled the same role, but the second guard's job was far easier. He could move his body a little and stretch his legs. The murderer couldn't stand any kind of movement. Supervising the guards was a duty commander; each in turn was so bored that they'd often doze off.

"Let's go eat," the duty officer called from the kitchen, jolting Abba's thoughts around the momentous encounter. Food arrived in a locked casserole sent from the main kitchen. Testing the food, the guards tasted the first portion: If it contained poison, they'd die first. Then they served Eichmann his food on a tray, as though serving an honored guest. Finally, they needed to wash the plates and cutlery, theirs and the prisoner's, and return them to a cupboard that was then locked.

The meal over, Abba was called for briefing prior to joining the first circle of guards. He was instructed on how to behave with the prisoner. The principles were based on taking full responsibility and performing every action with premeditated rationalism. In fact, thinking about it, the guards were also prisoners of a sort. The critical difference was that they were free men.

In the guards' room adjacent to the cell were several beds, a desk, a few chairs, and a radio. A detailed roster was hung on the wall. Abba noted that the next day he was listed for duty inside the cell with the prisoner. A cold sweat covered him, and a cloud of tension surrounded him; he counted the seconds until his turn came.

Abba and the Murderer

There he was, Shmuel, son of Avraham Yehoshua Heshel, son of Yehezkel the Scribe, scion of a family of rabbis and ritual scribes from Kielce and Chęciny, facing the oppressor, Adolf, son of Adolf Karl Eichmann, enemy of the human race, enemy of the Jewish people, and murderer of millions, including innocent elderly and children. As fate would have it, Abba was about to spend time together with Eichmann in the same space, breathe the same air, be surrounded by the same claustrophobia-inducing walls. That is what G-d determined. That is the fate, and at the same time the source of strength of a righteous person, as the innocent blood of the Jewish people called from their graves to Abba and to his fellow guards, and that call repeats the same thing: "Revenge! Revenge!"

There was Abba, standing just a mere meter from the heinous beast, approaching, standing face to face, their glances crossing. Abba, versus the oppressor who views himself as belonging to the master race, the chief architect of the twentieth century's most efficient, ruthless murder machine. There was Abba, progeny of a brutally murdered Chassidic family from a people persecuted for eons, a former slave, a forced laborer, a prisoner at Auschwitz, who through hundreds of miracles and coincidences, survived, barely saving his raw soul. In a single instant the prophecy of Ezekiel, in Chapter 37:14, came to life: "And I will put My spirit in you, and you shall live, and I shall place you in your own land."

As soon as the turn of the key in the heavy metal door sounded, locking Abba inside the cell, fear filled him as though he'd fallen into the lion's den. This was a slave's instinctive reaction, he knew, embedded in him on the Nazi extermination assembly line. A person can definitely be taken out of slavery, but the enslavement mentality is far harder to take out of the person. Terrible fear suddenly filled him. His legs felt as though they would no longer support him.

It was the first time Abba had seen the oppressor in his behind-bars location. His hands and legs trembled just as they had when the Kraków Ghetto had been eradicated, and when Göth had ordered that the children's house be emptied, the children shot down in a massacre of thousands of innocents in Zgoda Square. His heart raced, threatening to burst out of his chest, just like back then when he passed Furnace 3 and heard the death cries of victims. He had seen the flames spurting upwards, Herr Eichmann standing nearby in his splendid SS officer's uniform, commanding people to go to the crematoria. From the thick plumes of smoke and ash, millions of hands pointed at the murderer accusingly: Here he is, that officer, that robber of our youth, our lives, our families.

The evil oppressor, by comparison, now sat quietly on his chair next to the table. His feet rested on the soft rug. Only his eyes moved, staring at the plastered white walls. Abba brought the empty chair next to the door, intended for his use as Eichmann's personal guard, closer. Even though his first experience of Eichmann was not that long ago, it seemed to Abba that an infinite amount of time had passed before bringing him to these circumstances. He barely managed to sit down calmly and turn his gaze to the murderer.

And the murderer studied Abba. He bowed deeply as though he were totally innocent and greeted Abba. "Good morning, Guard, sir."

Abba felt as though a loaded gun jabbed at his heart. The oppressor had gotten mixed up; he seemed to think Abba had adopted some unfamiliar innovative tactic. He repeated his greeting but Abba was busy with the oddness of the situation. Abba studied each part of the room, checking to see if anyone was there and noticing the storm of emotions surging through him. He stared but saw nothing. His heart sent a prayer to G-d: Please don't let him faint here, G-d forbid! The oppressor was indeed confused, and therefore did not notice Abba's frightful emotional distress: Abba was experiencing a post-trauma attack as the Shoah's events raced through his mind's eye, threatening to capsize him.

And so the prisoner must have become convinced that the guard had adopted a particular type of method that he, the prisoner, had not yet worked out; therefore he repeated himself: he bowed to Abba a third time, smiling faintly, just as Abba had bowed to the SS officers in Birkenau. Back then, the faint curve of a smile merited the repeated slapping of Abba's cheeks until the sound rang in his ears.

Slowly Abba's traumatic reaction subsided, as did the slave-instinct fear, and instead pride flooded him, lifting his spirits. That is "Herr Eichmann?" That is the person he dreamed about so often in Auschwitz-Birkenau? Abba, realizing the weight of this situation, vowed to watch this oppressor keenly: Let our enemies never think that Jewish victims are nothing but bloodthirsty avengers. We will prove to the world that we do not seek revenge, but justice, he thought, and my fellow guards and I will watch over this monster until a just verdict is handed down, putting an end to this Satan's life.

Abba is clearly moved by this memory. From his perspective it is one of the highlights of his life; the role of prisoner is reversed and he becomes the guard in charge of the imprisoned. There's a stark difference, of course; Abba was a prisoner lacking any rights, whereas Eichmann is entitled to certain rights. I think of the long journey that Abba has been on since 1941, when the extermination of the Jews first began as part of the "Final Solution," and up until 1961, when Eichmann's verdict was handed down. There's an important moral here, and for that alone it was worth filling page after page with ink, so that every reader could learn and internalize the message for the future.

"Abba," I ask, "what in your view allowed you to survive the horrors? What's the secret to being able to overcome that immense hardship?"

Abba thinks before answering. "Three factors contributed to my ability to survive the Shoah. The first and most important was my promise to my mother to safeguard my bones and my Jewishness. That promise became an obsession. At the bleakest moments, on the verge of despair, of giving in, that promise urged me on. Despite knowing that my mother had been murdered in the gas chambers at Belzec, she nonetheless became a kind of living image that led me, guided me. When I was liberated, I raced off to Proszowice to prove to her that I'd upheld my promise to her."

Abba falls silent for several seconds. "Even now when I fly to Proszowice, I imagine meeting my mother, imagine her waiting at the front door, imagine saying to her, 'Look, Mama, here I am, I'm back. I did keep these bones together.' But of course I'm disappointed each time when I don't find her in Proszowice."

"And the second factor?" I prompt.

He answers without needing to think about his response. "My ability to take an active stance and influence my fate. Most prisoners didn't know how to calculate their chances, nor did the Germans really have a solid logic to their decisions. It was sadism and insanity for its own sake. That's why sometimes, when it looked like people were going off to work, they were actually led to their death. Other times it seemed as though you were being taken to die, and then it'd actually turn out to be for work. No logic at all, so my ability to align with my fate often saved my life." Abba smiles before adding the aspect which, in my view, is the most important. "Luck! Yes, don't be surprised by that. In Auschwitz, a kilo of luck was worth more than a ton of intellect. If all three were aligned, your chance of survival increased."

The Oppressor's Daily Schedule

At 6 a.m. the first signal came: An electric bell rang, calling all prisoners in the general prison to rise and begin their day. This call included Eichmann. In the general prison it'd take several long minutes before the prisoners dragged themselves out from under their blankets. Usually shouts, and yanking the blankets off, were needed to get them up.

In Eichmann's special cell there were no such problems. The light went on at the same time as the first bell. Eichmann was standing on the soft rug next to the bed within seconds. His first words were "Good morning, sir" or "Good morning, guard." Then he'd put on his woolen socks to avoid catching a cold, and the dressing procedure would begin. The duty officer would take his glasses and his abdominal belt out of a metal closet. Each regular or irregular action was recorded immediately and meticulously in the diary.

Next, Eichmann received a plastic cup containing hot tea. After drinking it, he dressed slowly. He had no reason to hurry; with so much time on his hands, he drew out routine actions, always at a relaxed pace. He meticulously straightened the abdominal belt's long laces; order, in his very DNA, needed to be maintained. Then he would pull the undershirt down and tie the abdominal belt over it. Finally, he put on his slippers, made of soft flannel in cream and brown checks.

Nothing of all these actions is out of the ordinary, or requires special attention, yet when he picks the slippers up to put them on, Abba's skin bristles. Oddly, Eichmann's slippers are identical to those his mother wore on the last day that he saw her, when she walked him to the door of their house in Proszowice an instant before he fled for the last time.

"Das Bett bauen" is another nightmarish phrase for Shoah camp survivors, especially in Auschwitz-Birkenau. Not "building" the bed correctly meant that the specific prisoner could expect harsh punishment. Even though the beds were made correctly, it could be a cause for any commander to find reason to shout, abuse, and terrorize a prisoner. That's when Abba recalled Fritz, the blockhalster from Auschwitz and Jawiszowice: Fritz, who loved his role as block supervisor and semi-commander, Fritz of the dog-bark voice and the harsh penalties over 'bed-building.'

For Eichmann, though, there in prison, Bett-bauen was a way to pass a little more time. First, he carefully folded the sheet, then spread out the blanket and covered the mattress, sliding it smooth until the mattress looked like a wrapped rectangular box. He would then fold the red pajamas and place them under the pillow. One more blanket was placed at the top of the bed, and the second was spread out, so that in the end he went around and around the bed, smoothing it out to perfection.

Then the process of arranging the cell began. It held a plastic water container and bowl. "If the room is clean or not, it makes no difference to me," Eichmann would say. "Cleanliness or filth, they're for you," he added, referring to the wardens. First, he swept the room with a brush. Every morning he used the same order and method. If he changed anything in his customary actions, it was a sign that something untoward was going to happen that day.

He began by putting his corner in order, then that of the guard. If he didn't like the look of the guard, he'd refuse to clean the guard's station; that was his kind of quiet protest. Guards never reacted because Eichmann's cleaning actions were in the range of voluntary rather than compulsory. On the other hand, no one dared upset him, since his life was far too precious to us all. Eichmann never did anything he didn't want to do, but on the other hand, he tried to present himself at every opportunity as the innocent victim sitting in prison for the sins of others, constantly hoping that his time there would be temporary. He displayed the typically courteous nuances of a European, not only when eating, but in all other daily activities.

By contrast, he would regularly complain about and denounce the guards to the head guard, and even purposely lie or exaggerate events to gain his objectives. During a routine daily medical checkup, the physician asked how he felt. Eichmann asked for cotton wool. The doctor asked if something was wrong with his ears. Eichmann answered that all was well but the guards talk among themselves and make noise when they walk on the floor.

Reaching the bathroom required a series of actions due to the need to leave the cell in handcuffs and ankle cuffs, provide soap and a towel, and the routine registration of every action in the activities diary, while noting any irregularities. One morning while conducting the daily cuffing, Abba was on duty when such an irregularity took place. The shift leader handed the hand and ankle cuffs to my father before heading for the toilets and shower. Precisely then and without warning, the unit commander appeared to spot- check the situation, entering the cell to ensure matters were being correctly handled. Abba had just cuffed Eichmann's ankles but as he was about to stand up, it turned out that he didn't have the key to lock the cuffs. A cold sweat covered his body. If he were to say anything to the duty officer, it would disclose the procedural mishap and he would later be rebuked by his own commander. If on the other hand he remained silent, matters might end up even worse. In short, Abba began riffling through his pockets in search of the key.

Meanwhile, the unit commander lost patience. "What's going on here? Why is it taking so long?" he asked impatiently. Help came from an unexpected source. Eichmann himself noticed that Abba was feeling incredibly stressed and realized that he was looking for the handcuff key. He saw that it was still in the ankle cuff lock. Not wanting the unit commander to bawl Abba out, he shifted his foot and winked at Abba. To this day, Abba is convinced it was the first and only time that Eichmann helped a Jew.

The cell and the bathroom were barely a step away from each other, and they were separated only by an iron door. Also beyond that door was the corridor where the prisoner could walk back and forth. Three guards accompanied the prisoner to the bathroom; one stayed inside with him, the second stood at the door, and the third waited in the cell. When he used the toilet, Eichmann would let the water run to cover his indignity of being so closely watched. The situation required that the prisoner's wardens be present at the prisoner's most intimate moments, thereby becoming the prisoner's shadow.

Eichmann would then undress and wash half his body in lukewarm water, brush his false teeth for 30 minutes or so just to use up the time of yet another day that would be wasted. His pocket handkerchief was brought to the prison in the daily pack of soap. Time was something he had far too much of; from the time he awoke until the ritual of washing the handkerchief, several hours would pass. This became the norm twice a day. When he had underwear that needed laundering, it provided him with a full day of activity.

While all this abundant time was slowly being messed about with, guards from the general kitchen brought breakfast into the kitchenette designated for the prisoner and the A1 guards. Food arrived in a locked dish. The duty warden served the prisoner on a ceramic plate. Serving involved respectfully putting out breakfast, which included herring, salad, oatmeal, and a soft-boiled egg. The menu was decided according to the physician's instructions. There were also four slices of bread, some margarine, fruit jam, and tea or coffee with sugar. A spoon, fork, and teaspoon, all of plastic, were provided.

These were all set out on a tray before Adolf, son of Adolf Eichmann. And the serving was carried out by a forearm tattooed according to the prisoner's own instructions in the Auschwitz-Birkenau extermination camp. The amount of food Eichmann ate at a single breakfast was more than an Auschwitz prisoner received during an entire week. Showing that arm every time he served Eichmann should have given Abba some small sense of revenge for the suffering and loss of his family, a reminder of Eichmann's action.

However, there was some small satisfaction in looking around at Eichmann's wardens. Most had been former walking skeletons on whom Eichmann and his cronies passed a death verdict without any fair court hearing. Herman, a Shoah survivor who opened the cell door, was a concentration camp prisoner with a tattooed number; Tzvi, who sat in the cell with him, was a Warsaw Ghetto survivor; Arieh, who entered the actions into the daily logbook, was a death camp survivor; and the duty commander was a Sosnowiec Ghetto survivor. Almost all the Shoah survivors worked the same shift, making them feel safer, as though they were partners to a shared fate. Any conversations among them were directed to their ultimate aim: carefully guarding the prisoner.

Now Abba picked up Eichmann's food tray. Even though several issues pertaining to Eichmann's care were not to Abba's liking, he always respectfully abided by the instructions he received. The log entry showed that Abba and the duty officer entered the cell with breakfast, and that Abba personally set it down on the prisoner's table. As soon as Eichmann heard the door open, he was ready in the "stand-at-attention" posture, greeting them with "Good morning, my masters!" as they entered, a smile playing lightly on his lips. Then he arranged the plates and cutlery on the desk and handed the tray back to Abba.

He would thank Abba again, and remained standing until the serving wardens departed, leaving him alone with only his personal guard. Eichmann carefully spread margarine on the bread and ate with enjoyment. Everything he did was carried out as slowly as possible; after all, the prisoner was in no hurry to get anywhere.

Wardens of Mizrahi origin who'd immigrated from Arab-speaking countries would repeatedly ask the incomprehensible: How could such a refined man have conducted such terrible crimes? Indeed, his behavior in prison, his table manners, and the way he slept, made it hard to understand how such a decent, polite, and relatively quiet man could carry out such extremely evil acts, as the numbers on the Shoah survivors' arms attested to. It took Shoah survivor wardens a great deal of effort to explain that this criminal operated with white silk gloves as his guise.

During the Holocaust, Eichmann sat in an office, but his instructions were cruelly implemented by his subordinates. Don't look at him the way he is here, now, the wardens would say, but judge him by what we experienced.

Among no small number of prison guards, it was assumed that the final verdict would be extradition to Germany. Eichmann himself developed an illusion of amnesty. Up until the final moment, he never believed that anyone would actually put him to death. Until you're actually dead, he convinced himself, do not believe it will take place. Only when you die, can you be sure. And why spend one's days without a sense of hope? Better to hold on hopefully to even the most minuscule shred of being freed. When you die, clearly there's no hope, but until then, what can you lose by hoping?

On rare occasions Eichmann left food on his plate. He had a tremendous appetite and little wonder that week by week, his weight rose by half a kilogram. Food was followed by cigarettes. Smoking was the prisoner's greatest pleasure. It appeared that he'd once been a chain-smoker. When smoking, he would sit up straight, placing one leg over the other the way he did in his chambers in Budapest from which he sent out his mass extermination plans. He drew in deep breaths, and let the smoke out in long, curling whiffs, watching them rise with clear enjoyment.

It would seem that fire, smoke, and ash provided his sadistic nature with gratification. He constantly glanced from the cigarette's burning end to the guard on duty, and back. No doubt he was thinking what a shame it was that his guards in Israel had somehow slipped past the Auschwitz furnaces. He seemed deeply sorry not to have destroyed all the Jews in the world.

A cigarette was provided every 90 minutes and logged in a specific notebook. Right after his first cigarette he was handed a small, round, pre-charged shaving machine of German manufacture. He was allowed as much time as he wanted to caress his skin with the shaver. One day it broke down during his shave. He dismantled it without requesting permission. The guards reacted instantaneously. Eichmann quickly apologized, showing the guards that the spring had come out of its place.

Shaving was followed by the ritual around books. First came a drawn-out procedure of changing to his reading glasses. It was such an elaborate set of movements that the only thing missing was an orchestra's dramatic fanfare. The unit commander collected hundreds of books in German, and each, when offered to Eichmann, was disdainfully glanced at, eliciting the comment that he'd read it. Finally, he requested Goethe's poems. Yes, they can always be reread. He was not at all interested in reading the New Testament, which a Canadian minister had brought on one of his visits. Of that book, he would say to his guards that it reeked of Judaism.

Every day in the late morning, the prisoner underwent a medical checkup. At 1 p.m. he was served lunch. Later it was time for an afternoon walk in the courtyard. Since he was required to take his walk while hand and ankle cuffed, he usually tried to avoid it, initially claiming that he felt unwell, but as time passed, he gave in and took his cuffed walk.

After breakfast, Eichmann would wash again, laundering his pocket handkerchief once more. Then he would shake it out to help it dry quickly. Finally, he folded it meticulously, smoothing it with his palms. Over time the guards picked up his habits, doing the same. It became a way to pass the shared, boring time.

On the bell's final ring, Eichmann's daily routine ended. Moments earlier he could feel bedtime approaching and would begin preparing for sleep.

In one of his conversations with Abba, Eichmann described how he set his internal clock according to prison life. When the first guard arrives, Eichmann registers that it's 6 a.m. According to Eichmann's calculations, the guard rosters change every two hours. The clang of keys in the last shift indicates bedtime. He brings his chair closer to the bed and readies himself, folding his clothes with military precision. He wears the red pajama top over his sweater. Had an Auschwitz prisoner gone to sleep in his sweater, the next day he would have had to work to his death or stand naked in the snow. But Eichmann was protected by Israeli law and could do that if he wished.

Next, he placed his warm slippers on the soft rug. If he changed even the slightest of his habits during the day, the night guards knew that they needed to be on the lookout because he was planning some kind of provocation. Then he would peel his socks off, smooth them out and tie them to the chair. He plumped his pillows dozens of times before nodding with approval. Finally, he would remove his abdominal belt and glasses and hand them to the duty officer before lying down with a "Good night, Mr. Guard." He would turn his back to the guard. That act signaled the end of Eichmann's waking day.

Attorney Robert Servatius

Eichmann had been imprisoned for several weeks but had not requested pen and paper to write his memoirs or prepare his appeal. This clearly indicated instructions he'd received – a calculated tactic to delay the procedure against him. From time to time he received letters from his family in Vienna containing words of encouragement and consolation. As the new year drew closer, he received a postcard sent by his brother and sister. On it was a picture of two lit candles adorned by droplets of wax. His siblings sought to encourage him, describing how everyone in Austria was sure he was innocent of any crime, and how he was suffering because of the sins of others, just like Christ did at the time. "But keep strong, do not break, for justice will win, and it will not be long before you will be strolling the city of Vienna as a free, proud citizen," they wrote.

"You are permitted to respond to the letters you've received," Abba said to him on handing Eichmann his mail. With a somewhat angry response, Eichmann answered that "Tomorrow is another day," adding that he had no need to rush.

A few days later, Attorney Robert Servatius's deputy visited the prison. Servatius was to be Eichmann's legal representative. At that meeting, Eichmann voiced very serious complaints. He shouted, he fumed – to the extent that Servatius himself was called in. The lawyer sought to keep Eichmann's spirits up, telling him that hope was not yet lost, that the distance between Ramle Prison and Israel's airport in Lod was no more than a 15-minute drive, and that he hoped that with the help of the Lord, he would soon see his client a free man.

Eichmann repeated his complaints, emphasizing that he would not betray his commanders or subordinates, but why did the dirty laundry need to be washed abroad, and in Israel of all places, and why was Hans Globke wandering around freely through the corridors of the German Bundestag? Globke was a senior jurist during the Third Reich period, known for formulating the Nuremberg Laws, among other things. After the war he enjoyed a prestigious position in West Germany's government. Servatius assured Eichmann that he would send him a book about that, recently published in Germany, which unequivocally stated that the architect behind the anti-Jewish laws was Globke and Globke alone.

The unit commander and Abba accompanied Servatius to the exit gate, bidding him goodbye.

The Stain on the Wall

During the long days of seemingly endless shifts during which Abba sat facing Eichmann in his cell, Abba's thoughts continued their historic reckoning with Eichmann.

He, Herr Eichmann, persisted in claiming his innocence, repeating the claim that he was no more than a small cog in the massive Nazi death machine, and Abba was nothing but a sliver of the great Jewish sacrifice. Any time they reached the bottom line, Eichmann summed up that he was innocent, and holding him in prison was illegal. He would then straighten in his chair, pleased and convinced of his own claims, surrounding himself with a cloud of cigarette smoke, rolling the smoke out in his unique manner, and stating very confidently that the Jews would not dare hang him.

Several days prior to this conversation, Eichmann was visited by the Canadian minister and his wife. "Merciful madam," Eichmann addressed her, "why are you so sad? Are you going to the gallows, or am I?" he smiled.

"May justice win," the woman replied.

Abba sat quietly off to the side, listening, swallowing hard, keeping his anger hidden, thinking: What justice? Where were you both 15 years ago? The entire world was silent as the Jews were being massacred!

Eichmann called his regular way of sitting, where one leg crossed over the other as he stared at the wall, "plank facing the eyes," but he never explained the term. On one particular day when the physician, during the daily medical checkup, asked why he had no sense of humor, Eichmann answered, "How can a man who has a plank before his eyes have a sense of humor?"

Eichmann's thoughts and complacent manner were suddenly disrupted by a fly buzzing around. What the guards hadn't managed to do to Eichmann in his meditative state, the fly did: Eichmann tensed up. Until then, the atmosphere in the cell had been quite easy-going, the cell being well heated, which added to the pleasantness, unlike the wild storm outside with its downpour, lightning, and loud claps of thunder.

As Abba sat in Eichmann's cell filling his role as the prisoner's guard, the prisoner's eyes followed every move Abba made. Abba's gaze was for the most part glued to him, too; he tried to read his thoughts. A battle of minds between the prisoner and the guard. Eichmann had long since concluded that among all the guards, Abba was the most burdensome. For some reason he was more curious than the others, gazing intently with his gray-blue eyes, examining every move the prisoner made, walking around Eichmann's table too much, watching the prisoner closely from the moment the shift began. Noting whether Eichmann's letters were neatly placed. Too polite when serving Eichmann his meals. Too courteously holding a cigarette out for him. The protocol required that the guard take a puff first and then hand the lit cigarette to the prisoner, but Abba gave him an unlit cigarette and held up the match like a true gentleman, not like the other guards.

Eichmann also noticed that Abba cuffed his wrists and ankles with great sensitivity. Often Abba would bring him hot tea. But when Eichmann needed the bathroom, Abba would, in Eichmann's view, "give him no headroom" as he deserved. During Eichmann's morning walk, Abba was not as distanced as the other guards, but gazed right into the prisoner's face.

Unexpectedly, Eichmann remembered having mentioned to Abba some days earlier that the ankle cuffs were bothering him and had asked if he was permitted to remove them. Abba answered firmly, "Eichmann, remove the cuffs, and let them jangle, that all shall remember you murdered 1,000,000 Jewish children, among them my brothers and sisters." He also remembered that when the shaver had stopped operating, he took it apart without permission. At the time, Abba responded emphatically, "Eichmann, remove your blood-stained hands from it." When Eichmann said he was "requesting forgiveness" and that he wouldn't do it again, Abba again said, very clearly, "A murderer of children can have no forgiveness or reprieve!"

Then he remembered something else. Abba bumbled along too much in German; when Abba served the food his sleeves were rolled up, revealing the Auschwitz-Birkenau tattooed number 108006. When Eichmann looked at it, Abba stated that it is a real, original Auschwitz number "made in Deutschland." Abba's answer ruined Eichmann's appetite. Although the prisoner tried to ignore the tattoo, Abba would mention it frequently. Even when Abba handed Eichmann a cigarette, he made sure to do so using his left, tattooed arm, his sleeve rolled up to make it fully visible.

Abba is certain that Eichmann knows his name and that he is a victim-survivor of Auschwitz. Eichmann knows the names of all his guards. He speaks Spanish, understands Yiddish, hates Jewish cantorial music, and understands a little Hebrew. He pricks his ears up, trying to understand the guards talking among themselves. He is not above asking them to turn the radio off when it annoys him.

Abba understands that Eichmann prefers the guards of Mizrahi origins to those of German-speaking European origins. With the Mizrahi guards he can brush up on his Spanish. They treat him as though sharing in his sorrow. Before them he can show his niceties when eating or washing and play the innocent victim. They weren't overly bothered by who he was. But Abba, the blond Polish guardian whose number is blatantly tattooed on his arm, is far harder for Eichmann to fool. Eichmann is aware that Abba gives him no slack, never lets him forget the horrors. Abba is conducting an ongoing reckoning vis-à-vis the suffering of all his fellow Jews in Auschwitz, Jawiszowice, and Ramsdorf.

Eichmann puffs curlicues of smoke from his cigarette and continues staring at the wall. Suddenly he notices the annoying fly. He flares into a fury, in an instant loses control, yanks his slipper off his foot, and rages at the cheeky flying critter that has sneaked into the warm cell. Initially, Abba couldn't make out the reason for Eichmann's outburst. "Here again!" the prisoner roars, "but this time I'm onto you, I've got you!" The sole of his slipper slams loudly, like a gunshot, and the fly is squashed. And what's left is a stain. The dead fly's blood.

Abba leaves his chair, goes over to Eichmann and asks, "What's this? What's gotten into you?" In response, Eichmann points to the wall and mutters, "That fly was driving me nuts."

Abba is surprised by the situation. He takes Eichmann on. "Herr Eichmann, are you murdering again?" Eichmann's lips curl into a faint smile and his face has the visage of a child caught red-handed. "After all," Abba drives his point home, "you claimed in court that you'd never hurt anyone, not even a fly on the wall. And look! You've just killed a fly!" Abba didn't need to say anything more; the logic was obvious to Eichmann.

Several days later Eichmann noticed a stain on the wall. The hot water boiler in the room had sprung a leak. The water stain spreading through the plaster had the shape of a human skull. For some reason it seemed to really frighten Eichmann. He quickly found a way to get someone to do something about the stain: he began to cough loudly. The noise reached the duty officer's room, where it was heard by him and the special unit's commander. At first the commander didn't realize who was coughing. A warden? Plenty of others could replace someone coming down with a cold. When the coughing grew louder, he asked the commander, in a concerned tone, who was coughing in Eichmann's cell.

"The accused," Abba answered.

"Eichmann? Really?" Confused, the commander scratched his head. That presented a problem, because unlike prison employees, there was only one Eichmann. A doctor was immediately called in to see the supposedly ill prisoner.

Eichmann continued his skillful coughing, realizing that he was achieving his objective. With every cough he glanced at the wall, indicating it was the source of his suffering. Abba, having noticed by now what shape the stain had taken, asked the prisoner what bothered him so much about it? After all, he had seen so many smashed Jewish skulls without fear; could he be afraid of an image on the wall?

"It's from the stain," Eichmann said. "It's the devil's skull. It's a real sickness. Under no circumstances can I sleep next to a wall like that." He paused. "Sir," he addressed Abba, "do you know what cement is? I am a professional in that field. Cement by nature absorbs moisture," he detailed his concern.

Medical bag in hand, the doctor quickly entered Eichmann's cell. The prisoner immediately noted that this wasn't a routine checkup since the visit was earlier than usual. He stood at attention next to his bed, greeting the doctor, a very decent, gentle person liked by all but who knew nothing of Eichmann's past. He was only interested in the prisoner's good health, unlike Eichmann's horde of extermination camp doctors.

Since this was early January, the doctor held his hand out to Eichmann to wish him a happy new year before checking his blood pressure, politely adding, "It's odd how on every Sunday your blood pressure is normal. Please open your mouth again. What about your teeth? Would you like a dental examination?"

"No thank you," Eichmann answered. "In the time I have left, these teeth will hold up just fine." A moment later, he added that he was at the dentist in Argentina when he was captured by the Jewish secret service and brought to Israel.

The thorough checkup showed nothing unusual. The doctor realized that Eichmann was harboring a specific request. "And other than that, is everything all right?"

"No," Eichmann answered. "I would like warm inserts in my shoes. My feet are cold." Then he pointed to the wall. "And what worries me the most is that stain on the wall. The wall, Herr Doktor, is made of cement and absorbs water. When the heater is on and the air becomes moist, it actually poisons me," he claimed.

Having completed the checkup, the doctor left instructions: a glass of warm milk, a soft-boiled egg because the prisoner doesn't like hard-boiled eggs, warm linings for his slippers, an orange to promote metabolism, move the bed away from the wet wall, and repair the leaking boiler. And in his thoughts, Abba corrected: Move the bed and change the water drum that accurately weeps bitter tears into Eichmann's prison cell over the destruction of the Jewish people.

The Appeal

Eichmann was represented by his German lawyer, Robert Servatius, heading the defense team. Servatius had previously represented other Nazis put on trial in the Nuremberg courts. Eichmann and Servatius met in a small visitor's room about 10 square meters in size and split in half with a glass divider that separated them, but allowed them to converse.

Eichmann told his attorney that "Eichmanns" like him can be found in abundance in Germany; he just had to ask Kurt Ernst Becher, a Nazi colonel who testified at Eichmann's trial and was himself saved from being tried due to his helpful testimony about Rudolf Kasztner's part in saving Hungarian Jews. Now Abba guarded in the room where Eichmann and Servatius were discussing the case. Abba sat shoulder to shoulder with Eichmann, like two old friends, taking in all the details of Servatius's line of defense for his client.

Servatius brought Eichmann the book as promised. It was a clear sign from the lawyer to his client that it was time for Eichmann to begin writing his appeal vis-à-vis the death sentence to be delivered by the court. Until then, other than letters, the prisoner had refused to write anything at all, in protest. Or, in other words, the idea was that if his life is mercilessly spared and he is allowed to live, he would write a book and perhaps even ask forgiveness from the Jewish people for his part in their extermination, but under the threat and pressure of the gallows, how could he leave a legacy that included a written apology?

Having received his lawyer's green light, Eichmann examined the book thoroughly. The front cover bore a photo of bespectacled Dr. Hans Globke, secretary of Chancellor Adenauer, himself a Nazi. Globke placed all blame on Eichmann: "Here he is, that pig, that smart aleck, architect of the race laws against the Jews. Why does he not speak up, rather than hide beneath old Adenauer's cloak?" Eichmann wanted to share his impressions with someone, and turned his face towards Abba as though hoping to share a secret, seeking a little empathy, but his voice suddenly caught in his throat. Abba's exposed arms rested on the table, the tattoo clearly visible. Eichmann wanted to lie yet again, removing all responsibility from himself, but right there in his line of sight was a living testimony of his actions.

"Yes," he sighed, "this book is my last hope. This book proves clearly who invented the rules of race. And this man, Globke, is a pensioner receiving a monthly German stipend of hundreds of Deutschmarks. It makes little difference to me either way, but why did Globke refuse to testify in my favor? Mr. Guard," he said, facing Abba, "please give me a pencil so that I can mark important facts which may assist me in preparing my appeal."

Eichmann's request was met immediately. The pencil was authorized; he continued thumbing through the book, each page carefully inspected. He spent longer gazing at the photos, and caressed the image of Hitler, may his name be forever obliterated. That photo was surrounded by images of Hitler's right-hand men, Eichmann's superiors. "Wansee Conference, Berlin, 20 January 1942," he muttered to himself, sighing. Abba also takes a look at the photo as though it were an album of events that he and Eichmann had shared.

"That's Heidrich, and among them is Herr Obersturmbannführer Adolf Eichmann," Abba identified the prisoner in one of the photos. In his heart, Abba noted that this was the date when "The Final Solution" was devised as a method of annihilating the eternal Jew, which is why the conference attendees departed with laughing faces.

The prisoner looked again, and again, over and over, at the photos, rubbing his own bald head as though in disbelief, as though wondering, "Where was I then, and where am I now?"… When his hand was not rubbing his head, it was smoothing out his prisoner's uniform, recently changed from red to gray, the outcome of Knesset Member Menahem Begin's fierce opposition. Begin had pointed out that the Warsaw Ghetto fighters had gone to their deaths in red clothes, as heroes, for their people's sake, and it would desecrate their honor for this vilified murderer to wear that color.

Changing the color actually gave Eichmann hope. He knew the rules well and concluded that his death penalty was not being taken seriously. It charged him with energy. If not for Abba, whose bare arms forced Eichmann to confront his past every time Abba came on shift, he might even have stood at attention, called out "Heil Hitler!" and saluted. Instead, he underlined an important sentence in pencil, and marked where Hans Globke ordered that every Jew with Christian-sounding names should be listed with the addition of "Israel" for men and "Sarah" for women.

Every so often the prisoner and Abba would study each other, a chill passing through Abba's bones as he still couldn't fathom that he was sitting with Eichmann and reading the book simultaneously with him. How sad. What a bitter situation. It was no easy matter for a "katzetnik," as concentration camp prisoners were called, to sit shoulder to shoulder with Adolph Eichmann and have to contend with the facts of that evil Nazi's life. What is white to Eichmann is black to Abba. Eichmann sees himself as innocent; Abba sees 6,000,000 Jewish dead in massacres, furnaces, forced labor, beatings. It annoys Eichmann intensely that Abba is reading the book together with him. So Eichmann tries to distract Abba through various ploys. "Sir Guard, the electric light is bothering me," he says to Abba, and adds, "After all, you wear glasses so of course you will understand that."

Meanwhile the leaking water drum was being replaced in Eichmann's cell in accordance with the doctor's instructions. Ironically, the new water drum also "wept" over the destruction of Europe's Jews. The skull on the wall expanded, grew a beard, and looked more and more like a Hassidic G-d-fearing Jew of pre-war Europe. Eichmann was beside himself when Abba pointed out that the stain was no longer the shape of the devil, but had become a bearded Jew, likely the very same one who would accompany him to the gallows.

The Real Eichmann

Eichmann studied the book over several sequential days. Eventually he turned his attention to preparing his appeal. In the cell was a vastly different Eichmann than the prisoner the guards had dealt with until then. No longer the man who sat calmly reading books; in his place was the real Eichmann, bursting with energy, restless, the same one who ran the Final Solution meant to wipe out Europe's Jewish population with utmost precision.

Eichmann requested a pencil and lined paper and began furiously copying sections of the book. He wrote so quickly that sparks seemed to fly from his fingers. Every few minutes the prisoner asked Abba to sharpen the pencil and provide additional pages. For several days this was the norm – until Eichmann came to the chapter on the Belzec concentration camp.

Here he began to scratch his head and squirm in his chair. It seemed that his appeal was bogging him down in complexities. The entire time, he kept a close watch on Abba. Eichmann was clearly uncomfortable, as though wanting to ask something but not sure about whether he should. Eventually he turned to the documents he'd written while under police arrest. He stood suddenly, a very unusual movement for him since he usually requested permission, but this time he went over and took out one of the documents. "Stop, Herr Obersturmbannführer. What's going on here?" Abba stopped him. "After all, you are a man of order. Where is your request for permission?" Abba half asked, half rebuked Eichmann.

"But it's mine!" Eichmann answered, acting innocent.

"Once, yes, it was yours, but no longer," Abba corrected.

"But I want to be sure that a certain fact is written correctly." Eichmann attempted to justify his spontaneous action.

"If what you wish to write is correct, simply write what you think. If it isn't correct, or if you're not sure, request permission from the commander. There are rules and regulations here," Abba persisted.

Eichmann's concerns were clear to Abba. The prisoner was unsure at that moment about the best next move, and the issue of what to write was disturbing him: Should he write what he thinks now, or should he write what he thought then? It was the first time that Abba heard the murderer fume. "That's unfair," he claimed, trying to threaten Abba by saying that he would complain to the commander.

Although there's no state of 100% justice in this world, some justice was achieved nonetheless. The former "katzetnik" was guarding him, and that disrupted Eichmann's ability to write smoothly; the number on Abba's exposed arm constantly reminded him that no matter what he writes or how he tries to defend himself, all his words are lies and fabrications. Abba agreed with Eichmann when the latter said that it's difficult to present himself in a positive light while the victim is "at his jugular," or, so to speak, "constantly in his view." Eichmann felt that Abba was watching him with 100 eyes, which made Eichmann keen on somehow getting rid of Abba.

Eichmann marked his goal: to get Abba out of the guards roster. How? As the architect of European Jewry's eradication, he began planning his steps towards having Abba removed from the special unit.

Kurt Gerstein, Nazi, Exposes the Truth to the World

After Eichmann was not permitted to receive the documents he wanted, Abba watched him pencil in notes next to SS Officer Kurt Gerstein's declaration. Gerstein, an expert in providing Zyklon B, the gas used by the Germans to murder the Jews, wrote a report in which he admitted to his part primarily in the Belzec and Treblinka concentration camps. Despite his efforts, and despite conveying real-time information to the West, he was sentenced to an extended prison sentence for his actions, and committed suicide in his prison cell after his verdict was handed down.

Gerstein, whose conscience began to bother him in 1942, sought to expose the mass murders to the world. Eichmann shrugged as though in disbelief. Could Gerstein really have betrayed Eichmann's trust by not providing the gas on time? Nor could Eichmann believe the first time that Abba suddenly agreed with him over something after having confronted Abba over countless issues on which their opinions conflicted, as could be expected. Abba would not accept the extenuating premise that some Nazis were imbued with human decency; on the contrary, he rejected the premise altogether.

Looking at Abba, seated at the desk where Eichmann was writing, the latter noted Abba reading what he'd just written. Had this happened during Eichmann's glory days in his Budapest office during the Third Reich, Abba would have been sentenced to "special treatment." Now, though, the prisoner had no power over Abba. Eichmann was no more than a shard.

Keen of eye, Eichmann noticed Abba's face flush red at the words "Belzec camp." Abba lowered his head. His eyes filled with tears, and not just because of Gerstein's revelations. Abba clearly remembered that on August 28, 1942, his parents and siblings were uprooted, along with 21,000 Jews from Proszowice and the region of Kielce. He remembered how they straggled along the 17 kilometers to the adjacent town of Slomniki. He remembered that horrific Shabbat, when massacred mothers and children lay in the streets and the town clerk loudly announced that all Jewish civilians must leave their town of birth forever. How could he forget the way his father carried his golden-curled children on his shoulders? His only sister was among the victims. His parents, along with all Jews in the area, were forced to wait on that grassy patch in Slomniki, under the bare skies, for five nights and six days because Eichmann, maestro of life and death, did not provide train carriages on time. To make sure no one was bored, the Germans and local firefighters hosed the patch of grass down every so often. The water was diluted by the Jewish community's tears.

And Abba remembered how at last everyone was loaded onto carriages caked with chlorine and lime and sent to Belzec. After a violent selection process at the Kraków Ghetto, Jews were sent to forced labor, consoling themselves with the thought that perhaps those sent to Belzec were nevertheless going to be given jobs inside the camp. But here was Gerstein, an SS officer, describing in detail just what the bitter end was for those Jews – including Abba's family. Abba's mother and his little brothers stood close together, hand in hand, and waited for 3 hours and 25 minutes until their souls left their bodies. Then Abba's mother cast her final curse on the murderer of children whose innocent blood was spilled.

Later, when Jews operating under forced labor opened the doors to the gas chambers, they saw entire families standing, hugging, forming columns of death. They were burned in the furnaces, their ashes scattered across Belzec's cursed land, but only after cutting off the thick black braids and golden curls, collecting it all and sending it to Germany. Gerstein affirms these details in his report. Eichmann, with one swipe of his pencil, marks a diagonal through that section as though erasing the words. "That's entirely unimportant," are the words that erupt from his mouth. As far as he's concerned, none of that has anything to do with him, and he bears no responsibility for those horrors.

* * *

Our visit to the remains of the Belzec concentration camp in the 1990s, where Abba's family was murdered, was a chilling experience. The many years that had passed since the camp was abandoned, Nazi crimes no longer blatantly visible, did not erase the ruins or conceal the disgrace. Abba's story was exacerbated by the region's general gloom, not to mention the delays that caused us to arrive there at night, making the visit even more strongly reminiscent of the camp's atmosphere of back then.

We direct the car's headlights onto the path leading to the monument. The area is pitch black. Dogs bark when they hear unexpected sounds. Ignoring them, Abba holds a memorial service as planned, playing a poem dedicated to his mother that he penned in Yiddish and saved on the tape recorder. He calls me and the others over to listen to "A Poem to My Mother Roza."

I am deep in thought about Abba, about the longing for his mother and family that I feel emanating from him here in this place where his family was gassed, then burned. What a strange way, I think, for G-d to choose innocent righteous folk from Abba's family, from his neighbors' families, to rise to heaven – not very unlike Elijah the Prophet, as described in 2 Kings 2:11: "*And it came to pass as they went on and talked that, behold, there appeared a chariot of fire, and horses of fire, which parted them; and Elijah went up in a whirlwind into heaven.*" The difference, of course, was that Elijah rose in a chariot whereas my grandmother, her children, and her neighbors rose, charred to cinders. I shiver.

Like Elijah's disciple Elisha, Abba has continued to accompany his mother and family ever since that day. Abba bends to the ground to scoop up a dusty layer of ashes left from 434,000 Jews burned in furnaces here in the Belzec death camp.

Among the handful of ash that Abba picks up is something hard. "Look!" Abba calls out. "A human bone!" It's dark, and I can't see a thing, but he's put the ash and bone into a small bag and then into his pocket. I am deeply moved.

On the long drive back we're mostly silent, me because of the shock of these events, and Abba because he's processing an idea that's come up. That's how Abba is: simultaneously living in the present, relating to and respecting the past, and plotting for the future.

At Birkenau, we stop next to Furnace 2, mostly destroyed by the Allies' bombing. Abba goes into the ruins, ignoring our pleas not to, and disappears from view. Others ask me what to do, clearly anxious. "Don't worry," I answer, "he knows this place like the back of his hand from the 1940s. He knows what he's doing." The truth is that I didn't know that for sure, but neither did I fear for him.

Once we're back home in Bat Yam, Abba takes several small cloth bags out of his suitcase. The name of each location is written on each bag with black marker. At my questioning stare, Abba answers. "I will bury this ash at the monument I'll build at the Holon Cemetery to commemorate the victims, since they have no gravesite. At least something of them should be buried here in Israel," he explains.

In the late 1990s, Abba initiated the establishment of a monument in the Holon Cemetery in memory of his town's Holocaust victims. At the ceremony attended by all the survivors of the town living in Israel, several items were buried on site: a parchment scroll containing the names of all the murdered Jews from his town, and the three sachets of ashes from the extermination camp furnaces brought back from that earlier trip.

As the years passed, and Abba and I began discussing what might happen when he passes away and eventually meets up with the family he has sought ever since that Friday when his mother made him flee from their home, Abba lifted his hand to stop me mid-sentence. "Arie, one second. I have something important to ask of you," he said, going over to the closet in his bedroom. He began to read his will. An awkward silence filled the room.

"When I die," he eventually said, "I want to ask that you bury me with these..." He turns to me, holding a cloth bag. The words in black marker say, "Ashes of righteous Jews from the concentration camps." The title is followed by names of the camps themselves in Hebrew and Polish: Auschwitz, Treblinka, Majdanek, Belzec, and Płaszów.

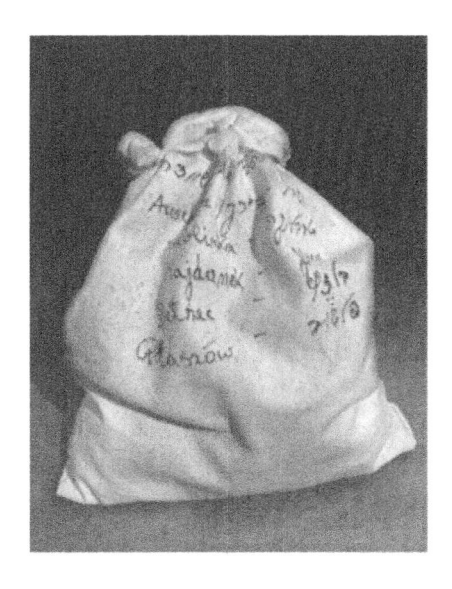

I don't react. I simply don't know what to say. Abba continues, ignoring me. "I couldn't be with them in their lives. At least I will lie at rest with them in my death." And he adds nothing more. The only way for me to handle this odd, emotional situation is to opt for humor, so I say, "Every other father leaves his progeny a will relating to money, to assets, but you leave me a will with instructions to bury little bags with you?" Abba just continues, "That's what I'm asking of you."

All I can think of is how appropriate this whole scenario is for a session with a psychologist. On the one hand, I can't fathom the concept of the day after Abba's passing, but on the other hand, let's be realistic: Abba's already more than 90 years old. I decide to opt for the strategy of postponement that I always go for in such situations, rather than face the dilemma head on. Okay, I think, meanwhile the little sachets will stay in the closet and I'll try to repress the knowledge that they're there until the fateful day arrives.

The Protest

For two months, Abba's been cooped up with the murderer on his guard shifts behind the same locked door. Days go by. Abba is already familiar with the prisoner's various "good" traits. Eichmann's sent his appeal to rescind the verdict and is waiting for a miracle. During his time in prison, procedures have changed. The roof above his cell has been covered with barbed wire, and inside the cell, sounds of hammering and building can be heard from the adjacent space where work is being rigorously carried out on constructing the gallows needed to implement the verdict once the green light is given.

The prisoner himself feels that his end is near, and both he and his cell are frequently checked. Over time, the guards have also experienced burnout, and many asked to be discharged from their role. Some were indeed replaced. The fear that Eichmann will try to commit suicide is increasingly perceptible. It was easiest to do shift changes at night because Eichmann snored, which helped Abba be certain that he was sleeping and therefore alive – which was the most important objective and helped the guards be a bit calmer.

But more recently, Abba noticed that Eichmann's shoes haven't been aligned as straight as they had always been. In Abba's view, that was a sure sign that the prisoner was about to carry out some kind of commotion to try and have Abba suspended from the guarding unit because in Eichmann's view, Abba was particularly tough on him. Abba was certain that Eichmann would try to oust him because Abba wouldn't let the prisoner access earlier documents, which forced Eichmann to write his appeal with somewhat less of his usual confidence and focus.

Eichmann's attitude actually developed after Abba had been very polite, fulfilled his obligations to the prisoner, did not harm him in any way, washed his eating utensils, served him respectfully out of his sense of mission on behalf of the nation ... and this was how the prisoner showed gratitude?

Abba entered Eichmann's cell as usual. He was greeted very coldly. Abba immediately caught on that the prisoner was angry, and remembered the previous day's incident, when the shift commander ordered the guard, Zvi, not to allow the prisoner to cover his face with his blanket. Eichmann protested and raised a ruckus, but in the end calmed down.

Eichmann was busy reading *Death Is My Love*. Baruch, the duty guard, prayed as usual inside Eichmann's cell. Saying

"Goodnight," Eichmann closed his day. "Guys," Abba said to the other guards, "I have a strong hunch that tonight he's going to try something. His clothes and shoes aren't lined up and folded neatly the way they normally are, and that's a red warning light for us."

The guards took up their positions. Abba was on the roster as Eichmann's personal guard. He sat in his usual spot next to Eichmann, who was having trouble falling asleep, even though his eyes were closed. Abba was afraid Eichmann would try to commit suicide by gnawing into his veins with his teeth, because he frequently pulled the blanket up to cover his face.

As part of his role, Abba went over and gently peeked under the blanket. Then he conveyed a message to the duty officer: The prisoner is not sleeping, so be ready with a key for any emergency that may arise and require that the cell be opened quickly. During the process of recruiting Abba to the task, Dr. Rozner asked Abba how he would behave if he needed to serve the prisoner. He didn't ask Abba how he'd behave if Eichmann attacked him. No one thought of that; it was a possibility that was never taken into consideration.

Abba stood and walked over to the foot of Eichmann's bed. That gave him a view of Eichmann's full body without disturbing the prisoner's sleep. Eichmann tossed and turned, writhing like a snake. At 5 a.m. the phone rang in the duty officer's room, and the unit commander's footsteps could be heard on his way for an unplanned visit. Eichmann heard the commander enter. It was as though he'd been waiting for this very moment. He bounded out of bed, furious. Anyone who hadn't experienced or seen that happen couldn't begin to imagine how frightening he looked. His eyes burned with sparks of fire. He stood, his entire body trembling, in front of his victim: my father. In a voice shaking with fury, he began screaming in the direction of the commander's room like a crazed man.

"Better not to sleep at all than that kind of sleep. Every night he..." he raged, his thumb gesturing at Abba, "fusses around me and rattles my brain! You've turned this room into a house of worship!" he screeched, pointing at the religious guard, "and the stain on the wall!" He jabbed his finger at the moist stain. "I'm just human!" he pointed at himself.

"You're human?" Abba thought. "Isn't that what I said in Auschwitz? We're just humans. But there you were, the Master of Death, and I was the accused, and now it's the other way around, so shout as much as you want," Abba thought.

But indeed, Abba was afraid — afraid that the commander would ask, or worse yet, order him to leave the cell. How shameful that would be, and just to placate this important prisoner. It could all end up being the worst insult Abba had ever been delivered, providing yet another resounding victory for Eichmann. Abba's body froze. He wasn't even able to move a finger. He was taken aback, surprised, and paralyzed. But not for long.

Gathering his wits, he ordered Eichmann in his own language, German, and in a calm but firm voice, "Get back into bed. It's far better that you maintain a low profile because this provocation that you're stirring up is not in your own best interest." The commander, who arrived at the door just then and must have heard the exchange, clearly trusted Abba and adopted the principle that an improper reaction to an improper situation is the correct behavior. He signaled to the guard at the door that everything was alright, and the guard signaled to Abba to continue his efforts at keeping Eichmann calm. A weight was lifted from Abba's heart.

Eichmann was surprised by Abba's constrained reaction, translating Abba's firm, yet quiet tone, as a position of power. Eichmann stood there, wondering what to do, and not knowing what his next move should be. Abba, on the other hand, was praying in his heart, "G-d, save me from these dire straits."

As always in situations like these, Abba imagined his own mother advising him, "Son, with patience, not with force." At that moment, millions of souls, Eichmann's victims, hovered over Abba, or so he felt. If only he could have, Abba would have transfused his own blood into their veins to bring them back to life, that they see the prisoner shaking in fear before one of his victims, who'd never stopped fighting to preserve his miserable life, just as they'd all wanted to live.

At this point, Abba rolled up his sleeve, exposing the tattooed number. Knowing that his commander relied on him, Abba looked straight into Eichmann's eyes while pointing to the number on his forearm and speaking with extreme, but assertive politeness to Eichmann. "Herr Eichmann, you are not in your office in Budapest, Hungary. You are now in the office of Shmuel Blumenthal, in the Ramle Prison, in Israel." Abba took hold of Eichmann, standing stock still as though paralyzed, sat him down on the bed near where Abba had sat observing him, and for quite a few minutes looked straight into the murderer's eyes.

The ringing bell heralded the night's end. Lights went on in Eichmann's cell, marking the end of this battle of wits and patience. Eichmann rose, and wished a "Good morning, Herr Guard" to Abba as though nothing had happened. That day he adopted sanctions against Abba: to punish him, he didn't sweep the spot where Abba had stood. When the doctor arrived to conduct the routine visit, he complained that the guard had angered him and made him feel unwell. A few days later an item appeared in one of the London newspapers that Eichmann had lodged a formal complaint against Abba for his conduct at the Ramle Prison.

The Legendary Satan's End

Mrs. Eichmann's visit to her husband in prison made it clear to the prisoner that his days were numbered, even though she consoled him and tried to boost his spirits. He continued his routines in the prison as though nothing had changed. It was his way of showing that he was a military man and would die with honor. Outwardly he appeared calm; inwardly, he was a big coward and refused to believe that he'd die at Jewish hands.

The legendary Satan's last days in prison looked like ordinary prison days. He ate, shaved, smoked, and read books. He looked through the cell bars at the sunset, the dusk, the night. But he did not know exactly when his last night and day would be. He received his cigarette and dinner as he had on every other day. Everything was normal.

The door to his cell suddenly opened. The commander and duty officer entered. "How are you?" they asked politely.

"Fine, thank you. Dinner was very tasty," Eichmann answered courteously, without any notion of this visit's importance.

After a few minutes of quiet, the commander spoke. "Eichmann," he said, while taking a printed letter from the President of Israel out of his pocket. Eichmann straightened. "The President of Israel, Mr. Yitzhak Ben-Zvi, has rejected your request for clemency. The President has decided not to use his power to pardon criminals and reduce their penalties relative to Adolf Eichmann." The duty officer translated these words into Austrian German.

Eichmann indicated his thanks for the appeal having been given consideration, and asked when the verdict would be enacted. The commander paused before answering. "The next time I arrive with handcuffs, you'll know that's the end. Meanwhile, you can lie down to sleep." Eichmann thanked him again. And Abba thought, "Tonight there's a good chance he won't sleep at all."

"Do you have a last request?" the commander asked.

"To shave, shower, smoke without limitation, and to drink some wine."

"Red or white?" the commander inquired, wishing to ease the tension.

"Truth be known, I was never a drinker. I just want to be humored a bit. Let it be red."

The number of guards throughout the prison was increased. In Eichmann's cell, the atmosphere was charged. For months the guards had waited; finally the moment was at hand. But time crawled slowly. The prisoner finished writing his last letter and waited to be taken at any moment. He frequently glanced at the door. Meanwhile he chain-smoked, filling the cell with an acrid odor.

The gallows room was ready and waiting to carry out the verdict. The key persons had arrived: the Prison Service Commissioner, the prison commander, the doctor, a court representative, two police officers, the Canadian minister, and journalists.

Hearing the clink of handcuffs being taken from the cupboard, Eichmann straightened out his bed, positioned the chair in its place, and stood at attention. The commander and duty officer entered to cuff his wrists and ankles. He asked to finish the half-empty glass of wine. Then he stood. "Sirs, I wish to thank you for your courteous attitude towards me. I have no complaints against you." His lips curled into a slight smile. "In any event, we'll all meet up quite soon on the other side."

Then, in Spanish, he thanked the man who opened the door leading to the gallows room.

The commander and duty officer gripped Eichmann's arms just under his armpits and led him like a groom to his bridal canopy. The murderer held his head high all the way. Behind him, several guards were at the ready for any eventuality. At the doorway, Eichmann stopped for a moment and requested that his nose be wiped. The two men leading him to the gallows could feel Eichmann's body trembling so hard that they barely managed to hold him upright.

At the gallows, they cuffed his arms and legs. He asked for the leg cuff to be loosened a little, saying that it was uncomfortable. Behind the gallows stood several officers, among them the officer from Sosnowiec who had survived the camps. He had been the one to sign the documents confirming Eichmann's entry to the prison at the time. Now he, and so many others, waited with bated breath for the murderer's final "jump," reminding those present that after the war Eichmann had said that he would gladly have jumped on the survivors' graves, knowing that he'd solved Europe's "Jewish problem."

"Long live Germany, Argentina, and Austria!" were Eichmann's last words before his last breath. And thus the life of one of the cruelest humans ever to have lived came to an end. The hatch beneath the gallows opened. Eichmann plunged. The rope lengthened. A few minutes later the prison doctor announced that Eichmann, architect of European Jewry's slaughter, massacre, and incineration, was dead. Abba had fulfilled his vow to keep Eichmann whole and well until he breathed his last breath.

Abba stepped outside of the prison and went to the place where he'd catch the van that took him home, recalling Dr. Rozner's words. The psychiatrist had claimed that guarding Eichmann would benefit Abba, releasing the pain and suffering, and that the nightmares would slowly dissipate.

"Wrong, Dr. Rozner, you're wrong," Abba muttered to himself. Guarding Eichmann has solved nothing for me. On the contrary, it has only deepened the scarred pit in my wounded soul. On seeing Eichmann the prisoner, anxious and miserable, Abba could not fathom that it was the same despicable, murdering Eichmann who engineered Auschwitz and other camps. "The voice of my brothers continues calling out from the earth," he thought, "and will never stop. May their memories be a blessing."

The Last Visit to Proszowice

The last day of our trip has come and we're off to Proszowice for the last time. It's another opportunity for Abba to make his farewells from the city, from his family's home, and mostly, from the cemetery that has become a symbol of Jewish presence in the region. But the official rationale for going there again is to meet up with Hieronim the artist, son of Abba's family's landlord before the Shoah.

Entering the city, the well-maintained Jewish cemetery is on the right; its three Magen David ornamentations are painted stark white, a bold statement against the black metal fence encircling the cemetery and the green spaces within the fencing. I can't help thinking how ironic and how tragic that everyone entering the city on the road from Kraków sees the Jewish cemetery first, and cannot ignore the fact that there used to be a vibrant Jewish community here, even though no Jews have lived here for over 70 years.

Abba's Home in Proszowice

The Wikipedia entry on Proszowice describes the Jews' deportation in August 1942: The Jews were gathered in the town center while being ferociously beaten, loaded onto carts, taken to Slomniki, and from there to the Belzec extermination camp. During the expulsion, as the church bells rang, the local town crier announced that the town had rid itself of its Jews for eternity.

Two things gnawed at me over the years, based on Abba's stories.

The first related to the Torah scroll that was most probably written by his grandfather and kept as part of the display at Golda's restaurant. We'd seen that exhibition of items on our first day of the trip. I felt that its rightful place was here, in Israel.

The second was where Abba's father had hidden various items, burying them in the yard before the family's deportation. For years I'd been trying to convince Abba to carry out a search and find whatever the family's treasure was, but Abba, aware of the difficulty involved, would wave my questions away with various excuses, such as the items have no value, or there isn't really anything there, or perhaps Tateh took them out himself at some point, and so on. Abba's answers were geared at unmotivating me from taking ridiculous or problematic actions. Now, when I suggest we start to dig, and he should just tell me approximately where to look, he answers, glancing to the sides to be sure no one's watching and lowering his voice to a whisper to be sure no one's listening.

"Arie, if you bend down now and start digging in the ground, tomorrow all the neighbors will be overturning this cursed earth, and if they do find anything, we'll never be allowed close, not even to see what it is." That's Abba's perspective: Just be grateful for what we have, before even that disappears.

But this trip is marked by a particular atmosphere that hadn't been evident on other trips: Abba also seems to be aware that this is his last chance, and if we don't do something now, probably nothing will ever be done. So we find ourselves meeting Hieronim.

Hieronim Cęckiewicza is a convivial guy, an artist of international renown who lives in Berlin and earns his living from church paintings, wall murals, and street illustrations. He tells me that his father passed away several years ago and transferred the property to his sister. When I ask why the sister was made the heir rather than the son, he explains that his father asked him, before passing away, if Hieronim wanted the plot, but because he is familiar with the townsfolk and knew he'd never come back to live in Proszowice, he suggested making the sister the inheritor. Meanwhile the sister, too, had passed away and her son, Hieronim's first cousin, was made heir.

Hieronim's cousin joined us. He turned the key in the gate. Hesitantly, Abba entered the yard itself for the first time since fleeing in 1942. Abba was visibly moved. He and Hieronim restructured the house's boundaries, which had deteriorated since the war and never been reconstructed. Based on Abba's descriptions, they mark out the small area where my grandfather likely buried the family's beloved items before being expelled from Proszowice.

Hieronim is as excited as a kid. A very emotional fellow, he also reminds us that his heart and soul were intricately linked to Abba and the other Jews living there. When I ask why they did nothing with the plot of land, why they left it empty and neglected despite its being a mere 100 meters from the city center, Hieronim explains apologetically, "Yes, I'd planned to rework this stone wall with the window as a monument to the

Jewish families who'd lived here." But I'm still curious. "Why didn't you build a house here, though? Surely there's a demand for houses so close to the heart of the city?" Hieronim and his cousin ponder the question but have no answer. And yet, all the houses around them are standing, rebuilt, and only this one is crumbling, and the land desolate, since 1942. It would seem that no logical explanation can be found.

Right then, Abba gets cold feet and apologizes. "Maybe the family's things were taken. Maybe they're worthless…"

But Hieronim encourages, is enthused, and has a strategy. "We'll put up a fence that will block this spot from view, dig only here, and bring a metal detector," he excitedly suggests.

Just then the church bells begin to ring, the same ones I'd heard on our earlier visits, but right here in the yard of Abba's Proszowice house backing onto the city's main church, the pealing is incredibly loud. Nor do they stop for several long minutes.

It brings to mind a history book I once read, as well as stories Abba related of that brutal expulsion. When the town's Jews set out – miserable and humiliated – their Christian neighbors lined the streets to mock them and rejoice at having gotten rid of them forevermore, and the church bells were rung to show the town's joy at the Jews' deportation. And here they are, once again ringing, but I could swear that this time I heard them announcing: "Mr. Shmuel has returned… Shmuel has returned…"

Or perhaps I just dreamt it.

Does it matter?

Another circle has closed.

And the bells continue ringing. I could swear I heard them ringing, "Mr. Shmuel has returned... Shmuel has returned..." Or perhaps I just dreamt it.

The Cemetery

We drive to the Jewish cemetery with its monument to Proszowice's Jews murdered in the Shoah. At age 92, Abba walks in slowly. He seems to understand that this is likely to be the last time he'll visit. He stands deep in thought, saying a silent prayer of departure from this place. I watch him, concerned. I can feel how difficult the idea of never returning is for him. His forehead is furrowed as he worries about who will continue looking after the cemetery, who will continue remembering the victims, and who will visit this wretched patch of earth. My heart is torn over my inability to help him.

Taking a deep breath, I keep my own emotions under control, sealing them up inside me. There's an old principle in our family: Crying is only for the weak. We don't cry.

My hand comes down gently on Abba's shoulder. I kiss his wrinkled forehead the way he used to kiss mine when I was a kid. "Don't worry, Abba," I whisper in his ear, "I'll carry on your legacy."

Shmuel Blumenfeld's Memoirs

Transcribed from Abba's handwritten notes

My camp father

The following lines are dedicated to the memory of my "camp father," Yankel Miller, son of Pincze and Rahel Reizels. Pincze, born in Pińczów, was a man whose life was steeped in Torah. He worked as a merchant and ran a fabric store in the town of Przytyk.

One day Pincze was returning from the fair in Radom, where he'd purchased merchandise for his business. He was traveling on his cart, bundled up in his heavy fur coat, when a bullet hit him. The cart rolled into town with its dead merchant on board. The incident aroused a storm throughout Przytyk, a Polish-Jewish township some 20 kilometers from Radom. The killer was never caught, and the event remained shrouded in mystery.

As a young boy, Yankel had already displayed his skill in trading. Maturing, he devoted his time to business, traveling to various cities to buy merchandise. On the other hand, he never neglected his Torah study. He married and had four children by the time the Germans reached Przytyk and the Jews there met the same fate as elsewhere, the Miller family among them.

Early in 1942, Yankel was caught by the Gestapo and sent to Auschwitz as a political prisoner. That was something of a protected status and brought him to Jawiszowice. I met him for the first time at the Jawiszowice hospital. In fact, it was the first time on "Planet Auschwitz" that I met a fellow Jew, and such a noble one, who dedicated himself to helping the inexperienced young men, guiding us with advice on how to resourcefully conduct ourselves in the camp. He did all he could for us, intervening with kapos and doctors, and helped us by providing moral and emotional support.

Yankel Miller was known for saying, "You're all my children." From then on, I never left him. I went with him on the death march to Theresienstadt. Thanks to him I stayed alive, and we were both liberated from Theresienstadt on May 9, 1945.

When the war ended, we said goodbye to each other. Miller left for the USA, and I went to look for my family in my hometown. Yankel Miller passed away in New York at age 90.

May his memory be a blessing.

***

Zev Lehrer's speech at the 24th Memorial Ceremony (1966) for Proszowice Jews, May their deaths be avenged.

Written by Zev Lehrer

I, Zev Lehrer, brother of Moshe Shohat, may G-d avenge his death, eulogize the righteous deceased on behalf of the community's survivors.

Twenty-four years have passed so quickly since the expulsion from our town. It is impossible to forget that Shabbat night of bloodshed, a night we had never imagined. That last Shabbat we were no longer in our homes. The next day we languished in the mud and muck of Slomniki's fields. On Shabbat afternoon the Jews of Proszowice were herded like sheep to their slaughter and we, the handful of survivors, must give thanks and praise to the Sovereign of the Universe that not all of us lost our lives. The evil-doers of Proszowice, may their names be forever expunged from this earth, were glad to be rid of us so quickly. It allowed them to enrich themselves with our properties and our belongings.

Some of us ran to non-Jews in their fields, their villages and towns, but were met with rioting. There was also one among our townsfolk, like a princeling who mocked it all, who sang praises to the non-Jews, may his name and memory also be forever erased. History should remember him for helping those who hated us spill the blood of fellow members of the people of Israel.

Matters were very harsh at Slomniki. Day by day our numbers decreased. Our elderly were shot on the spot. Others, dear and precious to us, were forced into the train carriages, where Polish police shot them to death.

We, a handful of folks, stood with them, surrounded by Polish police, recruited into forced labor by three SS murderers: Gorniak, Beckman, and Berlein, may their names be forever erased. These three German killers chatted with each other and shouted to the Polish police: Don't shoot! The SS preferred to shove our innocent families into the carriages, torturing them by letting them suffocate to death. And that's what they did. May the righteous souls of the innocent find eternal rest.

They, the best among us, were not incinerated at Treblinka but brought on carriages to the Ukrainian murderers. We, at the Reisha camp, watched closely and knew full well that they were taken to Belzec. May their memories remain forever. We must never forget them.

And may G-d never forgive or forget the Germans and their helpers.

May G-d send them plague, flood, and fire.

The Final Chapter of Abba's Life

Almost three years have passed...

And in September 2021, I submit a request as I have for several years now: "Recommendation to Light a Torch on Yom HaShoah." Year after year I've recommended that Abba be chosen to light one of the torches, due to his unique life story and his work to memorialize Shoah victims, and particularly the community of Proszowice, murdered by the Nazi Regime in Poland.

I find it interesting that Abba is so admired by the leaders of modern Proszowice, is awarded an honor of merit for his actions there to commemorate the decimated Jewish population, but here in Israel he has not yet been acknowledged.

I remember the first time I submitted Abba's name for this honor, when he turned 90. I was phoned by Yad Vashem, Israel's Holocaust Center, and explained that there are only six torches and so many individuals who have done so much for Shoah survivors, although Abba's story is nonetheless quite unique. "Thank you for calling," I laughed, "and there's always next year." She asked why I chuckled. "Oh, knowing my Abba, he won't go to the world to come without first having lit a torch." And I couldn't help adding, "See you next year."

For the next few years I made sure to resend the recommendation request. It was nothing more than a simple action in my computer – a "copy-paste" of the same request from the previous year. I remember Abba teaching me that rule of thumb: If you repeat the exact same action, don't expect a different outcome. The recommendation request was repeatedly rejected. On the other hand, it filled me with hope that we'd all enjoy another year of having Abba with us. It reminded me of the end of the seder on Pesach that Jews have been repeating for centuries: "Next year in Jerusalem!" Well, many didn't, or couldn't go, but that didn't stop them from saying it the following year and remaining hopeful. I took on that foundation of belief with blind faith à propos Abba, too.

So, as I noted, in September 2021, I submitted the sixth recommendation form, but this time it included an additional comment: All his friends from the first generation of Shoah survivors had passed away and Abba, at 95, was the last of the Proszowice community. His health was deteriorating, and if such an honor cannot be given to him for his own sake, perhaps he can be given the honor of lighting a torch in the names of all who died.

Not long afterwards, Yad Vashem once again phoned me. I answered somewhat indifferently and was therefore taken by surprise by the ceremony manager's response. Indeed Abba had been chosen to be one of the torch-lighters at the main Holocaust Day ceremony in Jerusalem, to be held on April 27, 2022. The woman's voice was filled with joy. It gladdened me, too, so much so that I completely forgot my comment, years earlier, that Abba would not pass away until he'd fulfilled that honor.

Eventually the long-awaited day was very close. Although Abba had until then not shown any great excitement, he began to get emotional as Yom HaShoah, Holocaust Remembrance Day in Israel, approached. Yad Vashem sent a photographer to our house to take a few shots, and the production team prepared a clip to be aired at the main event, describing Abba's activities over the years. Abba and I talked a good deal about the event's importance. Everything was going just fine, handled professionally, and moving ahead under the team's experience.

And then... on March 30, 2022, I got a call that hit me like a bolt of lightning and changed our plans instantly: Abba had collapsed, I was told, and was being taken in critical condition to Wolfson Hospital following two rounds of prolonged resuscitation efforts.

My world imploded. I went into autopilot mode. First, all efforts needed to be focused on saving Abba. At the hospital's entrance I met the ambulance bringing him into the trauma room; he was in cardiac arrest. I pleaded with the attending doctor to do all he could, since Abba was slated to light a torch on Yom HaShoah!

The medical team fights to restart his heart. I call my sister abroad. "Come as soon as you can," I tell her. "Abba's heart has stopped and they're working on him," I add.

After that call to my sister, my brain slowly grasps the scope of the disaster. It's not about lighting or not lighting the torch – it's about Abba's life, which is now hanging by a thread!

Frustrated and helpless, I sit by the trauma room praying to G-d to save this good, decent man, praying for a miracle, praying that he remains alive at least until my sister arrives. I scream my words, silently. I come up with a tactic: I'll ask G-d for short-term requests. If they come to fruition, I'll know my prayers are being answered, and anyhow, small requests are easier to fulfill. Somewhere in that line of thinking was another thought: To show G-d that I'm not greedy, not asking for too much at once, there's just a small request: If my sister makes it on time, then I'll ask for the next one: that he live to light the torch. If that comes true, then I'll ask that he live long enough to see my son – his grandson – get married at the end of June. Then I'll go for the next milestone.

I can't get beyond the sense of helplessness I feel at my inability to help the current situation. Sitting there unable to do anything only increases my frustration. Deep-seated fear seeps into my awareness: Maybe wanting to extend his life is not the right request because it could bring on a long period of suffering due to my selfishness, my wish to have him live longer. The trauma doctor doesn't make things easier, either, when he tells me that he cannot know the degree of brain damage Abba might have suffered. He leaves the matter of deciding Abba's fate in my hands.

In sheer despair I call the number I have for emergencies: Dr. Tamara Koolitz, director of the "LeMa'anam" Association. LeMa'anam, which means "For Their Sake," is an organization of medical professionals who volunteer to assist with Holocaust survivors' medical issues. We met Dr. Koolitz back when Abba needed a medical intervention, and she and he had an instant "click." She recruited Abba to be a presenter to assist in fundraising for the association. They developed a warm, close relationship. Abba loved Tamara – for her volunteer work as well as for her expertise in the unique aspects of medical care for Holocaust survivors. She, on her part, related to him as her "special grandpa."

"Tamara," I click my cell phone message in. "Abba had a stroke and is in ICU right now." I was hoping to receive some support from her at this critical, lonely time, such as a word or two that could guide me to the right answers. And as Tamara always did, she took up the reins and professionally guided the emergency process Abba needed. A few minutes later she was already at the hospital, providing professional support. In fact, she was the significant factor behind Abba's being saved at those critical moments.

The following days were filled with stress and distress. Abba was in critical condition with his life at high risk, but his recovery was moving ahead well and filled us with hope that quite soon he'd open his eyes and we'd find there was no brain damage. He did begin to show good signs: He sat up, ate with assistance, got out of bed and even took a few steps, and we all smiled, pleased that he was improving. It looked like the steps taken to save his life had worked.

At the hospital, the doctors discussed rehabilitation with him. We were all so optimistic. We began to feel sure that at the end of the month he'd light the torch after all. The guest list was being worked on, Yad Vashem having informed us that that we were limited to 10 people. Things were definitely looking up.

Tension was easing, and I remember thinking how many good people Abba has been surrounded by, and how much goodness there has been despite the sad parts of his story, which looked a bit like the layer upon layer "Chad Gadya" song that we sing on Pesach. Our mother's nursing aide called the neighbor, who immediately came and stayed with Abba until the ICU ambulance came at lightning speed, bringing the medics and paramedic who began resuscitation and kept him alive all the way to hospital, where the trauma team took over and immediately continued resuscitation and stabilization. They were backed up by Tamara, who came in like a member of an elite forces unit to make sure that everything was operating correctly, coordinating with the doctors and nurses of the ICU, who worked not only professionally but with great sensitivity, thereby allowing Abba to make it through the episode.

Everyone was focused on one target: enabling Abba to have the great honor of lighting the torch on April 27th.

And then... on Shabbat, a surprising turn. Abba was not feeling very well. It was a sign, but we were still euphoric over his improvement so far. On our way to the CT scan, I told him very firmly, "Don't worry, Abba, you'll get to light the torch." I wasn't going to let any doubt creep in. "Do you think so?" he asked, and he made that small, familiar hand movement that says, "You don't know what you're talking about." I caught it from the corner of my eye but ignored it, believing, hoping, that in a moment it would pass. It didn't.

On the evening of Tuesday, April 12th, my sister and I sat in the room next to Abba's bed. The atmosphere was heavy and gloomy. He was having trouble speaking and he was also partially ventilated. "That's it," he said, making a large movement with both hands that meant "I'm done. It's over."

He blew us one kiss after another. He even tried at one point to speak to me, making some last-minute suggestions, but I found it hard to understand because of my own hearing impairment. I begged G-d. I called him "Gottenyu" the way Abba's family had in Poland. "Gottenyu, please give me good hearing just for now so I can fulfill this precious man's last wishes as he asks his children's permission to leave them forever." In my mind, I shouted this to G-d but I couldn't hear – or, more importantly, understand.

In a state of anguish, I sat far from Abba but still in his line of vision. He continued waving and blowing kisses as though seeking my confirmation that it was all right for him to leave. All the while, my sister was bent over him, beseeching, "No, Abba, you still have things to do... to light the torch... and we have a wedding in the summer. Ashley's getting married..." she cajoled.

The image of my sister bent over him, tears rolling down her cheeks, pleading, sent me back to that Shabbat of August 28, 1942: Proszowice, surrounded by Nazis, and Abba's mother bending over him, tears rolling down her cheeks, begging him to flee and save his life. I mull over the irony of the reversal of roles. I must do something; I can't just sit here lost in my own thoughts. My body tenses, my hair stands on edge, the veins in my neck are pumping so hard that they feel as though they could burst from the emotions that are running through me. I go over to Abba, kiss his forehead, covered in a fine coat of sweat, and speak loudly.

"Abba, I'm going to take Shosh home now. You need to rest." My voice is unwavering. "We'll come tomorrow morning. If you're here tomorrow we'll be so happy to see, and if you're not, we'll understand and continue loving you." Kissing him once more, I leave the room, giving my sister Shoshana a little time alone with Abba.

On our way out of the hospital, I was mostly silent; my sister mostly sobbed. I hugged her tightly. "Shosh, Abba wants to go. Let him." She cried, but nodded her understanding and agreement. The rest of the way home we were silent; I couldn't find the words to encourage my sister – or myself.

An hour or so later the hospital called: Abba had another cardiac arrest. We raced back to the hospital. Back to the events that first brought him here. Abba slowly left us, but Tuesday, described in the Creation narrative as "doubly good" (Gen.

1:10 and 12) must have seemed to Abba not the best of days for departures. The doctors consulted with us, and when we asked if we should say our goodbyes, they confirmed, adding that if they're wrong, we can always do it again, since they really have no way of knowing whether his dying will take days or weeks. But somehow I realize that we are close to the end, and the final time will be determined by G-d and Abba.

Another insight slowly surfaces: Abba won't be lighting the torch. I need to update Yad Vashem, even though I'd already advised them of Abba's health situation, but everyone still hoped that he'd make it. My letter to them explains that Abba will not be able to fulfill the privilege, but I suggest that his honor and life's work be recognized by having the torch lit on his behalf, and on behalf of so many others, by Dr. Tamara Koolitz. That way, his efforts will become known and acknowledged by Israeli society.

Two days pass. On Thursday, eight minutes before 9 p.m., his soul ascends to heaven. We are left with a gaping hole.

The next day, Friday, is an important date in the Jewish calendar. At day's end, Jews around the world will mark Pesach and conduct the Seder service. The verses from Exodus 12:5-7 come to mind: *"(5) A lamb without blemish...(6) you shall keep unto the fourteenth day of the same month, and the whole assembly of the congregation of Israel shall slaughter it at dusk, (7) and they shall take of the blood, and place it upon the two side-posts and on the lintel of their houses, in which they shall eat it."* On this very date, over 3,000 years ago, the Children of Israel set out on their journey from enslavement in Egypt to freedom. How symbolic that Abba's soul rose to heaven, to freedom from earthly constraints, when it did.

* * *

Despite being mere hours until the festival of Pesach, and short notice, a large number of people came to the funeral. Undoubtedly Abba was accompanied to his last earthly place by all the innocent souls from Proszowice whose names he worked so industriously and faithfully to memorialize. They are listed in his card file – approximately 2,000 cards – that contain the names of entire families, some including dates of birth, and the dates and places where they were murdered.

On the way to his burial plot in the Holon cemetery, everyone stopped for a few moments at the monument to Proszowice Jewry that Abba instituted in the late 1980s. There, together with Abba's final entourage, we recited a chapter of Psalms in his memory and the memories of his childhood neighbors who did not survive the Nazi regime. Abba's name would now also be part of the group of people formerly of Proszowice.

As Abba was carried on the stretcher to the grave, the sachets of ashes brought from the various concentration camps in Poland rested at his feet. "If I wasn't with them in their deaths, at least their ashes should be with me on my death," I recall him having said. Not forgetting his request, I asked my nephew to fulfill the request, and scatter the ashes in the grave.

At around 1 p.m. that day, Abba was brought to eternal rest. He was the last person buried that day, on the eve of Pesach, in the Holon cemetery. He was eulogized by the Israel Burial Society's representative. "May you find sweetness in this earth of the Land of Israel," he said, and with that, Abba's grave was filled, ensuring that he rest peacefully from then on.

The burial over, one of the many attendees came up to me. "The flame of his candle has indeed been extinguished, but his great light will illuminate the Yom HaShoah torch and serve as an example to others." I nodded and said, "Amen," but couldn't really absorb the words.

Despite being surrounded by a large crowd of people, I felt alone. My sons, my nephew, and my daughter were right behind me, clinging together: Abba's beloved grandchildren. They put their hands on my shoulders and kissed my forehead just as I'd kissed Abba's in the Proszowice cemetery when we made our final visit. "Don't worry, Abba," they said to me, "we'll continue Sabba's memorialization efforts, honoring his vows to do so."

Two days after Abba's funeral, Yad Vashem contacted me. They would be pleased if I'd agree to light the Yom HaShoah torch for the Jewish year 5782, corresponding to 2022, in Abba's stead.

And thus, Abba's life and life's work received the perpetuation of which they were so deserving.

Acknowledgment:

The English version of the book was produced with the support of Intelligent RF and Microwave Solutions, an Israeli company, managed by Oren Hagai, In loving memory of Shmuel Blumenfeld, a one-in-a-generation giant.

Printed in Great Britain
by Amazon